A Theory of Employment in Firms

Contributions to Economics

http://www.springer.de/cgi-bin/search_book.pl?series=1262

Jessica de Wolff
The Political Economy of Fiscal Decisions
1998. ISBN 3-7908-1130-0

Georg Bol/Gholamreza Nakhaeizadeh/ Karl-Heinz Vollmer (Eds.)
Risk Measurements, Econometrics and Neural Networks
1998. ISBN 3-7908-1152-1

Joachim Winter
Investment and Exit Decisions at the Plant Level
1998. ISBN 3-7908-1154-8

Bernd Meyer
Intertemporal Asset Pricing
1999. ISBN 3-7908-1159-9

Uwe Walz
Dynamics of Regional Integration
1999. ISBN 3-7908-1185-8

Michael Carlberg
European Monetary Union
1999. ISBN 3-7908-1191-2

Giovanni Galizzi/ Luciano Venturini (Eds.)
Vertical Relationships and Coordination in the Food System
1999. ISBN 3-7908-1192-0

Gustav A. Horn/Wolfgang Scheremet/ Rudolf Zwiener
Wages and the Euro
1999. ISBN 3-7908-1199-8

Dirk Willer
The Development of Equity Capital Markets in Transition Economies
1999. ISBN 3-7908-1198-X

Karl Matthias Weber
Innovation Diffusion and Political Control of Energy Technologies
1999. ISBN 3-7908-1205-6

Heike Link et al.
The Costs of Road Infrastructure and Congestion in Europe
1999. ISBN 3-7908-1201-3

Simon Duindam
Military Conscription
1999. ISBN 3-7908-1203-X

Bruno Jeitziner
Political Economy of the Swiss National Bank
1999. ISBN 3-7908-1209-9

Irene Ring et al. (Eds.)
Regional Sustainability
1999. ISBN 3-7908-1233-1

Katharina Müller/Andreas Ryll/ Hans-Jürgen Wagener (Eds.)
Transformation of Social Security: Pensions in Central-Eastern Europe
1999. ISBN 3-7908-1210-2

Stefan Traub
Framing Effects in Taxation
1999. ISBN 3-7908-1240-4

Pablo Coto-Millán
Utility and Production
1999. ISBN 3-7908-1153-X

Frank Riedel
Imperfect Information and Investor Heterogeneity in the Bond Market
2000. ISBN 3-7908-1247-1

Kirsten Ralf
Business Cycles
2000. ISBN 3-7908-1245-5

Michele Bagella/ Leonardo Becchetti (Eds.)
The Competitive Advantage of Industrial Districts
2000. ISBN 3-7908-1254-4

Frank Bohn
Monetary Union and Fiscal Stability
2000. ISBN 3-7908-1266-8

Jaime Behar
Cooperation and Competition in a Common Market
2000. ISBN 3-7908-1280-3

Michael Malakellis
Integrated Macro-Micro-Modelling Under Rational Expectations
2000. ISBN 3-7908-1274-9

Stefan Baumgärtner
Ambivalent Joint Production and the Natural Environment
2000. ISBN 3-7908-1290-0

continued on page 206

Josef Falkinger

A Theory of Employment in Firms

Macroeconomic Equilibrium and Internal Organization of Work

With 49 Figures

Springer-Verlag Berlin Heidelberg GmbH

Series Editors
Werner A. Müller
Martina Bihn

Author
Professor Dr. Dr. Josef Falkinger
University of Zurich
Socioeconomic Institute
Chair for Public Finance
and Macroeconomics
Rämistraße 62
8001 Zurich
Switzerland
josef.falkinger@wwi.unizh.ch

ISSN 1431-1933

ISBN 978-3-7908-1520-7 ISBN 978-3-7908-2649-4 (eBook)
DOI 10.1007/978-3-7908-2649-4

Cataloging-in-Publication Data applied for
Die Deutsche Bibliothek – CIP-Einheitsaufnahme
Falkinger, Josef: A theory of employment in firms: macroeconomic equilibrium and internal organization of work / Josef Falkinger. – Heidelberg; New York: Physica-Verl., 2002
(Contributions to economics)
ISBN 978-3-7908-1520-7

Originally published by Physica-Verlag Heidelberg New York in 2002

Softcover Design: Erich Kirchner, Heidelberg

SPIN 10887242 88/2202-5 4 3 2 1 0 – Printed on acid-free and non-aging paper

Preface

Production and competition in a modern economy require internal interaction of individuals in firms. This book provides a systematic theoretical treatment of the consequences of this fact for the macroeconomic equilibrium. The requirement of internal interaction implies that a firm's capacity of producing and marketing products is limited by the employed organizational resources. This is analyzed by introducing the concept of a two-stage decision process of firms into macroeconomic theory, with choice of organizational capacity at stage 1 and choice of activity level or price policy at stage 2. Unlike industrial organization theory with two-stage games, the presented macroeconomic theory leaves strategic interactions aside. It is based on a model of monopolistic competition in which organizational costs are endogenous at stage 1 but sunk at stage 2.

My motivation for pursuing this research was the conviction that being employed cannot be taken for granted. Not only the willingness but also the possibility to participate are required. For most people participation in work means to be integrated into the workforce of a firm. This is possible if a role is offered which one is able to play. That is, when there is a firm which provides, in a broad sense of the word, a work place at which one is employable. This employability is not an exogenous variable, given by nature. Apart from individual abilities, it depends on the number and the characteristics of the provided work places. The theory presented in this book works out the basic economic forces determining the number of work places organized in an economy and the minimum level of abilities required from a person to be considered as employable. The book explains how they vary if new forms of work organization are introduced or the competitive environment of firms changes. In general, the level of employment realized in the macroeconomic equilibrium of a market economy may be lower than the efficient level of employment. So there is room for policy.

The book developed from my research at the University of Regensburg between 1995 and 2000. I have benefited from many discussions and comments. In particular, I wish to thank Hartmut Egger, Volker Grossmann and Martin Summer who read the original manuscript and gave me very competent feedback and helpful advice.

Josef Falkinger

Contents

1. Introduction

An observer of current trends may be left with the impression that the *success of the winners* is all what economics is about. However, Adam Smith, Karl Marx, John Maynard Keynes and most other great economists were not concerned with the question of how some individuals or groups of individuals can get rich. On the contrary, the central purpose of economic reasoning has been to inquire into the determinants on which the *earnings opportunities of the mass of people* depend in an economic system. In this respect, two problems are of particular relevance: The rise in inequality during the last decades and the threat of unemployment or precarious employment. This study concentrates on the employment problem.

1.1 A new theory

In an economy human and non-human resources are transformed into final goods. This is not only a *technological process*, it involves also the (social) *interaction* of *human subjects*. Standard general equilibrium theory in the Walrasian tradition considers exclusively *external interactions* of individuals in markets. In contrast to this, there are some approaches in economics (e.g. Coase [19], Williamson [69, 70] and, of course, the business literature) pointing out that *internal interactions* within organizational units (firms) also play a central role in real market economies. However, the discussion remains restricted to the partial analysis of single transactions. There is no general equilibrium theory which would bring out the macroeconomic consequences of the fact that modern economies are characterized by the interplay of *individuals* and *organizations*. This study attempts to contribute to such a theory. For this purpose a model is presented in which *internal organization* is a *conditio sine qua non* for external market transactions. Economic interactions between individuals are only possible in or through organized forms. A worker cannot sell her or his labor service directly in the product market but must be connected to an organizational unit, called firm, in which the interaction of different individuals is organized and transformed into a marketable output. The concrete forms of organization change. Traditional hierarchical firms may be followed by decentralized networks. But this does not change the principal fact that the interaction of individuals involves organizational arrangements. The assumption that no market interactions are possible without organizational intermediation is of course an idealization, as is the opposite assumption of standard equilibrium theory that stylized types of individuals interact in markets. The general equilibrium of an economy cannot be analyzed without leaving facets of reality out of account. The question is what are the *essential* features of reality.

It is true that an individual can go to another individual and offer her or his service as a maid or servant. But such direct external interactions between individuals are certainly not the most typical market transaction in a modern economy. They may have been typical of feudal economies . But then one has to ask how much feudal work relationships have in common with the idea of a market economy. Likewise they may be characteristic of certain secondary labor markets for personal services and casual labor. But the interesting question is how work is organized in the modern sectors which distinguish present-day production and transaction of goods and services from former times. In the approach of this study, the relevant distinction is between an economy in which individual interactions are organized in firms and firms interact in markets, on the one hand, and an economy with interactions of single individuals in markets, on the other hand.

In the presented approach the essential feature of modern economies is that the transformation of labor inputs into saleable outputs involves internal organization. The new element of the developed theory is that firms must employ *non-production resources* for the internal organization of work. Thus, in addition to the usually considered employment of production inputs under a given technology of production, the firms' choices of their profit-maximizing organizational capacity must be modelled. And, in addition to factor prices, employment in production and produced quantities, also the level of non-production resources employed for the organization of work must be determined in general equilibrium. Formally, this is achieved by adding to the standard model of transforming inputs into outputs by means of a *production technology* the internal organization of interactions by means of an *organization technology* as a new element. The inputs employed in the organization technology (i.e. the non-production inputs) are a prerequisite to production. They create the capacity of organizing production work and have to be fixed prior to production and competition in the market. Figure 1.1 illustrates this new element of the presented theory in a simple diagram.

In reality, part of the non-production inputs required for organizing production work is provided publicly. This aspect is not analyzed. Only the private provision of the capacity to organize work is considered.

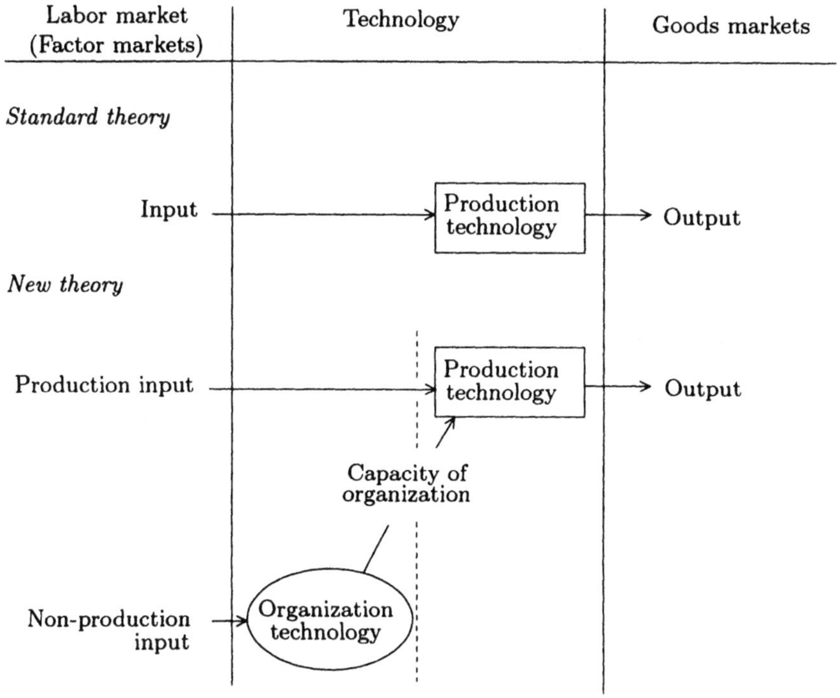

Fig. 1.1. Organization of internal interaction as a prerequisite to production.

1.2 (Un)employment

Unemployment is a large source of unhappiness (Clark and Oswald [17]). It is true that unemployment rates in some countries are substantially lower than in others. But it is not true that countries with flexible labor markets have no employment problem.[1] Even in the United States non-employment rates up to 35% are observed among low-skilled workers (Murphy and Topel [48]; see also Nickell and Bell [50]). And although the term non-employment suggests that some people have voluntarily left the labor force, there is a substantial share of workers who cannot find a job. Whereas any form of unemployment is or should be an important issue for economic policy, from the perspective of economic theory, the fact that involuntary unemployment is possible despite flexible wages is the biggest challenge. It is the purpose of this study to develop a theory which can explain involuntary unemployment as a macroeconomic equilibrium phenomenon in a flexible market economy.

[1] Saint-Paul [57] begins his book with Solow's [62] observation that "Essentially everywhere in the modern industrial capitalist world, unemployment rates are much higher than they used to be two or three decades ago."

The reason why employment is important for the well-being of people is that for those who have only their labor endowment, regular employment is the only possible source to earn a stable income. Casual labor and odd jobs help to survive but precariousness does not make people happy. Of course, highly qualified specialists and risk-loving people may prefer to be free-lance, although also they are anxious to be connected to well organized networks. In general, however, the observed trend away from employment at an organized work place to temporary employment and occasional labor has severe consequences for the workers. The question is what determines the level of employment at work places organized in firms and why is it possible that some people have an organized job whereas other find no or only precarious employment. The model presented in this study analyzes the equilibrium level of *organized employment*. *Unemployment* means *no organized work place in a firm*, and *involuntary unemployment* means that *people don't get such a work place although they would accept lower wages.* Since the equilibrium level of organized employment depends on the organization technology, the focus on organized employment allows also a rigorous analysis of the macroeconomic consequences of *changes* in the organization technology. In particular, it is possible to analyze the implications of the idea that new information and communication techniques radically change the way in which the interaction of individual workers is organized.

In the sixties when unemployment was relatively low in most developed countries the notion that unemployment is, at least partly, involuntary was taken for granted. It is hard to understand why, but the notion became more and more disputed in the seventies and eighties when unemployment rates increased. This induced Rothschild [56] to ask ironically "Arbeitslose: Gibt's die?" ("Is there such a thing as unemployment?"), to point out that the economic profession was going to ignore the obvious. In the mean time, the idea of unemployment as a supply side phenomenon is so widely accepted that one should not be sure that the question is perceived as an ironic one. People who have no employment are considered as having voluntarily withdrawn from the labor market or as being "unemployable". They are counted as non-employed or out of the labor force. But names are no substitutes for theoretical explanations. The fact that most people have a work place while others don't find an organized job in a firm requires an explanation. Moreover, a serious theory has to acknowledge the fact that many of those who have no work place would be happy to have one. From the perspective of the jobless worker this means involuntary unemployment.

Some economists seem to see the proof for the voluntary character of unemployment in the mere fact that people survive without employment. Fortunately, there are opportunities to survive outside the regular economy of organized work. The essential feature of involuntary unemployment is that these outside opportunities are less attractive than an organized job. A worker who is involuntarily unemployed does not prefer to live on transfers, servant-like personal interactions or casual jobs, but is forced to accept the possibilities to survive outside the world of organized work. Formally, the involuntary character of unemployment in the presented model is established by showing that some workers may find no work place even if they were ready to work at zero wages. No outside reservation wage prevents workers from working.

What is involuntary unemployment from the perspective of the jobless worker, may be unemployability from the perspective of the firm which does not employ the worker. But then we must explain what determines employability. The presented theory gives a precise foundation of the notion of *economic employability*. A worker is said to be employable, if (s)he can be *productively* integrated into organized work. Productively means that the aggregate output of the economy rises if the worker is employed. In contrast to this, a worker finds employment in the market equilibrium if (s)he can be *profitably* integrated into the work force of a firm i.e. if employment of the worker raises the profit of a firm. A worker is involuntarily unemployed if no firm is willing to employ him(her) even if (s)he underbids the equilibrium wage. This may happen although the worker would be employable in the defined economic sense. A clear theoretical distinction between the *equilibrium level of employment* and the *efficient level of employment* is provided by the presented model (see chapter 3.1). According to Lindbeck and Snower ([44], p.47), involuntary unemployment exists "whenever workers are willing to work at less than the prevailing wage for jobs that they could usefully fulfill, but are unable to find such jobs." The efficient level of employment which is derived in this study determines what workers could usefully fulfill, whereas the characterized equilibrium level of employment determines who can indeed find a job in the market.

1.3 Work organization and macroeconomic equilibrium

Weitzman [68] pointed out that a theoretically founded explanation of unemployment has to account for the fact that work is organized in firms. Not every piece of activity or each unit of service is exchanged through markets. There is also internal transaction and coordination. Although the boundary between market transactions and internal organization is changed profoundly by new management methods and new organizational structures like alliances, networks or "virtual firms" with quasi-self-employed workers, the essential point remains: Not isolated individuals but companies and corporations are the relevant "players" in a modern market economy. For earnings opportunities one has typically to be connected to a network, or put in more traditional words, work requires a place in an organization (called firm for short). The creation of work places, i.e. of earnings opportunities, requires employment of non-production resources. Development and design of saleable goods and services, permanent training[2] and integrating workers into the "corporate culture", management capacities for coordinating and supervising the work of different members of the organization, facilities for marketing the firm's output are prerequisites which must be arranged before firms can successfully enter competition in the market. The relevant macroeconomic question is: How large is the aggregate level of these non-production inputs which determine the *organizational capacity* in the economy and thus the number of organized jobs? This study answers the question by analyzing the *macroeconomic equilibrium* in a *two-stage model* in which profit-maximizing firms arrange work places by employing non-production resources in stage 1, anticipating the outcome of competition in stage 2.

New techniques of production and methods of organization have not wiped out the principle fact that besides competition in the market the internal organization of work is an important characteristics of modern economies. But, of course, the concrete characteristics of organizational methods and structures are changing. This change has an effect on the costs of organization and also on the skills required from the employed work force. Workers must be endowed with new abilities to be employable under modern forms of work organization. For instance, "customer-oriented teams require versatility, cognitive and social competence, as well as judgment" (Snower [61], p.9). Whereas many aspects and implications of the reorganization of work have been discussed at the firm level or in a partial equilibrium perspective (see, for instance, Snower [61]) for an extensive discussion of recent trends), the purpose of this study is to analyze *the role of the (re)organization of work in the general equilibrium*, in particular its relation to *aggregate employment*. From the perspective of a single firm or industry new forms of organizing work imply above all that careful selection of workers becomes more important. However, for any given stock of abilities in the population, the desired skills are going to become scarcer and scarcer if each firm tries to pick and choose workers with all the particular and general abilities which make flat hierarchies, decentralized teams, customer-orientation possible and allow for flexibility while guaranteeing reliability at the same time. As a consequence, firms may hesitate to employ more workers, or they invest more in their coordination, supervision and training capacity so that they can organize also work of less able persons. Put the other way round, an increase in aggregate employment means that firms employ also less able workers which raises the costs of organizing work. From a macroeconomic perspective, the central question is how rising skill requirements implied by new techniques of production and organization affect the average costs of organizing work and the aggregate number of work places organized by firms in equilibrium.

---

[2] In a modern economy training means not only embodiment of skills at the beginning but a permanent process. Whereas the single training at the beginning of employment amounts to turnover costs , continuous adaptation and learning requires of firms to arrange training capacities which are not bound to the entry of a concrete worker but to size and type of the employed work force.

This author has no ambition to contribute to a differentiated picture of work organization and reorganization strategies of firms as drawn by case studies and management science. What the presented study wants to bring out, at a general theoretical level, are the macroeconomic consequences of the fact that the costs of organizing work depend on the employed technology and, for a given stock of human capital in the economy, on the aggregate level of employment. The developed framework allows to analyze these consequences for a given technology but can also be used to endogenously explain the reorganization process induced by the availability of new technical and organizational methods. In chapter 4, the equilibrium pattern of reorganization and its consequences for the aggregate level of organized employment are determined for specific changes in the techniques of organizing work.

1.4 Skill bias and skill requirements

In the economic literature of the nineties, the most widely accepted reaction to the rise in inequality and unemployment has been the hypothesis of some form of skill-biased technological change.[3] In the usual theoretical models skilled and unskilled labor are used as factor inputs in a production function. Technical progress changes the marginal products of the two factors in favor of skilled labor so that relative demand for unskilled workers declines. Thus, in these models there is no direct link to the problem of how work is organized in firms and how non-production inputs for organizing work, skill requirements implied by the adopted techniques and abilities of the employed labor force are interrelated. In the *empirical literature*, however, the rise in the ratio of *non-production workers* to *production workers* is taken as evidence supporting the hypothesis of skill-biased technological change.[4] The justification is that non-production workers are relatively highly skilled compared to workers in production. In the model which is elaborated here, the distinction between non-production and production workers is not just an empirical proxy for skilled and unskilled labor, respectively, but is in the center of the theoretical argument, namely: Producing goods and delivering services requires a place in an organizational infrastructure which must be created by employing non-production resources in the development, design and marketing of products

[3] Bound and Johnson [12], Juhn , Murphy and Pierce [33], Berman, Bound and Griliches [8], Kahn and Lim [34] and many others. See Acemoglu [1] for a survey. Gregg and Manning [28] emphasize that not only the technology-induced change in the demand for skills but also the changes in the supply of skills must be considered. More recent studies try to endogenize both the biased technological change (see e.g. Acemoglu [2], Kiley [39], Vogt [66]) and the induced supply of skills (see e.g. Heckman , Lochner and Taber [31]). A broad discussion of the problem of inequality can be found in Atkinson [4, 5].

[4] Berman, Bound and Machin [9], Machin and Van Reenen [46].

and in the coordination, supervision and management of work.[5] As a result, this approach determines not only the range of skills which is employed in equilibrium but also the *equilibrium ratio of non-production to production work*.

For the explanation of rising wage inequality the central question is how the marginal productivity of workers with different skills has changed. Thus, the focus is on skill differentials which can be internalized and compensated by wage differentials. In this study, which focuses on the (un)employment problem, the emphasis is on ability dimensions which are associated with the workers' role as a member of an organization. "Social skills" or "interactive skills"[6] are current catchwords highlighting the importance of such abilities. Since the interaction of workers is a collective process involving many external effects, differences in the*interactive abilities* can *not* be *internalized*, at least not fully, by wage differentials reflecting the marginal impact of an individual worker on the performance of the organization.

How modern techniques and methods of organization shift the requirements toward this type of skills has been pointed out by Breshnahan [13] for the case of bureaucratic and organizational applications of computers. The argument in the study in hand is that generally modern production requires a certain quality of work which must be guaranteed by the non-production resources employed to organize production work. If workers are employed which are less autonomous, less reliable, less flexible or less able to communicate, the non-production resources required per unit of production work increase. Thus, the profitability of employment varies with the abilities of the employed labor force. Involuntary unemployment arises, if in the market equilibrium, it is not profitable for the firms to provide work places for all workers.

The explicit consideration of non-production work, as opposed to production work, also sheds new light on the traditional distinction between high-skilled and low-skilled labor. For this purpose, the basic model is extended to two types of labor in chapter 5. Whereas unskilled labor is only employed in production, high-skilled workers can be employed in *both* production *and* non-production work. The role of skilled labor in non-production work cannot be dealt with in standard models with skilled and unskilled labor as production inputs. The analysis in chapter 5 will show that the use of high-skilled non-production workers for the organization of work is the key factor through which aggregate employment and relative wage rates are related to the supply of skills.

[5] For another example of a skill-bias model which focuses on non-production versus production labor in an analysis of growth and distribution see Grossmann [29].

[6] Defined for instance by Howell and Wolff ([32], p. 488) as "the relative authority, autonomy, and degree of responsibility (for people and things) required on the job".

1.5 Other sources of unemployment

Unemployment has been the central issue in the macroeconomic tradition initiated by Keynes [37] and Kalecki [35, 36]. Their theory of effective demand has shown that income and employment may be rationed by pessimistic investment demand rather than by capacity boundaries.[7] This author has no doubt that effective demand remains an important source of employment fluctuations.

The organization of work and its impacts on the macroeconomic equilibrium are long-run phenomena. Thus, the relevant question is if there are structural reasons for why employment at an organized work place may be a problem also when effective demand doesn't fall short of the provided capacity. As is shown in chapter 3 (and, in a more general framework including capital and savings, in chapter 7) the unemployment equilibrium derived in this study represents a *best-case benchmark.* If the firm owners are pessimistic, additional unemployment arises in the macroeconomic equilibrium. The same is true, if other imperfections like wage rigidities or firm-owner rents distort the economy.

The equilibrium model of this study also disregards problems of asymmetric information or trading frictions which are central in other modern theories of unemployment. In contrast to efficiency-wage models, no selection or incentive problems are considered here. All firms have access to the same composition of labor force and there are no hidden actions of workers. The reduction of agency issues to a problem of asymmetric information takes it for granted that work quality is a question of monitoring in the sense of establishing incentive schemes. However, to integrate workers successfully into an organization requires coordination and supervision in the direct sense of non-production resources that have to be devoted to the support and control of workers and their interactions. The approach in this study is not to give the most realistic picture of a market economy but to bring out the macroeconomic implications of the idea that employment means a place in an organization as sharply as possible. For this methodological purpose, the theoretical framework of an ideal market economy with rational agents, no asymmetric information and no wage rigidities is used. Moreover, there are no transaction costs of individual employment contracts. No turnover costs of hiring or firing single workers are separating insiders and outsiders (Lindbeck and Snower [43, 44]). There are also no trading frictions in the labor market like in search equilibrium models (Diamond [21], Pissarides [53]). The internal interaction of different workers requires an organizational infrastructure which depends on the number and the types of employed units of labor. The employed non-production resources define a firm's capacity to organize

[7] The underlying coordination failure has been worked out by the so-called disequilibrium theories (Clower [18], Barro and Grossman [6], Malinvaud [47]) and quantity-constrained equilibrium models (see Drèze [23] for a survey).

work. Within the limits of a given organizational capacity employment can be freely adjusted (e.g. to unanticipated shocks) and workers can be hired and fired without costs. But the organizational capacity can only be adjusted by employing non-production inputs. Thus, the profit-maximizing choice of the organizational capacity determines how many and which types of workers can find a work place. The provision of work places rather than the mere act of connecting (or disconnecting) a concrete individual to (from) a given work place is the main issue of this analysis.

The theoretical reason why not all workers may have a work place in equilibrium is that only internally organized collectives of individuals, the firms, can compete in modern markets. It lies in the nature of a firm as internal organization of interactions that individual characteristics of workers, in particular their abilities!interactive, have spillovers on other workers employed in the same firm. As will be shown, this implies internal and external scale effects which cannot be fully internalized in market prices and wages. In particular, the costs of organizing work places for workers with low interactive abilities may not be covered by the market. These abilities are formed by primary socialization, education and work experience. Obviously, they also vary with age. Thus, concerning the structure of unemployment the equilibrium model developed in this study explains in a natural way why persons with poor education, young people who have not yet become acquainted with disciplining work, long-term unemployed who have lost their experience to work, or older workers who have difficulties to cope with new forms of work organization and communication are expected to be overrepresented among those who don't find a work place.

1.6 Main result and organization of the book

This is a theoretical work. That means it is an attempt to capture an idea in an abstract model and to work out its implications. The quality of a theoretical model is not to be a one-to-one picture of real world situations. This would imply an own model for each problem and situation which is the exact opposite of what theoretical reasoning is about. The quality test for a theory is whether it grasps essential features of the real world. The real phenomenon that this study wants to model is that work must be organized and business and competition take place between organized "players" (companies), not between isolated individuals. The idea is that an adequate analysis of this feature of economic reality requires a macroeconomic model in which the employment of non-production inputs in an organization technology is a prerequisite of production. The task of the theoretical analysis is to work out the logical implications of this idea and to see how far one gets in explaining macroeconomic problems, in particular joblessness. The claim is that the insights produced by focussing on work organization in the general perspective of a macroeconomic equilibrium model rather than from the partial view of single firms or industries are rich and worth to be studied.

The main result of the analysis is that despite flexible wages workers with low abilities may find no job in the macroeconomic equilibrium. This result is derived in chapter 2. Moreover, under fairly reasonable conditions, the equilibrium employment level is lower than the efficient employment level. This means, that involuntary unemployment does not coincide with unemployability from an efficiency point of view. Also workers who are employable in the sense that it would be productive to integrate them into the employed work force may remain jobless. This result is derived in chapter 3. Moreover, chapter 3 gives a detailed discussion of the relationship between the unemployment equilibrium explained by the presented theory and other sources of unemployment. Chapter 4 applies the model to the analysis of how changes in the organization of work affect the macroeconomic equilibrium. It turns out that it is important to distinguish between dominating and non-dominating reorganization technologies. In the first case, we have always total reorganization and aggregate employment is increased by reorganization. In the latter case, total or partial reorganization may result in equilibrium and aggregate employment in the reorganization equilibrium is lower than under traditional organization of work. Chapter 5 extends the analysis to a segmented labor market with high-skilled workers who can be employed in production as well as in non-production activities and low-skilled labor which can only be used in production. It is shown that an increase in the supply of high-skilled labor does not drive out low-skilled labor but allows a higher level of employment of low-skilled workers. Chapter 6 introduces capital and analyzes the role of capital for the creation of jobs. Moreover, the effects of market power of capital owners on employment and the impacts of international capital mobility are discussed. Liberalization of international capital markets may be good or bad for job creation. Whether world employment rises or declines and employment disparities are enhanced or dampened, depends on the reasons why the different locations are more or less attractive for firms. Chapter 7 addresses the role of savings and accumulation and works out the notion of a demand-constrained two-stage equilibrium. This provides new foundation of the role of pessimistic expectations of investors for the macroeconomic activity level. A detailed summary of the results is given in chapter 8.

2. The basic model

The model presented in this chapter is basic in two respects:[1] First, the model will be extended and applied in the following chapters. Second, it is parsimonious and concentrates on the minimal features that are necessary to capture the macroeconomic consequences of the idea that productive work requires an organized environment and employment means to have a place in this environment. These minimal features are: i) Two stages must be distinguished - a first stage at which the organizational capacity is established, and a second stage at which production and transactions are going on within the organized capacity.[2] ii) There must be some form of imperfect competition at stage 2 so that the non-production costs incurred at stage 1 can be covered by a mark up on production costs. iii) The costs of creating the organizational capacity for productive work must depend on the abilities of the available work force, as compared to the abilities required by the used technologies and methods of organization. iv) The quality of the available work force varies with the level of aggregate employment.

Moreover, the model is as close as possible to an ideal market economy: i) Firms are profit maximizers. ii) In equilibrium, they earn zero profits. iii) Wages are flexible. iv) And all expectations are fulfilled in equilibrium. Deviations from this benchmark are discussed in chapter 3 by considering wage rigidity, rents for firm owners, unanticipated shocks and pessimistic expectations.

2.1 Endowment, technology, demand and market structure

The economy consists of n symmetric firms. The number of firms will play no role for aggregate variables since both the production technology and the organization technology are linear in the inputs of the single firm. In contrast to models of innovation, in which profits are driven down by firm entry, here the expansion of aggregate employment increases the fixed costs of firms

[1] A first version of the model was presented in Falkinger [24].

[2] Section 5.1 will discuss the possibility that in some sectors, e.g. in the provision of services, there is no first stage.

due to external diseconomies of scale in the creation of work places. In the unemployment equilibrium profits are zero.

Firms are organizations which provide the infrastructure that is necessary to transform labor input into saleable products and services. The firm owners have access to an exogenously given technology. This technology consists of two components, an *organization technology* and *production technology*. The production technology describes how labor employed in a firm is transformed into output. Without connection to an organizational infrastructure (i.e. without "workplace in a firm") no production is possible. The organization technology describes how non-production input is transformed into the capacity to organize work for a certain size and quality of work force. The provision of capacity by employing non-production inputs in the organization technology has to take place at stage 1, before production can be started at stage 2 by choosing output and employing labor in production, according to the production technology.

The literature on labor division and coordination (see e.g. Becker and Murphy [7], or Bolton and Dewatripont [11]) emphasizes the interrelations between production and organization technology and focuses on the endogenous explanation of organizational characteristics like degree of labor division or depth of hierarchy. Here the focus is different. What are the macroeconomic implications, in particular for the aggregate level of employment, if firms use a certain type of work organization? And how is the macroeconomic equilibrium affected if there is a general shift in techniques of production and methods of organization, for instance, towards more multitasking of flatter hierarchies? For this purpose technology and technological change is considered as exogenously given. Moreover, the prevailing, i.e. the typical form of work organization is of interest. Therefore, firms are assumed to be symmetric. They cannot choose and pick a specific selection of workers like in the literature on optimal matching and teams (see e.g. Kremer [40, 41] or Lazear [42]). There is only one type of firms and their only choices are, how many work places they organize, how much they produce, and which prices they charge.

2.1.1 Labor supply

Each worker is endowed with certain abilities acquired by birth, general socialization and education. They are exogenous in the model.

Abilities can vary from worker to worker with respect to two dimensions. One dimension concerns individual productivity in the conventional sense of how many units of output a worker produces when (s)he is integrated into a firm. It is assumed that these differences can be transformed into homogeneous quantities and wages are uniform. Thus, in the basic model there are no skill differences in the usual sense. (The distinction between low-skilled and high-skilled labor is taken up in chapter 5.) Total labor supply L^S is normalized to one.

Heterogeneity of workers in this study always refers to the other dimension. This other dimension of abilities concerns those skills which are relevant for the non-production costs which must be incurred to provide work places, i.e. to install the capacity to integrate workers into the firm. Workers differ in their quality as a member of an organization or team. And this quality determines how much resources are necessary to organize work. If the available workers have high social competence and high skills in processing information and communicating with others, if they are versatile and able to take responsibility and to solve problems on their own, then less non-production input is required for coordinating their activities, for learning and training, or marketing the products and services. The variable $z \epsilon [\underline{z}, \bar{z}]$ will be used to measure differences in this dimension of abilities. As a short cut we may also use the label "social skills" or *interactive abilities*.

Symmetry of firms implies that the composition of potential workers is the same for all firms. It is assumed that workers are lined up according to their abilities. Workers with higher interactive abilities are more clever when looking for a job and are thus at the top of the queue. They are the first to find employment. If aggregate employment is $L\,(\leq 1)$, the ability range of employed workers is given by $[z_0(L), \bar{z}]$, where $z_0(L)$ denotes the ability level of the last employed workers. If aggregate employment is high, firms must hire also less able workers so that the quality of the employed work force declines. Thus heterogeneity of workers implies:

$$\frac{dz_0}{dL}(L) < 0 \;\text{ if }\; L < 1. \tag{2.1}$$

(For a homogeneous work force we would have $dz_0/dL = 0$ for all L.)

2.1.2 Organization technology

For being able to organize production work and to sell the output of this work, firm i must employ a certain amount of non-production work. Firms must decide about the employment of non-production resources at stage 1. This determines their organizational capacity. The units of labor employed for non-production activities cannot be used as production input. Production takes place at stage 2 by employing additional units of labor. The volume of production labor that can be employed is limited by the organized capacity[3]. Denote by m_i the units of labor required as non-production input for the organization of production work for $\bar{l}_i$ units of labor. Real examples

[3] This two-stage decision process is familiar in the industrial organization literature. Here it is introduced into a macroeconomic context with monopolistic competition. Although the organizational capacity is fixed at the stage of competition it is endogenously determined in a prior stage. A systematic analysis of endogenous sunk costs in the context of industrial organization was provided by Sutton[63, 64]

for non-production activities would be the hours of work spent on coordination, supervision, communication and training, or on any other efforts spent on generating a productive environment for production and good relationships to the customers. The important point is that, compared to production work, these non-production efforts are to be made on a longer-term basis. They determine the capacity of a firm.

The non-production requirements m_i depend of course on the used methods of production and organization. (Later, comparative static results about the impact of technological changes are derived.) But the requirements of organizing production work depend also on the interactive abilities of the employed work force. Organizing work of less able workers is more difficult, that means, it requires higher non-production resources. The crucial point is that by the nature of internal organization of interactions the interactive abilities of workers have many external effects on other workers. They depend on the characteristics of the whole workforce employed in the firm, for instance, on the average quality of the workforce or on other "aggregators" of individual abilities. In any case, since symmetry implies that each firm has access to the same composition of workforce and more able individuals were assumed to find employment first, the quality of the workforce available to firms declines if the range of employed workers is expanded. For any given distribution of abilities, the composition of the work force which is available for a firm is determined by the range $[z_0(L), \bar{z}]$, where z_0 decreases with L, according to (2.1). Thus, the non-production input m_i which must be employed to provide a capacity of $\bar{l}_i$ units of production work is an increasing function of aggregate employment L. Assuming constant returns to scale in the provision of capacity, we have, for a given distribution of abilities and a given type of techniques represented by γ, the relationship

$$m_i = g(L, \gamma)\, \bar{l}_i \tag{2.2}$$

with $\partial g / \partial L > 0$ if $L < 1$ and workers are heterogeneous. γ changes if for given abilities the skills required from workers change by a switch to different techniques of production and work organization, or if for a given technology the abilities of the labor force change, for instance, by education or for demographic reasons.

The linearity assumption in (2.2) will guarantee zero profits in the derived macroeconomic equilibrium. The level of employment of non-production input m_i is fixed ex post (at stage 2). But ex ante (at stage 1) it is proportional to the installed capacity. The individual firm takes the quality of the available work force and thus the non-production input coefficient $g(L, \gamma)$ as given independently of its own decisions. The diseconomies of scale resulting from $\partial g / \partial L > 0$ are external to the individual firm.[4] Section 2.1.5 will describe how the macroeconomic equilibrium is derived. The firms have correct ex-

[4] This is different from models like Calvo and Wellisz [16], in which rising internal transaction costs limit optimal firm size.

pectations about all aggregate variables and they base their decisions on the assumption that aggregates are not influenced by the individual behavior. Of course, the determination of the macroeconomic equilibrium does not depend on how the organization technology (2.2) is justified. The core element is a cost of generating employment capacity which is increasing in the overall level of employment. Heterogeneous interactive abilities are the reason given here. But any other justification of (2.2) leads to the same conclusions.

2.1.3 Production technology

Within its capacity a firm can vary employment of production work and output according to a linear production function

$$x_i^S = l_i/A \,, \tag{2.3}$$

where x_i^S denotes supplied output and l_i the amount of labor employed in production. $A > 0$ is the constant coefficient of labor. However, labor can be productively employed only to the extent to which the capacity to organize production work was built up by the employment of non-production inputs at stage 1. Thus, (2.3) is subject to the restriction

$$l_i \leqslant \bar{l}_i \,. \tag{2.4}$$

At the aggregate level, (2.4) together with (2.2) imply for employment in production, $L^x \equiv \sum_i l_i$, the restriction

$$L^x \leq \frac{M}{g(L,\gamma)} \tag{2.5}$$

where $M \equiv \sum_i m_i$ is employment in non-production and

$$L = M + L^x \tag{2.6}$$

is total employment (restricted by the supply constraint $L \leq L^S = 1$). The M units of labor employed for non-production activities cannot be used as production input. Thus, the total volume of employed labor is equal to the sum of non-production and production labor. It is assumed that employment of non-production labor M is productive in the sense that the possible level of employment in production, denoted by $\bar{L}^x$, increases with M. According to (2.5) and (2.6), $\bar{L}^x$ is implicitly defined by the equation $\bar{L}^x = M/g\left(M + \bar{L}^x, \gamma\right)$.[5]

[5] Implicit differentiation of $\frac{M}{g\left(M+\bar{L}^x,\gamma\right)} - \bar{L}^x = 0$ gives us the condition $\frac{d\bar{L}^x}{dM} >$ 0 if and only if $\frac{M+\bar{L}^x}{M} \left(= 1 + \frac{1}{g}\right) > \alpha$, where $\alpha \equiv \frac{\partial g}{\partial L}\frac{L}{g}$. Thus, g must not react too elastically to changes in L. We will come back to this condition in 3.1 when efficient employment is discussed. It will be seen that the condition is automatically fulfilled if only persons who are employable from a planer's point of view are included in the labor force.

2.1.4 Demand in the goods market

Since firms can make business only after they have arranged their capacity to organize work, the prices earned from selling the output of production work must also cover the costs of employed non-production work. These costs although variable at stage 1, are sunk at stage 2. This implies some form of imperfect competition in the goods markets at stage 2 with goods prices above marginal cost of production. A natural candidate is monopolistic competition which allows monopoly power of individual firms while retaining the competitive features that each single firm take aggregate variables as given and competition drives profits down to zero in equilibrium. As is known from Dixit and Stiglitz [22], monopolistic competition can be microfounded by assuming that preferences can be represented by a CES-index

$$U(x_1, ..., x_n) = \left[\sum_{i=1}^{n} x_i^{\rho}\right]^{1/\rho} \tag{2.7}$$

where $0 < \rho < 1$ and x_i denotes the consumed quantity of the good supplied by firm i.

Let Y be aggregate money income which is exogenously determined by the money supply and the velocity of circulation of money. Then, for given goods prices $p_1, ..., p_n$, maximization of (2.7) subject to the budget constraint

$$\sum_{i=1}^{n} p_i x_i = Y \tag{2.8}$$

gives us for the aggregate demand of good i the function

$$x_i^D(p_i) = \left(\frac{p_i}{P}\right)^{-\sigma} \frac{Y}{P} \tag{2.9}$$

where $\sigma \equiv \frac{1}{1-\rho}$ is the elasticity of substitution between products of the different firms and $P \equiv \left[\sum_{i=1}^{n} p_i^{1-\sigma}\right]^{\frac{1}{1-\sigma}}$ is a price index.

If all firms charge the same price $p_1 = ... = p_n = p$, equation (2.9) reduces to

$$x_i^D = x^D = \frac{Y}{np}. \tag{2.10}$$

2.1.5 Firm behavior and equilibrium

The aim of the firms is to earn profits by hiring labor for producing output and by selling this output to the market. However, they have to employ non-production work at stage 1 for preparing the capacity to participate in the monopolistic competition at stage 2 . According to the notion of monopolistic competition, the individual firms assume that aggregate variables are not influenced by their decisions. In equilibrium, the aggregate values resulting from the simultaneous individual decisions must coincide with the expectations on which the individual decisions have been based.

In a loose formulation – the formal details of the two-stage equilibrium are elaborated below – the basic mechanism determining the level of employment is the following: At stage 1 each firm faces an "investment" problem when having to decide about m_i, the amount of non-production labor used to arrange the capacity for organizing production work. The cost per unit of employed non-production labor is wage rate w, the created capacity is $1/g(L,\gamma)$ in terms of work places for production labor, and $1/[g(L,\gamma)A]$ in terms of final output. The return is the profit earned in stage 2 from producing within the limits of the arranged capacity in a monopolistic way. Unit costs of production are wA and unit profits are determined by the constant mark-up factor $\mu = 1/(1-1/\sigma)$ implied by (2.9). They are $(\mu-1)wA$ per unit of sold output and $(\mu-1)w/g(L,\gamma)$ per unit of "invested" non-production labor. Comparing this return on the employed non-production input to its costs, firms will provide work places until $(\mu-1)w/g(L,\gamma) = w$. This determines the equilibrium level of aggregate employment L. The further analysis elaborates the details of this argument more formally.

The exogenous parameters of the model are: Money income Y, demand parameter σ, production technology parameter A and organization technology parameter γ. (Labor supply L^S was normalized to one). The macroeconomic variables which are endogenously determined by the model are: The price level P, the aggregate production level L^x (and thus total output $X = L^x/A$), the level of aggregate employment in non-production and total employment, M and $L = M + L^x$, respectively, and the wage rate w. Remember that in the basic model there is only one type of labor which is homogeneous as far as isolated individual productivity is concerned. The heterogeneity is bound to the interactive abilities affecting organization costs. However, this impact cannot be internalized in individualized wages since it is the average quality of the employees which matters. One may argue that nonetheless non-production labor may get a different wage than production workers. This would not change the conclusions provided that the wage of non-production workers does not fall below the wage of production workers (see chapter 5). Therefore, a uniform wage rate is assumed in the basic model. The equilibrium values of the endogenous variables P, w, L^x, M, and L are determined as follows:

Section 2.2 derives the goods and labor market equilibrium resulting at stage 2 for given levels of the firms' provision of non-production resources, m_i, and aggregate provision, M. Firms choose for given expectations about the aggregate variables P, w and L (and thus $g(L,\gamma)$) the profit-maximizing values of price p_i, production x_i and employment in production l_i, under the given demand-, technology- and capacity-restrictions. In the goods market equilibrium, the aggregate values of P and L resulting from the simultaneous decisions of individual firms must be equal to the expected values. This determines aggregate price and employment levels as functions $P(w, M)$, $L^x(w, M)$, $L(w, M)$ of the wage rate and the non-production resources invested at stage 1. In the labor market, wage is flexibly adjusted to supply and demand conditions. In equilibrium the wage rate is neither overbidden by firms nor underbidden by workers. This determines the equilibrium wage rate as a function $w(M)$ of aggregate investment M.

In section 2.3, the equilibrium provision of the non-production prerequisites for productive employment is analyzed. Firms anticipate that for a given M the aggregate equilibrium values $P(w(M), M)$, $L^x(w(M), M)$, $L(w(M), M)$ and $w(M)$ result at stage 2. They also know how their profit-maximizing choices of p_i, x_i and l_i at stage 2 depend on the non-production input m_i provided by them at stage 1. Thus, a firm's profit to be expected for stage 2 is a function $\pi^i(m_i, M)$ of own input m_i and aggregate input M. To earn this profit, the firm must incur the cost of m_i units of non-production work. The value of this work is not determined until business and trading take place at stage 2. Firms anticipate the equilibrium wage $w(M)$ and choose the level of m_i so that their expected net profits $\pi^i(m_i, M) - w(M)m_i$ is maximized.[6] In equilibrium, the aggregate value of M resulting from the simultaneous decisions of the individual firms must coincide with the expected M. In section 2.4, the macroeconomic equilibrium is summarized and the role of the exogenous parameters (Y, σ, A and γ) for the equilibrium values of employment, prices and wages is discussed in a systematic way.

2.2 Prices and production in the monopolistic competition equilibrium (stage 2)

Firms enter competition at stage 2 with non-production resources $m_1, ..., m_n$, fixed at stage 1 for creating their capacity to organize production work. According to (2.5) and (2.6), the maximal aggregate level of production work, $\bar{L}^x$, which can be organized by these resources, is implicitly defined by the equation

$$\bar{L}^x = \frac{M}{g(M + \bar{L}^x, \gamma)}, \tag{2.11}$$

with $d\bar{L}^x/dM > 0$. And the maximal possible level of total employment is given by the function

$$\bar{L}(M) = M + \bar{L}^x(M). \tag{2.12}$$

With respect to the maximally employable range of abilities, this implies that work of workers with abilities $z \geq z_0(\bar{L}(M))$ can be organized by the given non-production inputs.

[6] To avoid complications we assume that non-production work signed under contract at stage 1 is paid when cash is made at stage 2. Thus, no cash-in-advance or credit market problems are considered in the model.

We determine now which activity level is actually realized within the capacities provided by the investments $m_1, ..., m_n$. First, goods prices, production levels, and labor demand resulting under monopolistic competition in the goods market are derived for a given wage rate. Then the equilibrium wage rate resulting in the labor market is determined.

2.2.1 The goods market

Individual firms take the aggregate employment levels L^x and $L = M + L^x$ as well as the aggregate price level as given when making their choices. Since the costs of the non-production inputs $m_1, ..., m_n$ are sunk at stage 2, they maximize current profits subject to the demand and capacity restrictions $x_i \leq x_i^D$, $x_i \leq x_i^S$ and $l_i \leq \bar{l}_i$, given by (2.2), (2.3), (2.4) and (2.9). Thus, firm i's maximization problem is:

$$\max_{p_i, x_i, l_i} \pi^i = p_i x_i - w l_i$$

subject to

$$\begin{aligned} x_i &\leq x_i^D \left(= \left(\tfrac{p_i}{P}\right)^{-\sigma} \tfrac{Y}{P}\right) , \\ x_i &\leq x_i^S \quad (= l_i / A) , \\ l_i &\leq \bar{l}_i \quad \left(= \tfrac{m_i}{g(L, \gamma)}\right) . \end{aligned} \tag{2.13}$$

Setting up the Lagrange function

$$\begin{aligned} \pounds \left(p_i, x_i, l_i, \nu_i^D, \nu_i^S, \nu_i\right) = & \left(p_i x_i - w l_i\right) + \nu_I^D \left(x_i^D - x_i\right) \\ & + \nu_i^S \left(x_i^S - x_i\right) + \nu_i \left(\bar{l}_i - l_i\right) \end{aligned} \tag{2.14}$$

with non-negative multipliers ν_i^D, ν_i^S, ν_i, and differentiating with respect to p_i, x_i, l_i, we obtain the Kuhn-Tucker-conditions

$$x_i = \nu_i^D \sigma p_i^{-\sigma-1} Y / P^{1-\sigma} , \tag{2.15}$$

$$p_i = \nu_i^D + \nu_i^S , \tag{2.16}$$

$$\nu_i^S = A (w + \nu_i) , \tag{2.17}$$

and $\nu_i^D \left(x_i - x_i^D\right) = \nu_i^S \left(x_i - x_i^S\right) = \nu_i \left(l_i - \bar{l}_i\right) = 0$. Obviously, firms sell as much as they can, i.e. they choose $x_i = x_i^D$. (Formally, $\nu_i^D > 0$, according to (2.15), so that the corresponding restriction is binding). Substituting x_i^D from (2.9) for x_i in (2.15), we get: $\nu_i^D = p_i / \sigma$. Using this in (2.16), we have $\nu_i^S = p_i (1 - 1/\sigma) > 0$. This and (2.17) imply

$$p_i = \mu (w + \nu_i) A , \tag{2.18}$$

where $\mu \equiv \frac{\sigma}{\sigma-1}$ is determined by the degree of monopoly in the goods market.

ν_i is the Lagrange multiplier corresponding to the capacity restriction $l_i \leq \bar{l}_i$. Thus, as long as this restriction does not limit the firm's decision, we have $\nu_i = 0$ and

$$p_i = p = \mu w A \,. \tag{2.19}$$

This is the usual mark-up pricing formula.

How do we know whether the firm's optimal policy at stage 2 is limited by its choice of non-production resources at stage 1? This depends on the chosen m_i and on aggregate demand. If $\nu_i > 0$, then $x_i = \bar{x}_i \equiv \bar{l}_i/A$. In view of demand function (2.9), this capacity output can be sold if[7] $p_i = [D(P,L)/m_i]^{1/\sigma}$, where D defined by

$$D(P,L) \equiv \frac{AYg(L,\gamma)}{P^{1-\sigma}} \tag{2.20}$$

is an expression which summarizes the impact of aggregate variables on the firm's situation. Using this in (2.18), we have

$$\nu_i = \frac{[D(P,L)/m_i]^{1/\sigma}}{\mu A} - w \,. \tag{2.21}$$

Thus, $\nu_i > 0$ is only possible, if the wage rate is below a certain level, otherwise we have $\nu_i = 0$. Formally,

$$\nu_i = \begin{cases} 0 & \text{if } w \geq \widetilde{w}_i \\ \widetilde{w}_i - w & \text{if } w < \widetilde{w}_i \end{cases} \tag{2.22}$$

with $\widetilde{w}_i = [D(P,L)/m_i]^{1/\sigma}/(\mu A)$.

For non-symmetric firms with different m_i's it is not possible to calculate the equilibrium values of P, L^x and L explicitly (see Appendix A). However, in the analysis of profit-maximizing behavior at stage 1 (see section 2.3) it will turn out that all firms choose the same level of non-production input. Thus, ν_i, p_i, x_i and l_i are identical for all firms, and we have the following solution for the goods market:[8]

Goods prices are

---

[7] $\bar{x}_i = x_i^D$ is equivalent to $p_i = \left(\frac{Y}{\bar{x}_i P^{1-\sigma}}\right)^{1/\sigma}$. Using $\bar{x}_i = \bar{l}_i/A$ and (2.2), we can rewrite this in the form $p_i = \left(\frac{AYg(L,\gamma)}{P^{1-\sigma} m_i}\right)^{1/\sigma}$.

[8] Budget restriction (2.8) reduces to $pL^x/A = Y$. This gives us $p = AY/L^x$. For $w \geq \widetilde{w}$, (2.22) and (2.18) give us $p = \mu w A$ and thus $L^x = Y/(\mu w)$. For $w < \widetilde{w}$, the proof is as follows: Using $P^{1-\sigma} = np^{1-\sigma}$, $p = AY/L^x$ and (2.11) (with $M = nm$) in (2.20) and (2.21), we obtain on the one hand $D(P,L)/m_i = (AY)^\sigma (L^x)^{1-\sigma}/\bar{L}^x$ and $\widetilde{w} = w + \nu = \frac{Y(L^x/\bar{L}^x)^{1/\sigma}}{L^x \mu}$. On the other hand, $p = AY/L^x$ and (2.18) imply $\widetilde{w} = p/(\mu A) = Y/(\mu L^x)$. Setting the two $\widetilde{w}$-expressions equal, we have $L^x = \bar{L}^x$, $\widetilde{w} = Y/(\mu \bar{L}^x)$ and $p = AY/\bar{L}^x$.

$$p_i = p = \begin{cases} \mu w A & \text{if } w \geq \widetilde{w} \\ \frac{AY}{\bar{L}^x(M)} & \text{if } w < \widetilde{w} \end{cases} \tag{2.23}$$

and aggregate production (measured by the labor input $L^x = AX$, $X \equiv \sum_i x_i = nx$)is:

$$L^x = \begin{cases} \frac{Y}{\mu w} & \text{if } w \geq \widetilde{w} , \\ \bar{L}^x (M) & \text{if } w < \widetilde{w} , \end{cases} \tag{2.24}$$

where

$$\widetilde{w} = \frac{Y}{\mu \bar{L}^x} \tag{2.25}$$

and $\bar{L}^x (M)$ is determined by (2.11).

This characterizes price policy and production level as a function of M and w, the non-production resources employed at stage 1, and the wage rate resulting in the labor market, respectively. The intuition behind (2.23) and (2.24) is easy. If firms charge the mark-up price given by (2.19), aggregate demand is $nx^D = Y/(\mu w A)$, according to (2.10). If $w < \widetilde{w}$, this is more than their capacity $(n\bar{x}\bar{L}^x/A)$ allows to supply. Thus, higher prices are charged and capacity is fully used. As long as $w \geq \widetilde{w}$, existing capacity is not rationing the demand resulting at prices $p = \mu w A$. To the contrary, for $w > \widetilde{w}$, demand falls short of capacity so that less labor is employed in production than the installed capacity would allow.

2.2.2 The labor market

For a given wage rate w, demand for labor in production is equal to L^x defined by (2.24). In addition, there is employment M in non-production work. The level of M has been already chosen at stage 1 and cannot be adjusted in reaction to wage rate changes in stage 2.[9] Thus, total labor demand is given by

$$L^D = \begin{cases} M + \frac{Y}{\mu w} , & \text{if } w \geq \widetilde{w} , \\ \bar{L} \left(= M + \bar{L}^x (M)\right) , & \text{if } w < \widetilde{w}. \end{cases} \tag{2.26}$$

Figure 2.1 illustrates this labor demand function (with the nominal wage rate on the ordinate and total employment on the abscissa).

At wages higher than $\widetilde{w}$, firms do not fully use their capacity of organizing production work. Therefore, a decrease in the nominal wage rate increases employment (An increase in money income Y by expanding the supply of money would have the same effect). This is a familiar mechanism. However, if $\widetilde{w}$ is reached a further decrease of wages does no longer stimulate labor demand. The reason is that firms have provided no capacity to organize additional work. We could also say there are no additional places in the arranged

[9] When deciding about M at stage 1, firms take the equilibrium wage rate resulting in the labor market at stage 2 into account. But they cannot adjust the M-choice ex post. Moreover, it will turn out in section 2.3 that the equilibrium value of M at stage 1 does not depend on the value of the equilibrium wage rate.

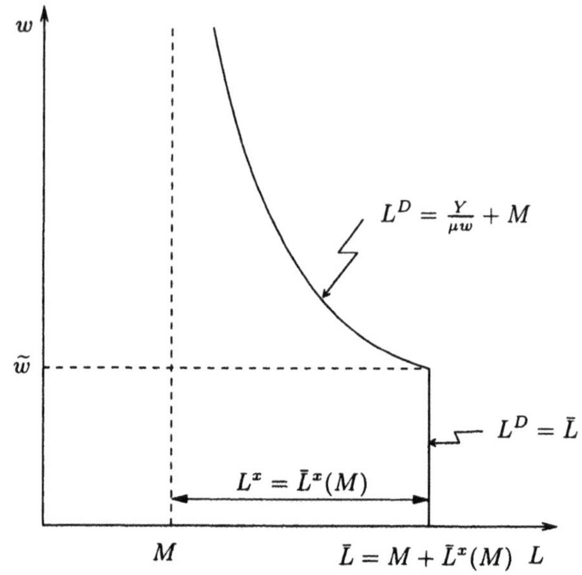

Fig. 2.1. Labor demand

organizations and networks called firms. Since such a place is essential for transforming labor input into saleable outputs, there is no productive use for labor units beyond $\bar{L}$, whatever their wage rate.

The vertical segment of the labor demand curve determines not only the maximal quantity of labor that is employed, but also the maximal range of employed abilities: $[z_0(\bar{L}(M)), \bar{z}]$, where $dz_0/dL < 0$, according to (2.1). Workers are employed in the order of their abilities (Remember that only differences which can not be individualized are considered). From the discussion of the organization technology in section 2.1 we know that the amount of labor which can be organized by a given volume of non-production inputs depends on the used technology but also on the quality of the employed work force. According to (2.11) and (2.12), an aggregate level of non-production work M allows total employment of $\bar{L}(M)$ units of labor with abilities of $z \geq z_0(\bar{L}(M))$. No provisions have been made at stage 1 to organize work of workers with abilities lower than $z_0(\bar{L}(M))$. This can mean the firms' provisions for training or, more generally, human resource development and corporate socialization programs are not prepared to deal with them. It can also mean that the arranged facilities of coordinating production activities or of marketing output are not prepared for labor of quality below $z_0(\bar{L}(M))$.

The equilibrium wage rate is determined by comparison of labor demand with labor supply. We start with the case of full employment and look then at situations with unemployment. Full employment requires that the resources M invested at stage 1 are high enough to allow an employment level $\bar{L}(M)$

which is not lower than labor supply $L^S = 1$.[10] This situation is illustrated in figure 2.2.

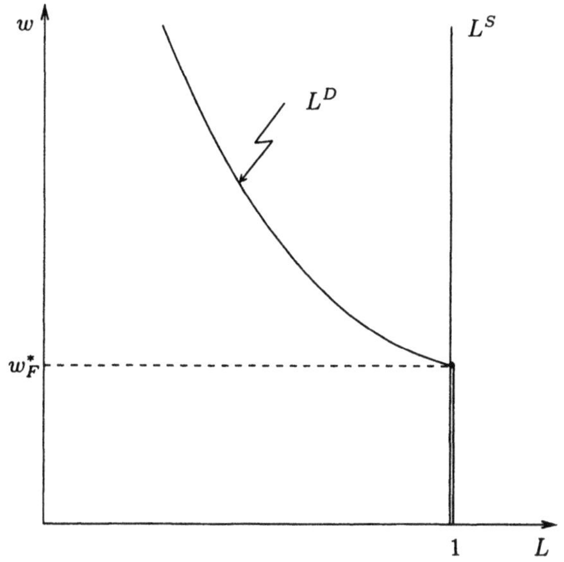

Fig. 2.2. Equilibrium wage rate (Full employment).

With flexible wages unemployed workers can successfully underbid wages as long as $w > w_F^*$. Since the firms have created enough work place capacity, they expand employment when wages decline. As soon as the wage rate w^* is reached, there is no worker left who could underbid the wage. Thus, w^* is the equilibrium wage rate.

The picture changes if $\bar{L}(M) < L^S$. This is shown in figure 2.3. Again, if wages are flexible, wage rates above $\widetilde{w}$ are underbid by unemployed labor. But as soon as $\widetilde{w}$ (defined by (2.25)) is reached, further underbidding is unsuccessful. Employment would not increase if wages declined below $\widetilde{w}$.

There is still unemployed labor willing to work at lower wages. But firms have provided no capacity to integrate this unemployed labor. No "work place" has been arranged at stage 1 for the job seeking units of labor beyond the level $\bar{L}(M)$. There is not only no place for additional workers but there is also no place for qualities outside the employed range $\left[z_0\left(\bar{L}(M)\right), \bar{z}\right]$. Thus, the unemployed labor force whose quality lies below z_0 cannot substitute employed workers. In sum, workers with abilities $z \geq z_0\left(\bar{L}(M)\right)$ are not willing to underbid $\widetilde{w}$, workers with abilities below $z_0\left(\bar{L}(M)\right)$ are not able

[10] Actually it will be equal, since firms do not provide work for a non-existing labor force $\left(\bar{L}(M) \leq 1\right)$.

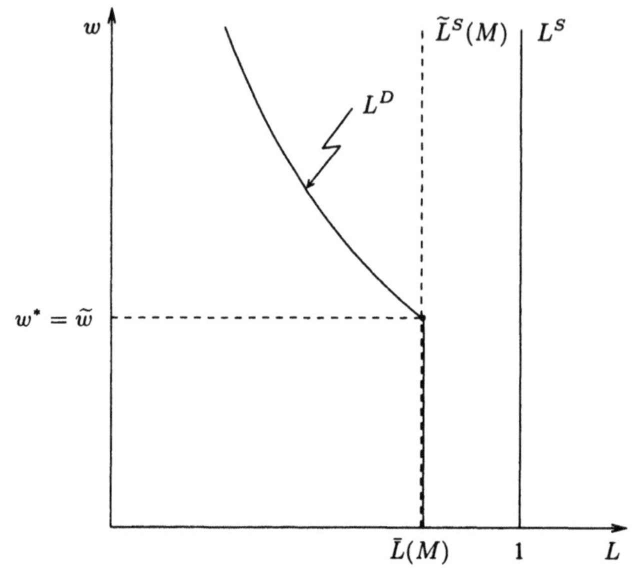

Fig. 2.3. Equilibrium wage rate (Unemployment).

to underbid $\widetilde{w}$ successfully, and firms have no interest to overbid $\widetilde{w}$. Therefore, the wage rate

$$w^* = \widetilde{w} = \frac{Y}{\mu \bar{L}^x(M)}, \tag{2.27}$$

is an equilibrium.

The reason why the labor market is not cleared at the equilibrium wage rate could also be formulated in the following way. The level of non-production labor M employed for the organization of work defines how much and which labor is employable in the sense that it can be integrated into the organized work. As a consequence, the effective labor force at stage 2 is not L^S, but that part which is employable in view of the firms' provisions at stage 1. In figure 2.3, this effective labor force is represented by the line $\widetilde{L}^S(M) = \bar{L}(M)$. With this line the picture is the same as in figure 2.2. The effective labor force is fully employed in the unemployment equilibrium with flexible wages. The important point is, that employability or effective labor force are not given by nature or voluntary choice of workers, but determined by the job provision decisions of firms. Ex ante, the whole labor force L^S is employable. Ex post, after firms have made their non-production provisions for organizing and marketing production work, those workers are employable for whom a place has been provided at which they can be productively employed. The next section analyzes how many such places are provided by profit maximizing firms.

2.3 The equilibrium provision of work places (stage 1)

Modern competition is characterized by the fact that companies and other forms of internal organizations interact in the markets rather than isolated individuals. Earning income in modern markets of products and services requires to be connected to such an organization. In this abstract sense, workers can sell their labor service only by being employed at a "work place" in a firm. Work places are provided by the firms' employment of non-production resources m_i, which determine the capacity of organizing work and making business in monopolistic competition. We first show that in view of the goods market situation analyzed in section 2.2 all firms choose the same level of non-production resources $m_i = m$. Then we derive the equilibrium volume of input m (and thus $M = nm$) under the assumption that firms anticipate the implied symmetric equilibrium at stage 2 correctly. Again, firms make their individual decisions under the assumption that the aggregate level of M is not influenced by their behavior.

When firms decide over m_i at stage 1, they anticipate the outcome of stage 2. According to the analysis in section 2.2, this outcome is as follows: For any $M \leq \bar{M}$, where $\bar{M}$ is the level of non-production input leading to full employment (i.e. $\bar{L}(\bar{M}) = L^S = 1$), monopolistic competition in the goods market leads to aggregate levels of prices $P(M,w)$, production and employment $L^x(M,w)$, $L(M,w)$ determined by the profit-maximizing behavior of the firm and the prevailing wage rate w. According to (2.18) and (2.21), the price that firm i realizes for its product when investing m_i is given by

$$p_i(m_i) = \left(\frac{D(P,L)}{m_i}\right)^{1/\sigma}, \tag{2.28}$$

where P, L are aggregate variables on which firm i has no influence.

The capacity output of a firm investing m_i is given by

$$\bar{x}_i^S(m_i) = \frac{m_i}{g(L,\gamma)A}, \tag{2.29}$$

according to (2.2) - (2.4). Since wages are expected to be flexible at stage 2, each firm can expect full capacity utilization, as long as $L < L^S$ (i.e. $M < \bar{M}$).[11] $L < L^S$ means that unemployed people are looking for a job and underbidding wages until all work places are occupied.

Thus, a firm which chooses m_i units of non-production work at stage 1 can expect gross profits

$$\pi_i = (p_i(m_i) - wA)\,\bar{x}_i^S(m_i) \tag{2.30}$$

[11] At $M = \bar{M}$, firms expect full employment and don't plan to expand capacity.

at stage 2. However, also the employed non-production work must be paid out of these profits. Therefore, net profits as a function of m_i are given by[12]

$$\pi_i^n = (p_i(m_i) - wA)\,\bar{x}_i^S(m_i) - wm_i\,. \tag{2.31}$$

Since all firms are confronted with the same macroeconomic variables P, L and w, maximization of (2.31), in view of (2.28) and (2.29), leads to identical choices of $m_i = m$ for all i. Thus, we have a symmetric equilibrium, in which, according to (2.27), $w = w^*\,(= \widetilde{w}) = \frac{Y}{\mu \bar{L}(M)}$ and thus, according to (2.23), $p_i = p = \mu w^* A$. Using this and (2.29) in (2.30), we obtain for the gross profits to be expected for stage 2 by a firm investing m_i at stage 1:

$$\pi_i = (\mu - 1)\,\frac{w^* m_i}{g(L,\gamma)}\,. \tag{2.32}$$

And net profit function (2.31) reduces to

$$\pi_i^n = w^* m_i \left[\frac{\mu - 1}{g(L,\gamma)} - 1\right], \tag{2.33}$$

where $L = \bar{L}(M) \leq L^S\,(=1)$ is determined by aggregate non-production input M, according to (2.12). This implies[13]

$$\frac{d\pi_i^n}{dm_i} >,=,< 0 \text{ if } \mu - 1 \;>,=,< g\left(\bar{L}(M),\gamma\right)\,. \tag{2.34}$$

Firms wish to expand their non-production resources m_i, as long as the real return $\mu - 1\left(= \frac{\pi^i}{w\bar{l}_i}\right)$ per unit of capacity $\bar{l}_i$ is higher than the input $g\,(= m_i/\bar{l}_i)$ of non-production work which is required to provide a unit of capacity. If return $\mu - 1$ is lower than cost g, then they reduce the investment m_i. An equilibrium is reached if for $M = \sum_i m_i = nm$ with $\bar{L}(M) \leq L^S\,(=1)$.

$$\mu - 1 = g\left(\bar{L}(M)\gamma\right) \tag{2.35}$$

so that no firm wants to change its capacity m, or if

$$\bar{L}(M) = 1 \tag{2.36}$$

---

[12] In chapter 5, a separate category of high-skilled workers is introduced. Only they can be employed in non-production and they get higher wages than low-skilled labor. This extension will not change the basic logic of the argument. The essential point is that the value of all work is determined by competition and business results at stage 2. If non-production workers get some agio over the wage w paid for production work, a relatively lower level of investment in job creation (M) results. But the way in which the equilibrium is determined is exactly the same.

[13] $g(0,\gamma) < \mu - 1$ is assumed. Otherwise there would be no activity in the economy.

so that full employment is reached and no firm can increase profits by creating additional work place capacity.[14] In the first case, we have zero profits in equilibrium since the square bracketed term in (2.33) vanishes if equality holds in condition (2.34). Moreover, if (2.35) holds for $\bar{L}(M) = M + \bar{L}^x(M) < 1$, we have an equilibrium in which not all people get a job despite flexible wage adjustment in the labor market. They are involuntarily unemployed and would supply their work even at zero wages. But firms are not prepared to integrate them into their organization. The properties and implications of this unemployment equilibrium are the central issue of the further discussion.

2.4 The macroeconomic equilibrium: Summary and discussion

Firms choose the level of non-production input at stage 1. This choice determines their capacity as "players" in the monopolistic competition taking place at stage 2. The aggregate variables are the result of the individual decisions, but firms take them as given when making their choices. An equilibrium is reached if the aggregate variables resulting from the individual decisions are those on which the individual decisions have been based. It has been shown that a symmetric equilibrium arises in the presented model.

At stage 2, the aggregate equilibrium variables are determined as functions of aggregate employment M of non-production inputs required for the organization of business. Equilibrium employment in production is $\bar{L}^x(M)$, determined by (2.11). The equilibrium wage rate is $w^* = \frac{Y}{\mu \bar{L}^x(M)}$, according to (2.27), and the equilibrium goods prices are $p^* = \mu w^* A$, according to (2.23). At stage 1, the equilibrium level of non-production work M^* is determined by the equations (2.35) and (2.36). Finally, total equilibrium employment is given by the sum $L^* = M^* + \bar{L}^x(M^*)$.

For the discussion of the comparative-static properties of the macroeconomic equilibrium we write the equilibrium employment level L^*, the price level p^* and the real wage rate w^*/p^* as functions of the exogenous parameters A, γ, μ and Y.

2.4.1 Equilibrium employment

By definition (2.12), total employment $L^* = M^* + \bar{L}^x(M^*)$ is equal to $\bar{L}(M^*)$. Thus, total equilibrium employment is implicitly defined by condition (2.35) or equal to full employment. We can write this in the form

[14] To find workers for the additional capacity a firm would have to overbid the prevailing wage. But according to (2.18) and (2.22), a wage above $w^* = \widetilde{w}$ implies a higher profit-maximizing price and a smaller market for the firm. Thus, the firm could not use its additional capacity and profits would decline.

$$L^* = \min\{L_O(\gamma,\mu), 1\} , \tag{2.37}$$

where $L_O(\gamma,\mu)$ is the implicit function defined by

$$g(L_O,\gamma) = \mu - 1 \tag{2.38}$$

with $\partial L_O/\partial\mu > 0$. If $g(L_O,\gamma) < \mu - 1$ for all L_O, we set $L_O(\gamma,\mu)$ equal to infinity.[15]

In an unemployment equilibrium, the level of employment increases with the degree of monopoly $\mu \left(= \frac{\sigma}{\sigma-1}\right)$ in the goods market. The reason is that with a lower elasticity of demand firms can charge higher prices and earn more profit per unit of organized production work. Thus, they have a higher incentive to invest in the provision of work places. A larger capacity of organizing production work means that also less able workers must be employed for full utilization of the capacity. But with a high μ, firms can afford the non-production resources which are necessary to organize work of people who are less "organizable".

The result that equilibrium employment increases with the degree of monopoly may seem surprising. To avoid misinterpretations two caveats are in order. First, the degree of monopoly reflects only changes in the price-cost margin. In reality, the increase in market power often goes hand in hand with other phenomena, in particular technological changes. For instance, the mergers and takeovers in the ongoing process of concentration in many industries are certainly accompanied by fundamental reorganizations of work. In our model, this would mean that parallel to an increase in the price-cost margin reflected in μ the parameter γ may be changed in a way that leads to a decrease of employment, since more complex companies require higher ("social") skills. A discussion of the principal role of organization technology for employment follows in the next paragraph and a more detailed analysis of observed trends in the reorganization of work can be found in chapter 4. The second caveat concerns the relationship between competitiveness and market power. The presented model is as close as possible to a competitive market economy. Firms earn zero profits in the unemployment equilibrium. Thus, any increase in gross profits due to a higher degree of monopoly in the goods market is invested in the creation of work places. In reality, market power is often related to rents. This means there is some market power *in addition* to the power of firms in goods market. Such market power may come from imperfect capital markets. So far there is no capital in the model (It will be introduced in chapter 6). But it is clear that a higher degree of monopoly in the goods market will not lead to the predicted increase in employment if the higher price-cost margin is used to pay more rents to the firm owners rather than to invest more in the provision of work places. Obviously, market distortions by rents induce deviations from the benchmark characterized by

[15] Obviously, we must have $g(0,\gamma) < \mu - 1$ in a viable economy. Otherwise equilibrium employment would be zero.

the equilibrium in the basic model. Chapter 3 analyzes such deviations more systematically.

The second parameter determining the equilibrium level of employment is γ, which represents, for a given quality of the labor force, the non-production requirements implied by the used organization technology. Figure 2.4 illustrates the employment equilibrium for two different organization technologies $g(L, \gamma)$ and $g(L, \gamma')$.

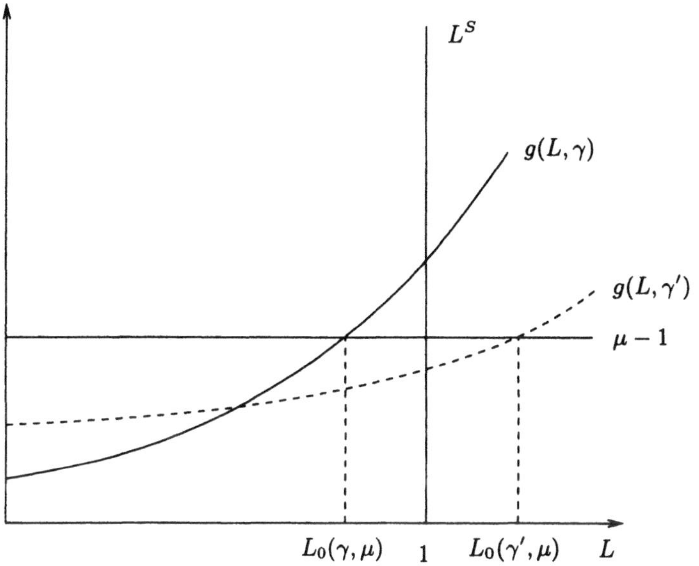

Fig. 2.4. Equilibrium employment.

With γ' we have $g(1, \gamma') < \mu - 1$ and thus a full employment equilibrium, according to (2.37).[16] With γ we have an unemployment equilibrium $L^* = L^0(\gamma, \mu)$. In this case, the organization technology is such that, given the abilities of the labor force, the least-able workers cannot be profitably employed by the firms. An employment level above $L_0(\gamma, \mu)$ would imply that, due to the lower quality of the employed work force, the non-production requirement per unit of production work $(g(L, \gamma))$ is higher than the return per organized unit of work $(\mu - 1)$. The fact that it is not profitable to the firms to organize work for less able workers does of course not mean that those who remain jobless are unemployable by nature or that providing jobs for them would be inefficient from a planner's point of view. The difference between an unemployment equilibrium, resulting according to this study in a

[16] If workers were homogeneous with respect to interactive abilities, the g-curve would be flat and full employment would arise.

market economy, and unemployability or efficient employment is elaborated in the next chapter.

The situations illustrated in figure 2.4 show that organization technologies cannot be ranked by the ratio of non-production to production work without reference to the aggregate level of employment. For instance, the technology represented by γ is a "lean organization" with relatively low non-production labor requirements as long as few and able people are employed under this organization technology. Such a situation may arise if single companies start to implement decentralized structures in which clever people are coordinated through sophisticated communication networks. But when the entire economy is reorganized so that also less clever people are to be organized in this way, then the coordination, supervision and training requirements may rise substantially so that the technology represented by γ requires relatively high non-production inputs and leaves individuals jobless whose employment under the new organization technology would be too difficult. Chapter 4 analyzes the macroeconomic implications of current trends in reorganizing work by considering such processes more carefully.

2.4.2 The ratio of non-production labor to labor in production

For any given technology, the ratio of aggregate non-production work M^* to aggregate employment in production $\bar{L}^x(M^*)$ is characterized by the equation

$$\frac{M^*}{\bar{L}^x(M^*)} = g(\min\{L_0(\gamma,\mu),1\},\gamma) \ . \tag{2.39}$$

(Use (2.11) and (2.37)).

This shows again that the organization technology influences the observed ratio of non-production workers to production workers in two ways: Through a direct channel γ, and indirectly via the implied equilibrium level of employment L_0. In particular, this ratio depends also on the degree of monopoly μ. Only under full employment the ratio is determined by the direct effect alone. Finally, the aggregate level of employment in non-production work can be calculated by solving the equation $L^* = M^* + \bar{L}^x(M^*)$. Substituting (2.11) for $\bar{L}^x$, we obtain

$$M^* = \frac{L^*}{1 + 1/g(L^*,\gamma)} \ . \tag{2.40}$$

where $dM^*/dL^* > 0$ for $dg/dL \geq 0$.

2.4.3 Equilibrium prices and wages

According to (2.23) and (2.27), the equilibrium price level is equal to

$$p^* = \frac{AY}{\bar{L}^x(M^*)} \ , \tag{2.41}$$

where $\bar{L}^x(M^*)$ is determined by (2.40), (2.37) and (2.11). Thus, the price level depends on how much money income Y is available in relation to aggregate equilibrium output $\bar{L}^x(M^*)/A$. The former is governed by money supply. The latter depends on production and organization technology (A and γ, respectively), and in the case of an unemployment equilibrium also on the degree of monopoly (μ).

The real wage rate is only a function of labor productivity and monopoly power. According to (2.27) and (2.41), we have

$$\frac{w^*}{p^*} = \frac{1}{\mu A} . \tag{2.42}$$

The interpretation is standard. A higher degree of monopoly allows firms to charge higher prices so that real wages decline. And an increase in labor productivity (i.e. a decrease in A) allows higher real wages. There is no direct link between employment and the real wage level. However, in an unemployment equilibrium an increase in the degree of monopoly (μ) leads to a rise in equilibrium employment (2.38). At the same time, it depresses the real wage, according to (2.42). Thus, although there is no trade-off between employment and real wages in this model, the same exogenous change may cause a rise in employment at the cost of a lower real wage, or vice versa.

3. Unemployability and involuntary unemployment

People differ in their abilities. They may be quicker or slower and make one or ten pins in a day, or rather one or ten units of specialized tasks in Adam Smith's pin factory. They may be more or less qualified in text processing and type one or five letters in an hour. Such differences produce wage inequality if labor is paid according to its individual contribution. But they do not lead to an unemployment problem as long as wages are flexible. If no worker is available who can carry out ten units of a task in a unit of time, firms employ two workers who carry out five units and pay them the half wage. However, modern production and organization of work is more complicated. Autonomous problem solving and non-routinized interactions with other members of the firm or with customers are required. Workers who are not able to do reliable work without permanent guidance, people who have difficulties to help themselves when confronted with a new situation, or individuals who find it hard to communicate or to use modern means of communication cannot be easily integrated into making business in modern firms. There is no principal limitation to employ these less able workers. The point is that their employment requires more supervision, training and coordination. Only to the extent that firms do not provide these prerequisites, the less able workers cannot be productively employed. Chapter 2 has worked out this point in an abstract model. It shows that indeed involuntary unemployment is possible in the macroeconomic equilibrium of a competitive economy, if the requirements of organizing work are taken into account.

In practice, the derived unemployment equilibrium can explain why people who are low-qualified with respect to general abilities like autonomy, versatility, or the capacity to learn and communicate don't find a work place. These abilities are formed by primary socialization, education in school and work experience, but they may vary also with age. Thus, the presented theory contributes to an explanation of specific categories of unemployment: Unemployment of persons with poor education, unemployment of young people who don't easily manage to behave in a well-organized way and to adapt to disciplining work, long-term unemployment of workers who have lost their experience to work, or unemployment of older workers who have difficulties to cope with new forms of work organization and communication. These examples suggest that unemployability rather than unemployment is explained.

The purpose of this chapter is to clarify the relationship between different notions of employability and different types of unemployment. It is shown that the model presented in chapter 2 allows a precise distinction between employability from the viewpoint of profit-maximizing firms in a market economy on the one hand and employability under economic efficiency considerations on the other hand. Secondly, it is shown that the derived unemployment equilibrium represents a best-case benchmark. If the market economy is distorted by wage rigidity, market power of firm-owners or by wrong expectations, then additional unemployment arises in the macroeconomic equilibrium.

3.1 Equilibrium employment vs. efficient level of employment

Any society must accept that some people are not able to work. However, the borderline is not drawn by nature but man-made. Therefore, notions like natural employment or natural unemployability are misleading. The ability level below which a person is not employable depends on how work is organized. This means two things: i) The cut-off level of skills below which a worker is not integrated into the work force employed in firms is determined by the used organization technology. ii) It depends also on the objectives of the decision makers. In chapter 4 we will consider the effect of changes in the adopted technology on employment. In this chapter the impact of the decision structure is analyzed. In a market economy *firms* decide about labor demand and thus employment for a given supply of labor. Their objective is to earn *profits* in the given competitive environment. In contrast to this, from the *social planner's* point of view the relevant objective is *efficiency*. The question is, if and how the efficient level of unemployment deviates from the unemployment equilibrium resulting in a market economy with profit-maximizing firms.

Since labor supply is fixed, economic welfare is an increasing function of the amount of labor $\bar{L}^x$ that can be employed in production. Now, according to (2.5), the organization technology (2.2) implies that employment in production is limited by $\bar{L}^x = M/g(L,\gamma)$ where the amount of non-production input is $M = L - \bar{L}^x$. Eliminating M and solving for $\bar{L}^x$, we have for the relationship between production capacity $\bar{L}^x$and total employment L:

$$\bar{L}^x(L) = \frac{L}{1+g(L,\gamma)} \,. \tag{3.1}$$

The social planner is interested in expanding the production capacity as far as possible. Thus, total employment L is increased as long as $d\bar{L}^x/dL > 0$. Differentiating (3.1), we obtain the criterion:[1]

[1] $\frac{d\bar{L}^x}{dL} = \frac{1+g-L\partial g/\partial L}{(1+g)^2} = \frac{g}{(1+g)^2}\left(\frac{1}{g}+1-\frac{L}{g}\frac{\partial g}{\partial L}\right)$.

$$\frac{d\bar{L}^x}{dL} >,=,< 0 \text{ if } 1 + \frac{1}{g(L,\gamma)} >,=,< \alpha(L,\gamma) \ , \tag{3.2}$$

where

$$\alpha(L,\gamma) \equiv \frac{\partial g(L,\gamma)}{\partial L} \frac{L}{g(L,\gamma)} \tag{3.3}$$

is the elasticity of non-production requirement g with respect to the aggregate amount of employed units of labor L. $\partial\alpha/\partial L \geq 0$ is sufficient for a unique efficient level of employment. It is defined by

$$L^+ = \min\left\{L_0^+(\gamma), 1\right\} \ , \tag{3.4}$$

where $L_0^+(\gamma)$ is defined by condition (3.2) holding with equality. As long as elasticity α is not too high, it is efficient to increase employment. (That this is the case was assumed in section 2.1.) In particular, $\alpha(L,\gamma) \leq 1$ for $L \leq L^S (= 1)$ is a sufficient condition for making full employment of the labor force efficient.[2] The reason is that from the efficiency point of view the relevant question is to what extent the integration of less able workers into the productive work force complicates the organization of work. An additional unit of labor in production produces $1/A$ units of output. However, additional units of labor can only be employed if more non-production resources are spent on the organization of work, since the non-production costs of organizing work places increase if the quality of the employed labor force declines. As long as these non-production costs don't rise too strongly, the integration of additional workers expands the production possibilities of the economy.

Comparing criterion (3.2) for efficient employment with condition (2.34) for profitable employment, we see a fundamental difference. The condition for profit-maximizing level of job creation was

$$\frac{d\pi_i^n}{dm_i} >,=,< 0 \text{ if } \mu - 1 >,=,< g(L,\gamma) \tag{3.5}$$

where $\mu = \frac{1}{1-1/\sigma}$.

For both the planner and the profit-maximizing firm expanding employment becomes less desirable if, ceteris paribus, the costs of organizing a work place rise (i.e. if the organization technology switches from $g(L,\gamma)$ to $g(L,\gamma') > g(L,\gamma)$). However, whereas the planner's decision depends only on the non-production input requirement $g(L,\gamma)$ and its elasticity $\alpha(L,\gamma)$, for the profit-maximizing firm also the competitive situation is relevant. In the basic model of chapter 2 this situation is characterized by μ, which according to (2.42) is equal to the price-cost margin $p^*/(w^*A)$ that can be achieved in the goods market. Under the market distortions considered in the next

[2] $\partial g/\partial L > 0$ and thus $\alpha > 0$ is a necessary condition for equilibrium unemployment. It is also sufficient in the sense that for any g with $\partial g/\partial L > 0$ a $\mu > 1$ exists so that $g(L,\gamma) = \mu - 1$ for $L < 1$.

sections additional factors play a role. Elasticity α, which is important in the criterion for efficient employment, is not relevant for the job creation behavior of firms in the market economy. The reason is that the effect of aggregate employment on the range of employed abilities and thus on the non-production inputs required for organizing work is external to the individual firm. The fact that with rising employment also less able workers must be employed cannot be influenced by the behavior of single firms. Which range of abilities is available to an individual firm depends on how much workers are already employed in the whole economy.

Regarding unemployability, the efficient level of employment gives a precise economic meaning to this notion. Without specifying the meaning of employability, one risks to talk about nothing but a view that somebody considers somebody as being not employable. If, in addition, the fact that people are not employed is taken as proof for their unemployability, the circulus is complete. The presented model provides a scientific basis for the discussion. Efficient employment means that all people who can be productively integrated into the work process are employed. If the efficient level of employment is lower than full employment, employing the unemployed workers would reduce the production possibilities of the economy. That means, the unemployed persons cannot be productively integrated into the work process. They are unemployable in this objective economic sense. Objective does not mean: given by nature.[3] The efficient level of employment is determined by the given abilities and the used organization technology (represented by the parameter γ in our model). This technology may change and if the abilities do not keep pace with the skill requirements implied by the current technology, the efficient level of employment is decreased. The question of who is productively employable is determined by the technology. This gives the notion of unemployability an objective meaning. At the same time, it remains necessarily a relative notion in being contingent upon the used technology.

In contrast to the borderline between employability and unemployability defined by the efficient level of employment, the question who is employable in the eyes of the firms and actually employed in the market equilibrium is answered by profitability considerations and competitive pressure. In the macroeconomic equilibrium all those workers find employment who can be *profitably* integrated into firms. In general, this range of workers will not be the same as the range of workers who can be *productively* integrated. Employing less able workers may depress profits but still increase output. In principle, the equilibrium employment could deviate in both directions from the efficient level of employment. But as we have seen in the discussion of (3.2), full employment of the labor force is efficient under the assumption that non-production requirements don't react too elastically to an increase in ag-

[3] The economic system is after all a "man made world" (Pasinetti [51]).

gregate employment.[4] Then equilibrium unemployment means that workers don't find employment although they are employable in the sense of economic efficiency. This conclusion remains true in the case that not all workers are productively employable provided that the price-cost margin μ and elasticity α are not too high. Formally, if $L^+ < 1$ condition (3.2) holds with equality. Substituting $g(L^+, \gamma) = \frac{1}{\alpha(L^+,\gamma)-1}$ into condition (3.5) and remembering (2.37), (2.38), we obtain

$$L^* < L^+ \text{ if } \mu < \frac{1}{1 - 1/\alpha(L^+, \gamma)} . \tag{3.6}$$

For given abilities, the efficient level of employment is determined by technology, whereas the equilibrium level of employment depends also on the market conditions. In a long-term perspective, however, the technology will also be affected by the competitive situation. The concrete impact of markets on the organization of work depends on the nature of technical progress. In chapter 4 a process of technology adoption is described in which competitive forces induce firms to choose methods of work organization which require more abilities. This change in the organization technology may not only imply higher unemployment in the macroeconomic equilibrium but also lead to a decrease in the efficient level of employment so that indeed market forces can increase the number of people who cannot be productively integrated into organized work. Maybe it is such a scenario which people have in mind when they raise their voice in warning of the way towards a "two-third-society".

3.2 Unemployment under wage rigidity

The analysis so far has shown that involuntary equilibrium unemployment can be explained in a model which reflects the requirement of internal organization in a stylized form but retains the features of a competitive market economy as perfectly as possible. In the real world markets may be distorted for many reasons, in particular by rigid wages, power of firm owners or wrong expectations. Such distortions cause unemployment also in the framework of standard equilibrium theory.[5] The following sections of this chapter clarify the relationship between these conventional sources of unemployment and the unemployment equilibrium derived in the presented alternative theory. In this section, the role of wage rigidity is introduced in the basic model of chapter 2.

[4] For a high elasticity α, equilibrium employment could be above the efficient level, since firms don't account for the external effect of the expansion of employment on the non-production costs of organizing work.

[5] The caused unemployment is involuntary since the distortions are not set up by the (individual) unemployed workers. This is obvious with respect to rents of firm owners or wrong expectations. With respect to wage rigidity it is true if wages are set by unions or minimum wage legislation.

With flexible wages the employment equilibrium is characterized by (2.37), (2.40) and (2.11). Firms employ M^* units of non-production labor for the organization of work places. This creates an employment capacity for $\bar{L}^x(M^*)$ units of labor in production. And total employment L^* is equal to the sum of M^* plus $\bar{L}^x(M^*)$. The equilibrium wage rate is given by $w^* = \frac{Y}{\mu \bar{L}^x(M^*)}$, according to (2.27). Any wage above w^* is underbidden by unemployed workers, whereas w^* cannot be successfully underbidden since firms are not ready to provide more than $\bar{L}^x(M^*)$ production work places. Wage rigidity means that the underbidding is stopped before w^* is reached. Formally, there is a restriction

$$w \geq \bar{w} > w^* \tag{3.7}$$

for some exogenous $\bar{w}$. Obviously, it is always possible to increase aggregate money income Y so that $w^* \geq \bar{w}$ whatever is $\bar{w}$. Thus, nominal wage rigidity can only be a binding restriction for a given level of Y (fixed by tight money supply).

Under flexible wages firms can be sure at stage 1 that at stage 2 they can fully utilize any level of production capacity $\bar{L}^x(M)$ as long as the labor force is not fully employed (i.e. for all levels M allowing total employment $\bar{L}(M) < 1$, where $\bar{L}(M)$ is determined by (2.11) and (2.12)). If wages are restricted by (3.7), this can no longer be expected.

Let $\bar{M}(\bar{w})$ be the implicit function defined by the equation

$$\bar{w} = \frac{Y}{\mu \bar{L}^x(\bar{M})} . \tag{3.8}$$

Since $\bar{w} > w^*$ and $d\bar{L}^x/dM > 0$, we have $\bar{M} < M^*$ and $d\bar{M}/d\bar{w} < 0$.

For any $M \leq \bar{M}$, labor demand at stage 2 is given by (2.24) with $\widetilde{w} = \frac{Y}{\mu \bar{L}^x(M)} \geq \bar{w}$. Thus, wage rigidity constraint (3.7) does not prevent wages from falling until labor demand equals M. So the situation is the same as under flexible wages. The labor market equilibrium at stage 2 is identical to the one analyzed in section 2.2.2. Unemployed workers will underbid wages until $L^x = \bar{L}^x(M)$ and the wage rate is equal to $\widetilde{w}$, as illustrated in the figures 2.1, 2.3 and determined by equation (2.27). Moreover, for any $m_i \leq \bar{M}/n$, firm i's profit expectation at stage 1 is the same as in section 2.3, since the firm can be sure that wages go down and employment in stage 2 will rise until the capacity installed by non-production input m_i is exhausted. Thus, according to (2.34),

$$\frac{d\pi_i^n}{dm_i} >,=,< 0 \text{ if } \mu - 1 >,=,< g\left(\bar{L}(M), \gamma\right) \tag{3.9}$$

as long as $m_i \leq \bar{M}/n$.

Since $\bar{M} < M^*$ and thus $\bar{L}(\bar{M}) < L^*$, we conclude from (2.37) and (2.38) that $\mu - 1 > g\left(\bar{L}(M), \gamma\right)$ if $M \leq \bar{M}$. Combining this with (3.9), we have

$$\frac{d\pi_i^n}{dm_i} > 0 \text{ if } m_i \leq \bar{M}/n \,. \tag{3.10}$$

The intuition behind (3.10) is straightforward. Since under flexible wages the profit-maximizing level of non-production resources m_i is equal to M^*/n, it is desirable for firms to expand m_i as long as the wage rigidity constraint does not distort the outcome at stage 2.

The next step is to show that firms do not expand beyond $\bar{M}$. To see this suppose that $m_i > \bar{M}/n$.[6] Then $M > \bar{M}$ and $\widetilde{w} = \frac{Y}{\mu \bar{L}^x(M)} < \bar{w}$ so that according to (2.24) and (2.25) employment in production at stage 2 stops at $L^x = \frac{Y}{\mu \bar{w}} < \bar{L}^x(M)$. Since the wage rate is blocked at $\bar{w}$, it is not profitable for the firms to hire more production workers. Moreover, according to (2.23) and (2.10), the demand for output of firm i is equal to $x^D = \frac{Y}{n\mu\bar{w}A}\left(= \frac{L^x}{nA} < \frac{\bar{L}^x(M)}{nA}\right)$. Thus, for any $m_i > \bar{M}/n$,[7]

$$x^D < \bar{x}_i^S = \bar{l}_i/A \,. \tag{3.11}$$

Demand at stage 2 is limited by the wage rigidity constraint so that capacities resulting from $m_i > \bar{M}/n$ cannot be exhausted. As a consequence, a firm's profit expectation for stage 2 is in this case not given by (2.32) but equal to[8]

$$\begin{aligned} \pi_i &= (p_i - \bar{w}A)\, x^D \\ &= (\mu - 1)\, \tfrac{Y}{n\mu} \,. \end{aligned} \tag{3.12}$$

And, instead of (2.33), we have for the net profit achieved by employing m_i at stage 1.

$$\pi_i^n = (\mu - 1)\frac{Y}{n\mu} - \bar{w}m_i \tag{3.13}$$

Thus,

$$\frac{d\pi_i^n}{dm_i} < 0, \text{ if } m_i > \bar{M}/n \,. \tag{3.14}$$

Combining (3.10) and (3.14), we conclude that firms expand their capacity to organize work until $m_i = \bar{M}/n$, is reached. Thus, the function $\bar{M}(\bar{w})$ which was defined by (3.8) characterizes the equilibrium level of non-production labor invested in the provision of production work places, if wages are constrained by $\bar{w}$. The provided employment capacity $\bar{L}^x(\bar{M})$ is then exactly exhausted at stage 2, and total equilibrium employment under rigid wages is given by

6 Since firms are symmetric, all firms or none choose $m_i > \bar{M}/n$.

7 According to (2.2) and (2.6), $\bar{l}_i = \frac{m_i}{g(M+L^x,\gamma)} > \frac{M}{ng(M+L^x,\gamma)}$. Moreover, $\frac{M}{ng(M+L^x,\gamma)} > \frac{\bar{M}}{ng\left(\bar{M}+\bar{L}^x(\bar{M}),\gamma\right)}\left(= \frac{\bar{L}^x(\bar{M})}{n}\text{, according to (2.11)}\right)$, since $L^x < \bar{L}^x(M) \leq \bar{L}^x(\bar{M})$ and $\partial g/\partial L \geq 0$. Thus, $\bar{l}_i/A \geq \bar{L}^x(\bar{M})/(nA) > L^x/(nA) = x^D$.

8 Use $x^D = \frac{Y}{n\mu\bar{w}A}$ and $p_i = \mu\bar{w}A$ at $w = \bar{w} > \widetilde{w}$, according to (2.23).

$$\bar{L}(\bar{w}) = \bar{M}(\bar{w}) + \bar{L}^x(\bar{M}(\bar{w})) \tag{3.15}$$

with $d\bar{L}/d\bar{w} < 0$, since $d\bar{M}/d\bar{w} < 0$ according to (3.8).

This result is illustrated in figure 3.1.

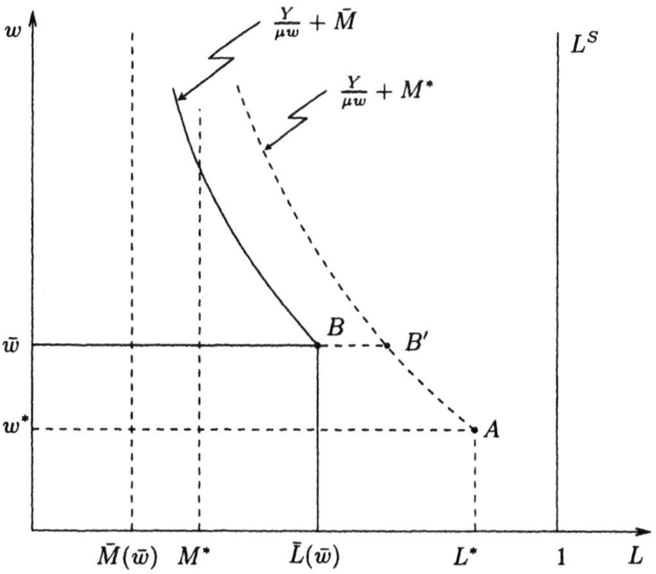

Fig. 3.1. Employment equilibrium under wage rigidity

Under flexible wages firms can expect that employment and production at stage 2 will adjust to the capacity provided by the invested non-production input at stage 1. This leads to the equilibrium values $L^* = M^* + \bar{L}^x(M^*)$ and w^*, as analyzed in chapter 2. Point A in figure 3.1 reproduces this equilibrium. The fact that the wage is stopped by $\bar{w}$ from falling to w^* reduces employment in production at stage 2. If firms had not anticipated constraint (3.7) and had installed an organizational capacity corresponding to M^*, then the stage 2 equilibrium would be shifted from point A to B' in figure 3.1.[9] However, this would imply empty capacities. Therefore, rational anticipation of the negative effect of wage rigidity on the level of activity in stage 2 induces the firms to adjust their employment of non-production resources at stage 1 from M^* downwards to $\bar{M}(\bar{w})$. This implies that total labor demand $L^D = M + L^x$ is shifted to the left so that not point B' but point B represents the equilibrium

[9] If the requirement of non-production resources is ignored (i.e. $\bar{M} = M^*$ is set to zero), figure 3.1 reduces to the conventional picture of labor markets with a minimum wage constraint.

achieved under rigidity constraint (3.7). Since $\bar{L}(\bar{w}) < L^*$, we have strictly positive profits in this equilibrium.[10]

3.3 Market power of firms and rents for firm owners

Standard partial analysis tells us that market power of agents tends to reduce the transaction level in a market. This suggests that market power in labor or goods markets depresses the macroeconomic activity level i.e. aggregate employment. How wage setting of unions affects the creation of work places and equilibrium employment in the presented model was the subject of the preceding section. In this section we turn to the role of the market power of firms and firm-owners.

A much debated issue in the literature of the seventies and eighties was the question of whether imperfect competition in the goods markets alone can generate unemployment (see Silvestre [60] for a survey). Whereas Hart [30] emphasized that in his model of imperfect competitions a non-competitive labor market was necessary to get underemployment, others have pointed out that Hart's conclusion is not robust and that under alternative assumptions involuntary unemployment may indeed be generated by solely noncompetitive goods market without any need to fall back on rigid wages (D'Aspremont , Dos Santos Ferreira, and Gérard-Varet [20], Silvestre [59]).[11] The approach presented in this study also explains unemployment in a model with flexible labor markets, in which firms and workers are allowed to over- and underbid wages, and imperfect competition in the goods market. However, the imperfect competition in the goods market at stage 2 is a necessary consequence of the requirement of internal organization of work. Without a mark-up on unit production costs firms could not finance the investment in the non-production resources which are necessary for organizing production. Thus, not the market power of firms but the organization technology is the root cause of the analyzed employment problem. As consequence, the degree of monopoly $\mu\left(=\frac{\sigma}{\sigma-1}\right)$ which determines the margin $\frac{p^*}{w^*A}$ of price to production cost per unit of output has even a positive impact on employment ($\partial L_0/\partial\mu > 0$, according to (2.38)). This may seem strange, at first glance. As discussed in section 2.4, the reason for the positive impact of μ on employment is that the market power in the goods market at stage 2 is

[10] Use (3.8), $m_i = \bar{M}/n$, (2.11) and (3.15) to calculate $\bar{w}m_i = g\left(\bar{L}(\bar{w}),\gamma\right)Y/(n\mu)$. Thus, according to (3.13), $\pi_i^n = \left[\mu - 1 - g\left(\bar{L}(\bar{w}),\gamma\right)\right]Y/(n\mu)$. Since $\mu - 1 \geq g(L^*,\gamma)$, according to (2.37) and (2.38), and $\bar{L}(\bar{w}) < L^*$, we have $\mu - 1 > g\left(\bar{L}(\bar{w}),\gamma\right)$.

[11] A model in which firms have monopsony power in the labor market while they are price takers in the product market was recently presented by Bhaskar and To [10]. Their model is based on the assumption that workers have different preferences over non-wage characteristics and different reservation wages.

only used to finance the organization of work places at stage 1. On the whole, firms earn zero profits in the basic model. Ex ante there is actually no market power at all. Thus, for an adequate discussion of the role of power of firms in the proper meaning of the word, the basic model must be modified so that strictly positive profits i.e. rents for the firm owners exist in equilibrium. The following discussion shows first that the effect of monopoly power considered in conventional models of imperfect competition in the goods market can be seen as a special case of the role of the degree of monopoly μ in the two-stage model presented in chapter 2. Secondly, the role of power that leads to rents for firm owners is contrasted with the role of μ.

3.3.1 The role of market power in a zero profit equilibrium

To see the role of a change in the degree of monopoly at stage 2, we make a comparative static analysis of the impact of an increase of μ from μ_1 to $\mu_2 > \mu_1$.

At stage 2, such an increase leads to a downward movement of the demand curve for labor in production L^x defined by (2.24). This movement corresponds to the usually considered effect of market power of firms (see e.g. figures 2.1 - 2.4 in Silvestre [60]). It is illustrated by the curves $L_i^x = \frac{Y}{\mu_i w}$ in figure 3.2, for a given level of M.

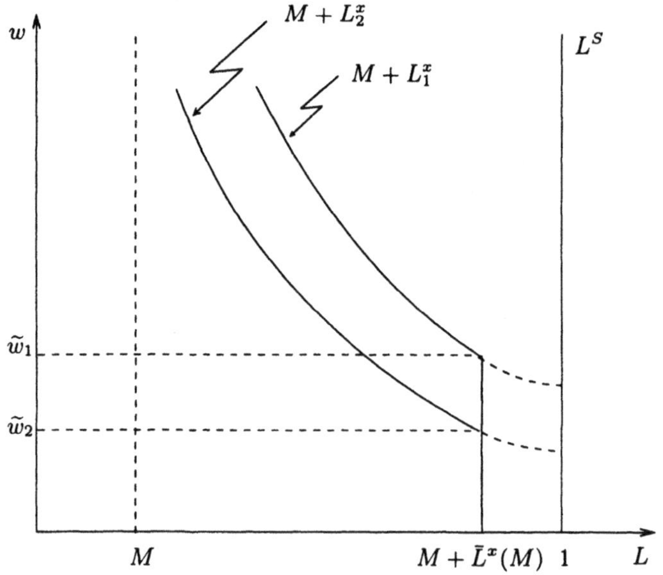

Fig. 3.2. The role of market power at stage 2 ($\mu_1 < \mu_2$)

Thus, ceteris paribus, at any wage rate above $\widetilde{w}_2$, in particular also at $\widetilde{w}_1$, employment in production is lower if market power in the goods market increases. In flexible labor markets the underbidding of wages by unemployed workers would lead to $\widetilde{w}_2$ so that (un-)employment would be the same as at $\widetilde{w}_1$.

However, this conventional look at the relationship between market power in goods market and labor demand neglects that resources are required to organize work within firms. An increase of the price-cost margin from μ_1 to μ_2 extends the possibilities to finance non-production work. If all profits earned at stage 2 are invested in the provision of work places at stage 1, then the increase of μ from μ_1 to μ_2 leads to an increase of M and thus to an expansion of the capacity $\bar{L}^x(M)$ of organizing labor in production. Combining the negative effect on labor demand which results if only stage 2 is considered with the positive consequences induced at stage 1, we obtain according to (2.37) and (2.38) that aggregate equilibrium employment rises from $L_1^* = L_0(\gamma, \mu_1)$ to $L_2^* = \min\{L_0(\gamma, \mu_2), 1\}$, if we start in an unemployment equilibrium with $L_0(\gamma, \mu_1) < 1$.[12] According to (2.40), the rise in L^* is accompanied by an increase of M^* from M_1^* to M_2^*. The two effects and its consequences for the macroeconomic equilibrium are represented in figure 3.3.

The labor demand curve not only moves downwards from $M_1^* + L_1^x$ to $M_1^* + L_2^x$. It is also shifted to the right from $M_1^* + L_2^x$ to $M_2^* + L_2^x$ because of the additional investment in the provision of work places. Thus, although at the original wage w_1^* unemployment would rise as a consequence of the increased market power (see point C), under flexible wages employment expands since more work places are provided for the job seeking workers. As a result, the higher profit margin in the product market stimulates employment at the cost of lower wages. (According to (2.42), also the real wage rate goes down.)

3.3.2 The role of rents for firm-owners

Proper power of firms means that pure profits i.e. rents for firm-owners exist in equilibrium. Such rents are possible if the organization of work in firms requires in addition to non-production labor a factor (e.g. capital as analyzed in chapter 6) which is imperfectly supplied by the owners of firms or if the acquisition of property rights in firms is tied to inheritance. The purpose here is not to explain *why* rents may exist but to analyze which effects rents have *if* they exist. The simplest way to model rents is to assume that firms must pay a royalty to their owners. We stick as close as possible to the presented framework and assume that the required fee is linear in the size of the firm (measured by the capacity created at stage 1). This guarantees that like in

[12] If we start in a full employment equilibrium, the only effect of the increase in μ is a decline in the nominal and real wage rate, according to (2.27) and (2.42). Graphically, in this case, the downward movement of the L^x-curve in figure 3.2 describes already the whole story, since M is fixed by the condition $M + \bar{L}^x(M) = 1$.

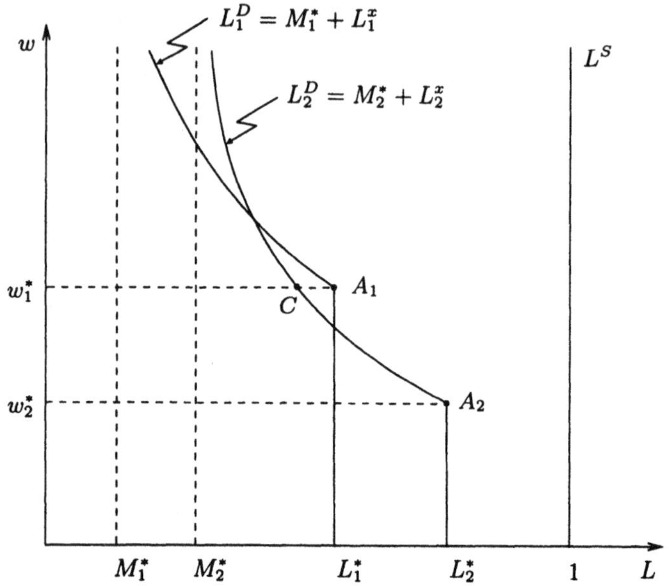

Fig. 3.3. The role of market power in a macroeconomic equilibrium with zero profits ($\mu_1 < \mu_2$).

the analysis so far no profits arise from internal economies of scale. Regardless of the number of firms, the amount of pure profits in equilibrium is equal to the fee paid to the firm owners. Formally let R be the fee (in real terms) that firms must pay to their owners per unit of production capacity installed at stage 1. The corresponding nominal fee in equilibrium is $p^*R = \mu w^* AR$. Then a firm creating a capacity of $\frac{\bar{l}_i}{A} = \frac{m_i}{Ag(L,\gamma)}$ by investing m_i units of non-production labor has to pay the sum $p^* R\bar{l}_i / A = w^* m_i \mu R / g(L,\gamma)$ to the owners of the firm. As a consequence, the net profit of the firm which is relevant when deciding about m_i at stage 1 is given by (2.33) minus this sum. Hence,

$$\pi_i^n = w^* m_i \left[\frac{\mu - 1}{g(L,\gamma)} - 1 \right] - w^* m_i \frac{\mu R}{g(L,\gamma)} \tag{3.16}$$

and

$$\frac{d\pi_i^n}{dm_i} >, =, < 0 \text{ if } \mu(1-R) - 1, >, =, < g(L,\gamma) \, . \tag{3.17}$$

The aggregate employment equilibrium is thus determined by

$$\widetilde{L}^* = \min\left\{ L_0(\gamma, \widetilde{\mu}), 1 \right\} \tag{3.18}$$

where $L_0(\gamma, \widetilde{\mu})$ is determined like in (2.38) with

$$\widetilde{\mu} \equiv \mu(1-R) < \mu \, . \tag{3.19}$$

Market power which yields rents to the firm owners decreases employment, since it reduces the profit which is available for the investment in the non-production labor required for the organization of work.

The negative effect of R on aggregate employment is illustrated in figure 3.4.

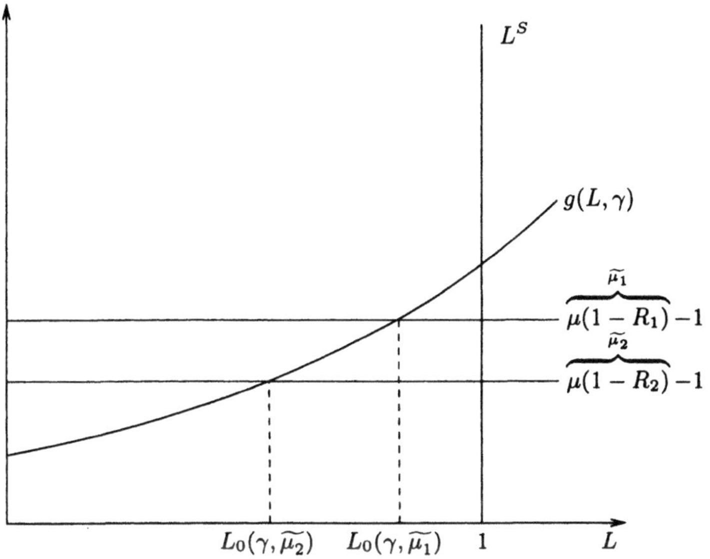

Fig. 3.4. The effects of firm-owner rents on employment ($R_1 < R_2$).

This brings out quite clearly that for the effective role of market power two opposing components must be considered: On the one hand, the profit margin μ allowed by the elasticity of demand in the goods market. On the other hand, the share $R\mu$ of this margin which is taken by the firm owners as a rent. Whereas an increase in the former is, ceteris paribus, positive for employment since it allows higher expenses on the organization of work places, the effect of the latter is negative, since it reduces the resources for providing employment.

For the real wage rate, the size of rent R is irrelevant. The reason is that the payments of royalties are fixed costs when competition takes place at stage 2. They can not be passed on to the price. Thus, the model shows a direct trade-off between pure profits and employment. If firm owners have the power to require rents, firms save other non-production costs by cutting work places for workers with low (interactive) abilities. Formally, this can be seen by evaluating (2.39) at $\widetilde{\mu} = \mu(1-R)$. The decrease of equilibrium employment from $L_0(\gamma,\mu)$ to $L_0(\gamma,\widetilde{\mu})$ brings down the ratio of non-production labor to labor in production. This "downsizing" allows firms to pay the rents to their owners.

3.4 Employment when firms have uncertain expectations

The unemployment equilibrium established in chapter 2 was derived under the assumption that firms have perfect foresight. They know what they can sell at a certain price at stage 2 as well as which profit they will earn at stage 2 when choosing a certain capacity at stage 1. Economists, in particular Keynes and Keynesian economists, have always emphasized that uncertainty and imperfect expectations are a central source of macroeconomic problems like unemployment. In the presented model there are two points at which uncertain expectations get involved in a natural way. First, the market situation at stage 2 may differ from the situation which firms expected when choosing their organizational infrastructure at stage 1. This is the case if the economy is hit by unanticipated shocks. Secondly, firms may perceive the future as not clearly foreseeable so that they base their decisions at stage 1 on crude tendencies rather than on sophisticated calculations concerning the equilibrium outcome to be expected at stage 2. This is what Keynes and Postkeynesian economists called true uncertainty. In this case the state of long-term expectations determines the macroeconomic equilibrium. The next two sections show that unanticipated shocks lead to *deviations* from the characterized unemployment equilibrium, whereas uncertain long-term expectations lead to *shifts* in the unemployment equilibrium itself.

3.4.1 Unanticipated shocks

Suppose that M^*, $\bar{L}^*(M^*)$ and L^* are fixed by the firms' decisions at stage 1, as determined by (2.37), (2.40) and (2.11). But then at stage 2 something in the goods or labor market is different from what has been expected.

For a given level of non-production resources employed for the organization of work the production capacity (measured in units of labor employable in production) is fixed at $\bar{L}^x(M^*)$. According to (2.23) - (2.25) the implied equilibrium values for goods prices p and employment in production L^x depend on the demand parameters Y and μ. Thus, unanticipated situations can arise if Y or μ fluctuate. The implications for employment can be easily seen by varying figure 2.1.

In figure 3.5 the equilibrium resulting at stage 2 for certain values μ, Y is shown by point $A = (L^*, w^*)$.

Suppose now that there is an adverse demand shock caused by a decrease in money supply dampening money income to Y_1 or by an increase of the firms' market power to μ_1 which pushes up the price level. This shifts the

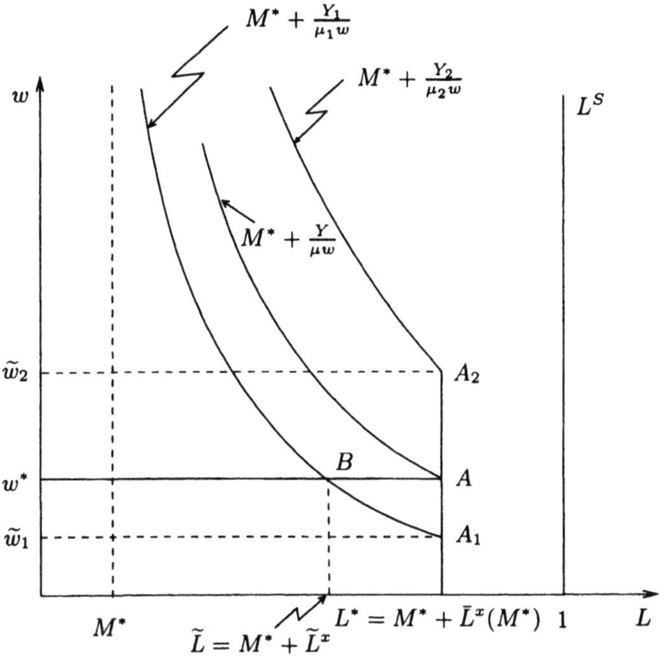

Fig. 3.5. Short-run demand fluctuations.

demand curve for labor in production down to $L_1^x = \frac{Y_1}{\mu_1 w}$. As long as wages are not adjusted downwards accordingly, goods prices remain high (see (2.23)) and demand for goods and labor is depressed. At the original equilibrium wage rate w^*, the goods market equilibrium defined by (2.23) - (2.25) for the exogenous parameters μ_1, Y_1 implies that $\widetilde{L}^x = \frac{Y_1}{\mu_1 w^*} < \bar{L}^x(M^*)$ units of labor are employed in production. This outcome is represented by point B in figure 3.5.

Compared with the (un)employment equilibrium at L^*, the unanticipated negative demand shock leads to a rise in unemployment which is not due to a lack of organized work places. To the contrary, firms fire workers and leave work places unoccupied, since underutilization of the installed capacity is the profit-maximizing short-run reaction to the deteriorating demand conditions. Figure 3.5 shows also that point B is a labor market disequilibrium which vanishes when wages are adjusted downwards. The new equilibrium wage is then $\widetilde{w}_1 = \frac{Y_1}{\mu_1 \bar{L}^x(M^*)}$, according to (2.27). At this lower wage firms expand current production and employment to the equilibrium level determined by their decisions at stage 1 (see point A_1).[13] This reaction to an unanticipated negative shock makes it very clear that not turnover costs are the source of unemployment in the presented model. Within the limits of the organizational capacity production labor can be freely adjusted without costs. Only the level of non-production labor required for the organization of work is fixed in the short-run. This fits well into the picture of modern labor markets characterized by flexible job relationships where labor, in particular production labor, bears the burden of shock absorption. If wages are not adjusted downwards in reaction to deteriorating market conditions the production workers with the lowest abilities are dismissed. If wages react flexibly also in the short-run, workers bear the burden in form of wage cuts.

A positive shock caused by an increase of aggregate money income to Y_2 or by a decrease of the firms' market power to μ_2 shifts the labor demand curve upward to $M^* + \frac{Y_2}{\mu_2 w}$. This has no real effects since an expansion beyond L^* is not possible if M^* is fixed. Thus, according to (2.23), prices rise till demand equals capacity. As long as wages remain at w^*, firms enjoy rising profits and the real wage rate declines. An upward adjustment of wages to the equilibrium value $\widetilde{w}_2 = \frac{Y_2}{\mu_2 \bar{L}^x(M^*)}$ (see point A_2) has no negative impact on employment but also no price-increasing effect, as shown by (2.23). Only the distribution of aggregate income between wages and profit is changed.

The shocks considered so far came from changes in money supply or market power of firms. In principle, also the organization technology could be subject to unanticipated variations. According to (2.11), $\bar{L}^x$ depends on M^* but also on the exogenous parameter γ. A technological shock means, it turns out at stage 2 that with the employed non-production resources M^* a lower amount $\bar{L}_1^x$or a higher amount $\bar{L}_2^x$ of production labor can be organized, coordinated and supervised than the amount $\bar{L}^x(M^*)$ expected at stage 1. The consequences of such an unanticipated technological shock can be seen in figure 3.6. Again, $A = (L^*, w^*)$ represents the equilibrium without shocks.

The effects are analogous to those which have just been discussed with respect to unforeseen demand shocks. A negative technological shock leads to a destruction of work places so that employment is reduced to $\widetilde{L}_1$. This effect is independent of how wages react to the shock. Since the destruction of work places means that those workers who lost the job have become unemployable with the given organizational capacity of firms, the wages of those who kept their job can rise to $\widetilde{w}_1 = \frac{Y}{\mu \bar{L}_1^x}$ without risking successful underbidding by the jobless. According to (2.23), the price level rises in any case, since with the decreased capacity $\bar{L}_1^x$ $(< \bar{L}^x(M^*))$ goods become scarcer. Thus, a negative technological shock produces at the same time rising unemployment and rising prices in the presented framework. A positive technological shock would allow to expand employment of production labor to $\bar{L}_2^x$ with the given level of non-production input M^*. However, this possible expansion of employment

[13] If wages were rigid in the long-run, firms would anticipate this rigidity at stage 1 and adjust their work capacity downwards as analyzed in section 3.2.

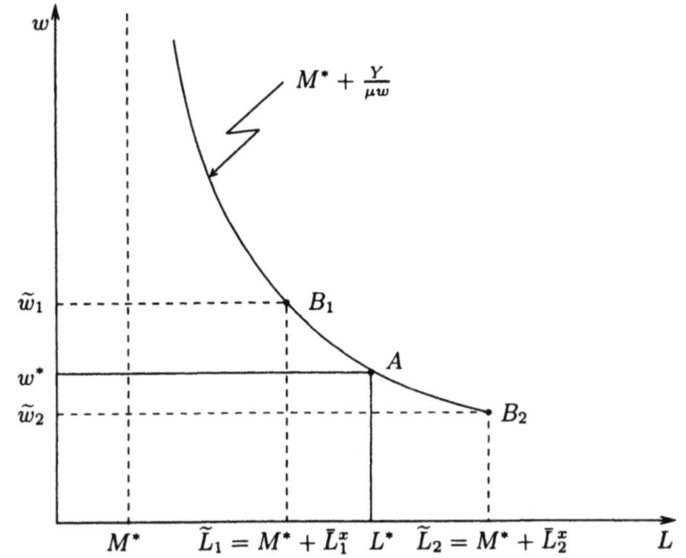

Fig. 3.6. Unanticipated technological shocks.

to $\widetilde{L}_2$ is only realized if wages decline to $\widetilde{w}_2$ so that labor demand moves from A^* to B_2. If wages remain at w^*, the positive technological shock has no effect at all. The unforeseen possibilities of organizing additional production work are not utilized.

This analysis of unanticipated shocks shows that traditional short-run considerations about price and quantity effects of exogenous shocks can be consistently integrated into the presented model as transient deviations from the established macroeconomic equilibrium. The deviations are transient in the sense that the underlying changes in the market situation are not reflected in the firms' decisions at stage 1. In contrast to this, the next section considers fundamental shifts in the firms' expectations which induce them to revise their behavior at stage 1. This leads to less conventional conclusions about the role of uncertain expectations for the macroeconomic equilibrium.

3.4.2 Macroeconomic equilibrium and the state of long-term expectations

Firms decide at stage 1 about the size and the quality of labor force they can manage in monopolistic competition at stage 2. The capacity to organize work is provided by employing non-production labor. The return on this employment only emerges when firms enter competition with the provided capacity. With perfect foresight firms can make optimal decisions by going back from the outcome at stage 2 to the stage 1 decision that optimizes this outcome. Ex post the results may deviate from the expectations if there are unanticipated changes. However, if at stage 1 the uncertainty about what happens at stage 2 is so fundamental that nothing can be anticipated, the idea of choosing the optimal level of non-production inputs m_i at stage 1, given the profit $\pi_i(m_i)$ to be expected at stage 2, becomes problematic. The intention of this section is not to go into the long standing debate about behavior under risk and uncertainty. The purpose of the following analysis is to show the macroeconomic implications which follow from the presented theory if an exogenous state of expectations determines the macroeconomic equilibrium.

In chapter 12 of his General Theory (see also Keynes [38]) Keynes emphasized that the level of investment depends on "the state of long-term expectations". Since investment determines effective demand and effective demand determines employment, we come to the Keynesian conclusion that pessimistic expectations of investors are responsible for involuntary unemployment. This conclusion is in sharp contrast to the classical view that, according to Say's law, supply determines demand and limits the macroeconomic activity level. In the model presented in chapter 2 of this study there is so far no savings and accumulation of capital. (Capital is introduced in chapter 6, and investment and savings will be considered in chapter 7.) But firms have an investment problem in the sense that they must make decisions about the employment of resources (non-production labor) which determine future profits. The question is therefore how the macroeconomic equilibrium at stage 2 is affected if the firms' decisions at stage 1 are based on some exogenous state of expectations instead of being endogenously determined as profit-maximizing choices in an equilibrium with perfect foresight.

Let, for a given state of expectations E, $M_E = nm_E$ denote the level of non-production resources which firms have decided to employ for organizing production work. Then, according to (2.26), total demand for labor is given by

$$L^D = M_E + L^x , \tag{3.20}$$

where employment in production L^x is limited by the employed non-production resources M_E. According to (2.5), the relevant constraint is

$$L^x \leq \frac{M_E}{g(L^D, \gamma)} . \tag{3.21}$$

Combining (3.20) with (3.21), we obtain

$$L^D \leq B(M_E, L^D) \tag{3.22}$$

where

$$B(M, L) \equiv M\left[1 + \frac{1}{g(L, \gamma)}\right] \tag{3.23}$$

describes the upper bound of employment levels which can be organized with non-production input M and a labor force with abilities $z \geq z_0(L)$. With flexible wages labor demand increases until the labor force is fully employed or (3.22) holds with equality. We have,

$$L^D = \bar{L}(M_E) = M_E \left[1 + \frac{1}{g\left(\bar{L}(M_E), \gamma\right)}\right] \tag{3.24}$$

in equilibrium (provided that $\bar{L}(M_E) \leq L^S = 1$. Otherwise we have a full employment equilibrium).

These equations show a multiplicator relationship between aggregate employment and the non-production resources employed in view of a given state of expectations. The relationship is illustrated in figure 3.7.

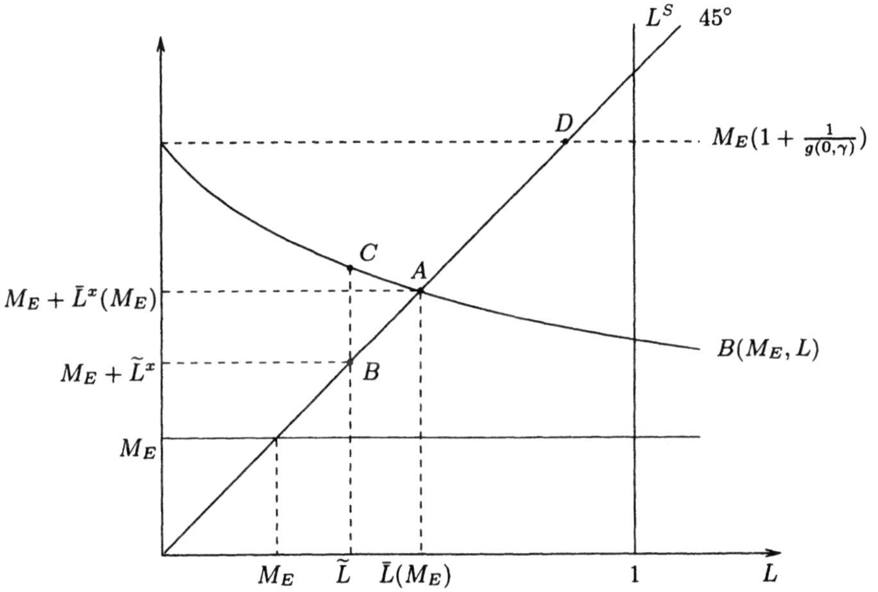

Fig. 3.7. Unemployment and the state of expectations.

The curve $B(M_E, L) = M_E\left(1 + \frac{1}{g(L,\gamma)}\right)$ represents the volume of work that can be organized with the non-production resources M_E if aggregate employment is L and the ability range of employment is thus $[z_0(L), \bar{z}]$, where $dz_0/dL < 0$, according to (2.1). As long as employment is below $\bar{L}(M_E)$, e.g. at $\widetilde{L}$, there are unoccupied work places (represented by the distance $BC = B\left(M_E, \widetilde{L}\right) - \widetilde{L}$). Such a situation corresponds to a short-run disequilibrium situation arising, for instance, from an unanticipated shock as analyzed in the preceding section. However, if wages are flexible the unemployed workers underbid wages and firms hire more labor in production. They are prepared to do so since they have unused resources for organizing work. Employment levels above $\bar{L}(M_E)$ are not feasible with the given non-production resources M_E and the organization technology represented by γ. At point A, the stage 2 equilibrium corresponding to M_E is reached.[14] If $M_E = M^*$, then the perfect foresight equilibrium analyzed in chapter 2 results.

Suppose now that first the economy is in an equilibrium with perfect foresight, in which employment in non-production is M^* and total employment is L^* as determined by (2.37) and (2.40). This equilibrium is represented by point A^* in figure 3.8. Then, firms turn pessimistic about future demand. The pessimistic state of expectations induces them to downsize their non-production inputs to $M_E < M^*$.[15] According to (3.23), this moves the B-curve down to $B(M_E, L)$ and the new equilibrium point is A_E with aggregate employment $\bar{L}(M_E) < L^*$.

The pessimistic expectations about demand are not disproved ex post. The activity level at stage 2 is indeed lower than without the pessimistic perception of the future, and demand is not rationed by the decreased capacity. Of course, if expectations about future demand would turn back to optimism the more optimistic expectations would be fulfilled in an analogous way. Optimistic firms employ more resources for the provision of work places, and with flexible wages the level of employment and production realized at stage 2 is high enough to utilize the increased capacity fully. The law of Say, according to which supply creates its own demand, is in operation at stage 2. However, at stage 1 expected demand determines the supplied capacity. Thus, the analysis may be interpreted as a possible synthesis of the two opposite views which have characterized the history of macroeconomic thought to a great extent: At the operating stage, when business takes place within the given organizational capacity of firms, the model reflects the classical view that supply determines demand if markets are fully flexible. But what is relevant is the firms' supply of capacity to organize work, not the supply of labor. At the more fundamental stage, when firms arrange their organizational infrastructure, exogenous expectations about unforeseeable future demand may determine the supply of the resources required to organize production work. We come back to this point in chapter 7 which analyzes the

---

14 Note that even with $g(L,\gamma) = g(0,\gamma)$ unemployment can arise if expectations are so pessimistic that $M_E\left(1 + \frac{1}{g(0,\gamma)}\right) < 1$ (see point D). This is in contrast to the equilibrium with perfect foresight, in which M^* allows full employment if the g-curve is flat.

15 Note that optimistic expectations leading to $M_E > M^*$ are not viable since, according to (2.33) and (2.38), firms make losses at $\bar{L}(M_E) > L^*$ provided that the labor force was not already fully employed (If $L^* = 1$, $M_E > M^*$ would mean that firms waste non-production resources whatever the future situation). The external effect of aggregate employment L on the quality of the available labor force increases the ratio of non-production labor to labor in production to a level that is not born by the market. In contrast to this, $M_E < M^*$ implies $\bar{L}(M_E) < L^*$ and profits are positive.

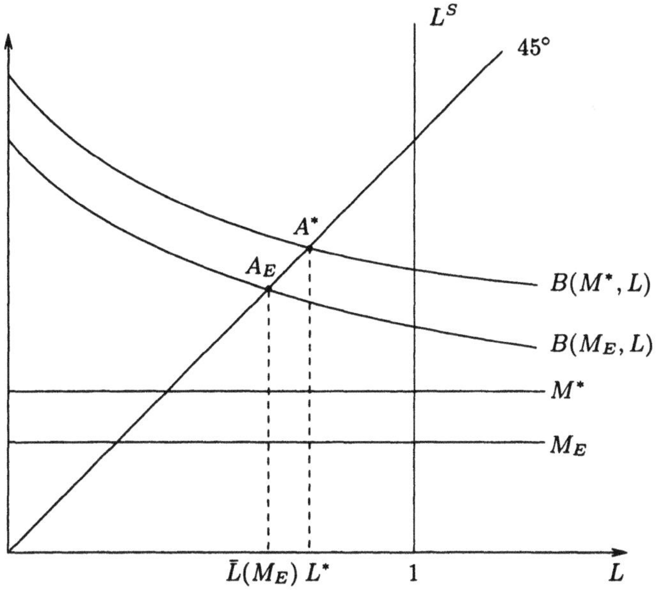

Fig. 3.8. Unemployment under pessimistic expectations.

role of investment and savings in the two-stage macroeconomic equilibrium framework developed in this study.

4. Equilibrium reorganization of work and aggregate level of employment

Modern mass production has been based on the principles of labor division and specialization. As emphasized by Adam Smith, the interaction of specialized workers within a factory allows to generate an enormous increase in labor productivity. Of course, the fragmentation of the production process must be planned and the interaction of the single operations must be coordinated. This requires appropriate forms of organization as developed by practitioners and management science (Ford or Taylor are prominent figures in this development). However, during the last decades new trends in work organization can be observed whose common features are the attempt to reduce central coordination costs by putting more weight on the workers' responsibility and on decentralized interactions. The dream firm seems to be a self-organizing network of highly apt, self-motivated, versatile and socially competent individuals. By this one hopes to bring down the non-production requirements for organizing production ("Lean management" is one of the many recent catchwords). A rich picture of recent trends of reorganizing work is given in Snower [61]. In the abstract framework of this study the manifold trends come down to a change in the production technology on the one hand, represented by the labor input coefficient A, and a change in the organization technology, represented by the function $g(L, \gamma)$, on the other hand. The implications of the change in A are straightforward. According to (2.42), the real wage rate increases to the extent that the reorganization of work increases labor productivity in production. The macroeconomic consequences of the process of reorganization are less obvious. It is the purpose of this chapter to analyze these consequences, in particular the employment effects. For this purpose two stylized forms of organization technologies are compared. To focus the analysis on the role of the organization requirements under different technologies, it is assumed that the labor input coefficient A is exogenously fixed in this comparison.

In an economy in which internal organization of work is essential the aggregate level of employment depends on which organization technology is used by the firm. This was shown in chapter 2. If all firms switch to a new technology $g(L, \gamma)$, the unemployment equilibrium $L_0(\gamma, \mu)$ changes as discussed in section 2.4. The open question to be addressed in this chapter is what are the incentives of firms to switch to a new way of organizing work and how many firms adopt the new organization technology in equilibrium. Since different modes of organizing work require different abilities of workers, the decision about which organization technology is adopted by a firm is not independent of the available range of abilities. And the range of abilities left over is not independent of which organization technology is used by the other firms. If only a few firms reorganize work they can pick up the most clever workers for their firms. If all firms adopt the new organization technology the whole employed labor force is to be organized in the reorganized way. This chapter determines the equilibrium adoption of organization technologies and analyzes the implied equilibrium level of aggregate employment. The availability of a new organization technology leads to an equilibrium with total or partial reorganization. In both cases it may have a negative effect on the aggregate level of organized employment.

Snower [61] delineates the many dimensions involved in what he calls "organizational revolution": Customer-orientation instead of task orientation, multi-tasking instead of single-tasking, decentralized decision-making instead of central coordination. Such reorientations require from workers multiple and social skills rather than highly specialized skills[1], permanent learning and adaptation rather than once for all acquisition of know-how. Lindbeck and Snower [45] presented a formal analysis of the change from firms in which workers are specialized in single tasks to firms in which workers fulfill multiple tasks to exploit information complementarities arising between different activities. By the distinction between specialized and holistic workers they explain rising inequality and changing patterns of wage formation. The focus of the present study is the impact of work organization on the equilibrium level of employment. In contrast to the multi-tasking aspect of modern forms of work organization, the new feature of the theoretical approach presented in this study is its focus on the fact that organization is related to the *interaction* of individuals within firms. To bring out the implications of modern management trends with respect to this basic character of organization we contrast an economy with firms in which interactions are organized by "central coordination" to an economy with firms in which interactions are organized by "decentralized communication".

In the presented model the mechanism connecting macroeconomic equilibrium and work-organization in firms is determined by the skill requirements implied by the used organization technology relative to the supplied skills. As the endowment of the labor force with relevant abilities improves, the organization technology can be changed accordingly without any consequences for aggregate employment. However, the reorganization of work is not only a reaction to changes in the supply of skills but also fostered by new technologies. The relevant question is then: What are the macroeconomic consequences of such a technological change for a given level and distribution

[1] Aghion, Garcia-Penalosa and Caroli [3] speak of "*polyvalent* agents, who can both perform varied tasks *and* learn from other agents' activities" (p. 76).

of abilities among the labor force? According to (2.1) and (2.2), for given endowments of workers with (interactive) abilities, the organization technology was represented by a function

$$g(L, \gamma) , \quad \frac{\partial g}{\partial L} > 0 \tag{4.1}$$

which describes the non-production resources required to provide the capacity to organize one unit of production work if aggregate employment is L and the used technology is labelled γ. Whereas the employed mode of organization (γ) determines the skill requirements, the aggregate level of employment L defines the range of abilities $[z_0(L), \bar{z}]$ which is available to firms. Since also less able workers must be employed if the level of employment rises ($dz_0/dL < 0$), the organization of work requires, ceteris paribus, a larger non-production input.

How are non-production resources to be invested into the organization of work affected if the prevailing mode of organization switches from "central coordination" to "decentralized communication"? For an answer to this question two types of effects must be considered. First, the range of abilities which is available to a firm depends also on the number of firms which have already switched to the new mode of organization. Second, the non-production resources required if decentralized communication characterizes the interaction of workers in a firm have to fulfill a function which is distinct from the one under central coordination. This implies that the $g(L, \gamma)$-curve is not only shifted when firms switch to new methods of organizing work but also changes its shape. The next two sections discusses these effects more formally. Then the decision of firms to adopt new organization methods and the macroeconomic implications, in particular the effects on aggregate equilibrium employment, are analyzed.

4.1 Employment under different organization technologies and the available range of abilities

Suppose that there are two methods of organization in an economy, a new one and an old one, represented by γ_d and γ_c, respectively. The new method of organization, γ_d, corresponds to "decentralized communication" and the old method, γ_c, corresponds to "central coordination". The concrete characteristics of the two organization technologies will be described in section 4.2. Which range of abilities is available to the firms operating under the different organization technologies? Since workers are heterogeneous with respect to their interaction skills, this depends on the level of aggregate employment and on the allocation of workers to the different types of organization technologies. It is assumed that workers have a preference for working in an environment organized by decentralized coordination. And workers with better interactive abilities are more successful in getting a work place they want.

They go to the firms which use the new technology.[2] Then, for given levels of employment, the range of abilities which is available to the respective types of firms is determined as follows.

Let $L = L_d + L_c$ be aggregate employment, where L_d is aggregate employment in firms using the new method of organization γ_d and L_c is aggregate employment in firms using the old method γ_c, respectively. Then the least able worker employed under organization technology γ_d has ability level $z_0(L_d)$ and the range of abilities available to firms operating under the new technology is given by

$$Z_1(L_d) \equiv [z_0(L_d), \bar{z}] \tag{4.2}$$

with $z_0' < 0$, according to (2.1).

Workers with lower interactive abilities are employed under the old technology. Since with aggregate employment $L = L_d + L_c$ the least able worker who finds employment has ability $z_0(L)$, the range of abilities available to firms which use the old method of organizing work is given by

$$Z_2(L_d, L) \equiv [z_0(L), z_0(L_d)[\ , \tag{4.3}$$

where $L = L_d + L_c$. Since $z_0' < 0$, the quality of the labor force remaining for old-type firms decreases with total employment but also with the level of employment in new-type firms.

A firm can attract the workers who are relatively versatile, autonomous and communicative by using a more decentralized mode of organizing interactions. But also all other firms which are switching to the new work organization attract them. Thus, it would be an illusion if each firm would think that its access to abilities is independent of the aggregate situation. According to the approach of monopolistic competition, firms take macroeconomic variables as given. In particular, they take the volume of labor L_d that is already employed under the new technology, the volume of labor L_c employed under the old technology, and the implied ranges of available abilities $Z_1(L_d), Z_2(L_d, L)$, respectively, as given when making their decision about whether to adopt the old or the new type of organization. By these simultaneous decisions the aggregate employment levels L_d and $L = L_d + L_c$ are determined in equilibrium (see below).

The fact that the range of abilities available for firms with technology γ_c does not only depend on L_c but also on L_d has an important consequence for the costs of organizing work with the old technology. As long as there is no new type of organization which attracts the relatively abler workers, i.e. if $L_d = 0$, the non-production input required for providing the capacity to organize one unit of production work is given by the function $g(L_c, \gamma_c)$, according to (4.1). However, if the best $L_d > 0$ units of labor are employed under the new technology, the work force remaining for old-type firms has relatively

[2] Remember it has been assumed that, as far as the dimension of individual productivity is concerned, labor is homogeneous.

low abilities. According to (4.3), the range of abilities which is available for firms adopting the old form of work organization is shifted towards lower interactive abilities if L_d increases. Thus, ceteris paribus, the non-production resources required to organize the interaction between workers rise. That means, the non-production input function shifts upwards if L_d is increased and the employment of L_c units of labor under the old technology starts at a lower ability level $z_0(L_d)$. Formally, instead of $g(L_c, \gamma_c)$ firms adopting the old mode of organization face actually a modified non-production input function, conditional on L_d. Let this conditional non-production input function be given by

$$g(L_c, \gamma_c | L_d) = \tilde{g}(L_d + L_c, L_d) , \tag{4.4}$$

where $\tilde{g}(L, L_d)$ with $\partial\tilde{g}/\partial L > 0$ and $\partial\tilde{g}/\partial L_d > 0$ is a function defined over $]L_d, L]$ which describes the non-production input required per unit of capacity organized in the old-type firm, if the range of available abilities is $[z_0(L), z_0(L_d)[$ and the distribution of abilities over this range is given.[3]

Obviously, for $L_d = 0$, the conditional function must coincide with the unconditional function, i.e.

$$g(L_c, \gamma_c | 0) = g(L_c, \gamma_c) . \tag{4.5}$$

Moreover, according to (4.3), for $L_d, L_c > 0$, the range $Z_2(L_d, L)$ is "strictly worse"[4] than the range of abilities $Z_1(L_d + L_c) = [z_0(L_d + L_c), \bar{z}]$ which would be available if $L = L_d + L_c$ units of work were organized with technology γ_c alone. Therefore, the conditional non-production input function must fulfill the inequality:

$$g(L_c, \gamma_c | L_d) > g(L_d + L_c, \gamma_c) , \tag{4.6}$$

for positive values of L_d and L_c.

The switch from $g(L_c, \gamma_c)$ to the conditional curve $g(L_c, \gamma_c | L_d)$ is illustrated in figure 4.1.

In contrast to this, according to (4.2) firms adopting the new method of work organization are not affected by employment level L_c. Thus, their non-production input function is only a function of L_d, as in the basic model:

$$g(L_d, \gamma_d), \quad \frac{\partial g}{\partial L_d} > 0 . \tag{4.7}$$

Taking (4.4) - (4.7) together, we see that two channels are important for the way in which the relative costs of organizing work under different technologies

[3] One should keep in mind that writing g as a function of employment levels is a short cut. Actually, the function depends on the composition of the abilities of the employed work force. For a given distribution of abilities, this composition is characterized by the range $[z_0(L), z_0(L_d)[$ of available abilities. And this range is determined by aggregate employment levels.

[4] That is, $Z_2(L_d, L) \subset Z_1(L_d + L_c)$ and, for all $z \in Z_1(L_d + L_c) - Z_2(L_d, L)$, $z > \max\{z | z \in Z_2(L_d, L)\}$.

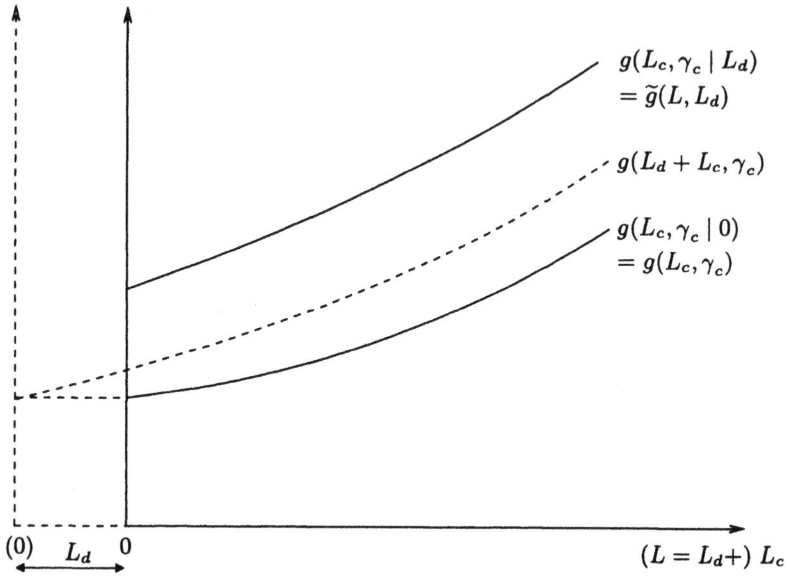

Fig. 4.1. The effect on γ_c - organization of an outflow of the best L_d units of labor.

depend on the volumes of employment organized in the respective modes. Function (4.7) shows that, ceteris paribus, the new form of work organization becomes less attractive (in terms of non-production requirements) if it is applied to larger parts of the labor force. What is easy for few is not so easy for all. The assumption of Lindbeck and Snower [45] that the costs of restructuring firms, from traditional Tayloristic work organization to modern "holistic" firms with multi-tasking, are increasing in the number of firms which have switched reflects a similar logic.[5] Whereas they are not explicit about what these switching costs are, here there are no exogenous switching costs but the change in organization costs arises endogenously from the fact that the range of available abilities changes if more workers are employed under the new model of work organization. However, (4.4) - (4.6), illustrated in figure 4.1, show us that this is only part of the truth if the aspect of firms as internal organization of interactions between workers is taken seriously. Also the traditional way of organizing work becomes more costly if the new type of organization is used more widely, since the quality of the labor-force remaining for old-type firms decreases. The demand by firms for workers

[5] Note that in Lindbeck and Snower [45] the size of employment per firms is fixed, where the "holistic firm is assumed to employ fewer people than the Tayloristic one" (p. 318). Thus, employment levels are simply a function of the number of firms operating under the two modes of organization. In contrast to this, the size of employment organized in the different types of firms is endogenously determined in the macroeconomic equilibrium derived below.

with high interactive skills exerts a negative externality on the other firms. This externality is ignored if the reorganization process is considered from the perspective of single firms. But for the macroeconomic equilibrium effects of the reorganization of work they are essential. Before we can turn to the analysis of these effects, we must take a closer look at the concrete nature of reorganization that we want to consider, namely, the change from central coordination to decentralized communication.

4.2 Central coordination versus decentralized communication

To bring out the essential difference between traditional forms of internal organization of the interaction of workers and new trends in the organization of these interactions, the following two stylized types of organization technology are considered.

4.2.1 Central coordination

This label is used to characterize a type of organization in which the predominant way of interaction is a hierarchical one, between non-production staff and production workers. Figure 4.2 sketches this type in a stylized scheme.

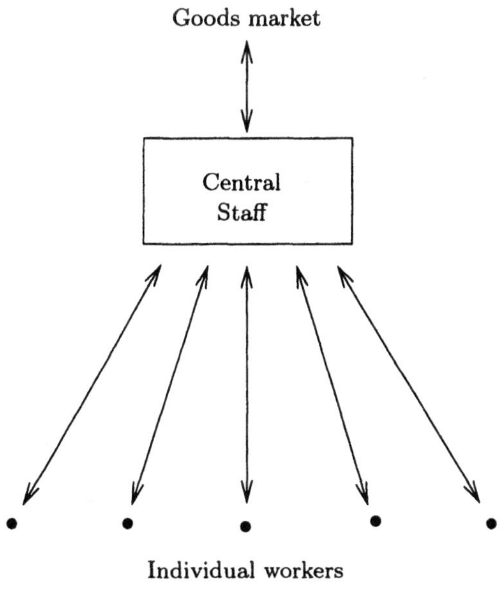

Fig. 4.2. Stylized scheme of central coordination.

This scheme is typical for strict labor division between specialized workers fulfilling a single task. The design of the different tasks and their combination to a saleable product is exclusively carried out by specialized non-production workers summarized under the heading central staff.[6] The function of non-production staffs are to coordinate and to supervise the individual workers. On the one hand, this requires certain basic interactions with each worker regardless of his/her abilities. The corresponding non-production inputs vary with the size of the organized work force not with its quality. On the other hand, the design, coordination and supervision of routinized single activities will be probably less easy if the work force to be organized contains less able workers. Thus, under central coordination (CC), the non-production input requirement per organized work place may be decomposed into a fixed component CC_0 and a component $CC_1(L)$ reacting to the quality of the organized work force. Denoting the central coordination technology by γ_c, we can write: $g(L, \gamma_c) = CC_0 + CC_1(L)$ with $CC_1' > 0$. The two components are illustrated in figure 4.3.

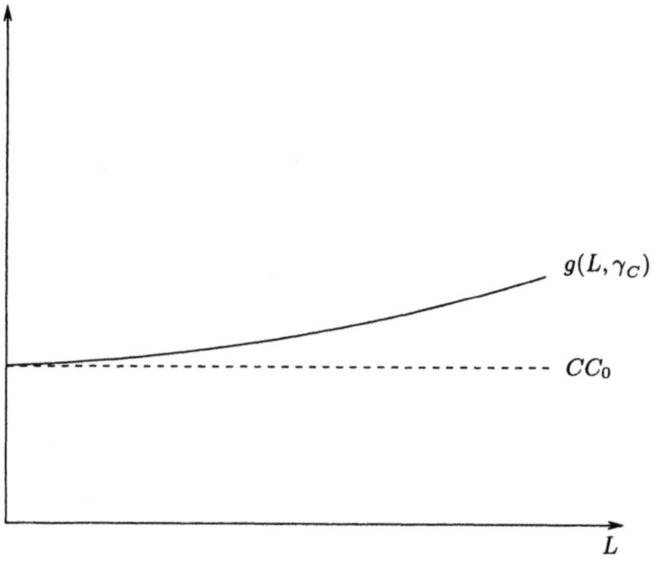

Fig. 4.3. Organization requirements per work place under central coordination.

[6] Since the purpose of this study are macroeconomic questions, the focus is on the fact that there is hierarchical interaction. Specific complexities of its structure, in particular multi-level hierarchies as considered in organization theory, are avoided. As already mentioned in section 2.1, possible internal diseconomies of scale arising from such complexities are also neglected.

4.2.2 Decentralized communication

Modern information and communication technologies allow lean management with flat hierarchies and autonomous workers or teams of workers who organize their work in a more or less decentralized way. This idea is addressed here under the label decentralized communication. To bring out the idea in its clearest form it is assumed that there is no hierarchy at all and interactions among workers and between workers and customers are entirely organized by direct communication between the involved subjects. This communication is supported by an *IT* infrastructure IT infrastructure. A stylized scheme of this type of organization is sketched in figure 4.4

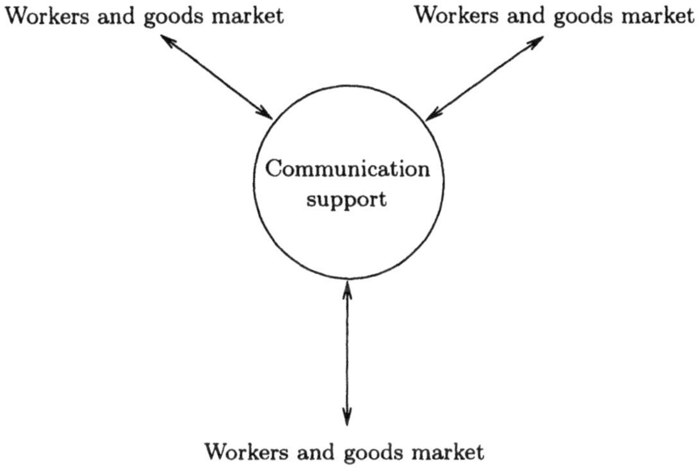

Fig. 4.4. Stylized scheme of decentralized communication.

Of course, such a decentralized network requires from workers much higher social and communicative skills than centralized coordination.[7] Provided that the employed workers have these skills they are quasi self-organizing. But what about individuals who have difficulties to handle the information and communication tools, to design their work or to fulfill both the task to produce and the task to coordinate themselves with coworkers and to deal with customers? An extreme assumption would be that these workers cannot be organized in the decentralized form. In terms of the non-production costs of organizing work such an assumption would mean that non-production inputs are zero as long as aggregate employment is below a certain level so that only workers are employed who have no problems to organize themselves

[7] Quite generally, the degree to which a new technology can be exploited depends on the abilities of the workers who work with the technology. See Walther [67] for an attempt to formalize this idea.

in a decentralized way. But increasing employment beyond this level implies prohibitive non-production costs since decentralized communication does not work if subjects with poor interactive abilities are included in the work force. This dichotomic view corresponds to a g-curve like represented by the broken line in figure 4.5.[8]

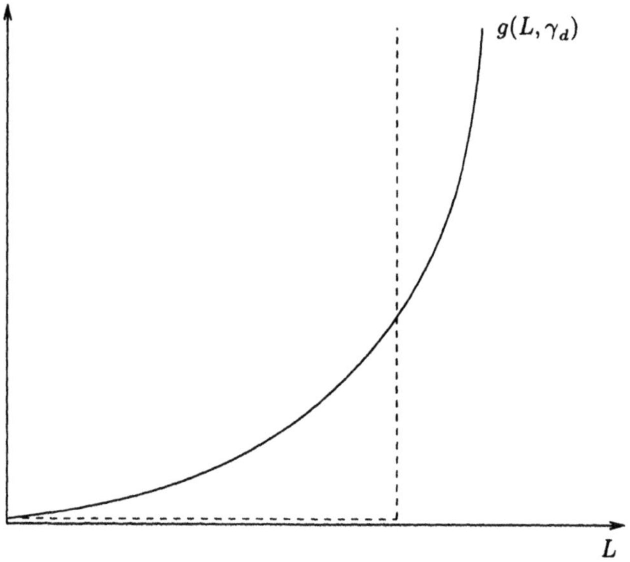

Fig. 4.5. Organization requirements per work place under decentralized communication.

More realistically, there is not a sharp line dividing the labor force into a group of perfectly able workers on the one hand and a group of workers who are organizable in a network. The point is that with less able workers more and more non-production inputs are required for supporting the communication network, i.e., time for intervening in critical situations, for guiding and helping those who are less capable of handling the network tools or performing the interactions with members or clients of the organization. Thus, the non-production requirements for supporting a work place in a decentralized network when the range of available abilities is $[z_0(L), \bar{z}]$ are represented by a function like $g(L, \gamma_d)$ in figure 4.5 rather than by the broken line (Parameter γ_d stands for decentralized organization technology). It is certainly true that a work force which consists only of able workers can be properly organized

[8] For instance, Lindbeck and Snower [45] assume that a certain fraction of workers is versatile (i.e., capable of working in a "holistic firm" with multitasking) whereas the other workers are non-versatile (i.e. capable of working only in "Tayloristic firm" with specialized single tasks).

in a decentralized way. However, it is also true that a work force containing workers with very low interactive skills can be more easily organized in a centrally coordinated and supervised firm with strict labor division and routinized tasks. Formally, it is assumed that there is an aggregate employment level $L_T > 0$ with corresponding range of abilities $[z_0(L_T), \bar{z}]$ so that

$$g(L, \gamma_c) \lesseqgtr g(L, \gamma_d), \text{ if } L \gtreqless L_T . \tag{4.8}$$

Condition (4.8) does not mean that decentralized communication is dominated by central coordination if aggregate employment surpasses the threshold L_T. It only states that this would be the case if all L units of employment were organized either in the one way or in the other way. But in principle different firms may adopt different technologies so that the more able workers are organized in the decentralized way while the others are centrally coordinated.

The next section asks which of the two types of organization technology is adopted by a firm, for given levels of aggregate employments L_c under technology γ_c and employment L_d under technology γ_d, respectively. In section 4.4 the macroeconomic equilibrium resulting from this adoption behavior is analyzed.

4.3 The adoption of organization technologies by firms

Suppose that of n symmetric firms with production capacity $\bar{x} = \bar{l}/A$ a certain number $n_d \leq n$ of firms use the decentralized organization technology (γ_d), whereas $n_c = n - n_d$ firms organize work by the centralized organization technology (γ_c). That means, $\bar{L}_d^x = n_d\bar{l}$ units of production labor can be employed in firms with decentralized communication and $\bar{L}_c^x = n_c\bar{l}$ units of production labor can be employed in firms with central coordination.[9] And total work place capacity in production is $\bar{L}^x = \bar{L}_c^x + \bar{L}_d^x = n\bar{l}$. With flexible wages all organized places are occupied[10] and all firms produce the same amount of output which implies $p_i = p = \mu w A$, according to the analysis in chapter 2.[11] The profit earned by a firm in the goods market at stage 2 is then

$$\begin{aligned} \pi &= p\bar{x} - w\bar{l} \\ &= (\mu - 1)\, w\bar{l} \, . \end{aligned} \tag{4.9}$$

[9] n_c, n_d as well as $\bar{L}_c^x$, $\bar{L}_d^x$ will be endogenously determined in equilibrium.

[10] Otherwise unemployed workers would successfully underbid wages.

[11] Firms are identical in the operative business at stage 2. They have the same linear production technology, given by the labor input coefficient A. That means, a unit of labor is equally productive in all types of firms and earns the same wage rate, provided that it can be organized at all. What differs across the two types of firms are the non-production resources they require for being capable to organize a certain volume of production work. These requirements are relevant at stage 1 when the size of the firms and their organizational design are determined.

The question to be decided by a firm at stage 1 is now not only how large the arranged production capacity should be but also in which form it should be organized. When deciding these questions each single firm takes the macroeconomic variables as given, in particular the ranges of abilities which are available to a firm adopting organization technology γ_d or γ_c, respectively. According to the analysis of section 4.1, these ranges depend on the aggregate levels of employment under the two technologies. According to (4.4) and (4.7), we have for the non-production input required for organizing a work place in a firm of type γ_c the conditional function

$$g\left(L_c, \gamma_c \,|L_d\right) , \tag{4.10}$$

and for a work place in a firm of type γ_d the function

$$g\left(L_d, \gamma_d\right) , \tag{4.11}$$

where L_c and L_d are the aggregate employment levels in γ_c-type firms and γ_d-type firms, respectively.[12] They are uniquely related to the production capacities $\bar{L}_c^x$, $\bar{L}_d^x$ by the conditions

$$\begin{aligned} L_d &= M_d + \bar{L}_d^x \\ &= \left[g\left(L_d, \gamma_d\right) + 1\right] \bar{L}_d^x \end{aligned} \tag{4.12}$$

and

$$\begin{aligned} L_c &= M_c + \bar{L}_c^x \\ &= \left[g\left(L_c, \gamma_c \,|L_d\right) + 1\right] \bar{L}_c^x , \end{aligned} \tag{4.13}$$

where $M_k, k = c, d$ denote aggregate non-production labor required in the respective types of organization.

A single firm, taking the described macroeconomic situation as given, faces the following profit options: When adopting organization technology γ_d, it has to invest $m = g\left(L_d, \gamma_d\right) \bar{l}$ units of labor as non-production inputs into the organization of $\bar{l}$ units of production work. Together with (4.9) this implies that the corresponding net profit function (after deduction of non-production labor costs wm) is given by[13]

$$\pi_d^n = \left[\mu - 1 - g\left(L_d, \gamma_d\right)\right] w\bar{l} . \tag{4.14}$$

[12] The convention in section 4.1 was that workers with relatively high interactive abilities are matched with the new type of organization. That means, according to (4.2) and (4.3), for each firm of type γ_d the range of the abilities of the employed work force is $[z_0\left(L_d\right), \bar{z}]$, whereas the range of abilities employed in a firm of type γ_c is $[z_0\left(L_d + L_c\right),\ z_0\left(L_d\right)[$. No work place is provided for workers with abilities $z < z_0\left(L\right)$, $L = L_d + L_c$.

If the decentralized communication technology γ_d would not attract the relatively able individuals but had to be operated with low interactive abilities it would probably never get adopted by firms in view of (4.8).

[13] In the case of firm-owner rents R, considered in section 3.3, we would have $\tilde{\mu} = \mu\left(1 - R\right)$ instead of μ. (Use $m = \bar{l}g$ in (3.16)).

In contrast to this, the firm has to invest $m = g(L_c, \gamma_c | L_d)\bar{l}$ units of non-production labor for providing the organizational capacity for $\bar{l}$ units of production labor, if it uses the central coordination technology γ_c. In this case, the achieved net profit is given by

$$\pi_c^n = [\mu - 1 - g(L_c, \gamma_c | L_d)] w\bar{l} . \tag{4.15}$$

Clearly, the firm will adopt that type of organization which yields higher profits. Thus, the firm adopts the decentralized form of organization γ_d if $\pi_d^n > \pi_c^n$ i.e., if

$$g(L_c, \gamma_c | L_d) > g(L_d, \gamma_d) . \tag{4.16}$$

It adopts the central coordination technology γ_c if

$$g(L_c, \gamma_c | L_d) < g(L_d, \gamma_d) \tag{4.17}$$

and is indifferent between the two modes of organization if

$$g(L_c, \gamma_c | L_d) = g(L_d, \gamma_d) . \tag{4.18}$$

Regarding the volume of employment which the firm wants to organize with the adopted organization technology, we obtain from (4.14) the decision criterion

$$\frac{d\pi_d^n}{d\bar{l}} >, =, < 0 \quad \text{if} \quad \mu - 1 >, =, < g(L_d, \gamma_d) \tag{4.19}$$

for a firm which adopts γ_d. And for a firm adopting γ_c the criterion is:

$$\frac{d\pi_c^n}{d\bar{l}} >, =, < 0 \quad \text{if} \quad \mu - 1 >, =, < g(L_c, \gamma_c | L_d) . \tag{4.20}$$

In the macroeconomic equilibrium, the aggregate employment levels L_d and L_c resulting from the simultaneous decisions of firms about the adopted technology and the volume of organized work must coincide with those levels on which the firms have based their decisions according to (4.16) - (4.20). Moreover, the production capacity ($\bar{x} = \bar{l}/A$) organized by different firms must be identical in the equilibrium so that the assumption of a symmetric goods market equilibrium, on which profit expectation (4.9) was based, is fulfilled.

4.4 Equilibrium employment after reorganization

Two situations have to be compared: i) The equilibrium before new techniques made the reorganization of work feasible. The corresponding aggregate equilibrium employment level, derived in chapter 2, is denoted by L_{AR}^*. (AR may be remembered as "ante reorganization".) The ratio of non-production to production work in this equilibrium is given by (2.39). ii) And the equilibrium resulting after the new techniques of organization have become available to firms. This equilibrium results from the adoption behavior analyzed in section 4.3. It is derived in this section. Section 4.5 discusses the employment effects of the "organizational revolution" by comparing the two equilibria.

Denote by L_{PR}^{*}, PR like "post reorganization", the aggregate employment level resulting in the PR-equilibrium. By definition, it is equal to the sum

$$L_{PR}^{*} = L_{d}^{*} + L_{c}^{*} \tag{4.21}$$

of total employment L_{d}^{*} in reorganized firms and total employment L_{c}^{*} in firms which do not adopt the new mode of organizing work. If $L_{c}^{*} = 0$, we have *total reorganization*, else the reorganization is only *partial*.

The equilibrium values L_{c}^{*}, L_{d}^{*} and L_{PR}^{*} are derived from (4.16) - (4.20) and (4.21). With L_{c}^{*}, L_{d}^{*} and L_{PR}^{*} also all other variables are determined. The decomposition in production work $\bar{L}_{k}^{x}$ and non-production work $M_{k}, k = d, c$, follows from (4.12) and (4.13). And the symmetric equilibrium in the goods market implies that the equilibrium ratio of the number of non-reorganized firms, n_{c}^{*}, to the number of reorganized firms, n_{d}^{*}, is equal to the ratio $\bar{L}_{c}^{x}/\bar{L}_{d}^{x}$ organized in the new and old way, respectively.[14] The first important observation is that there is always some reorganization of work. Formally,

$$L_{d}^{*} > 0\,. \tag{4.22}$$

This follows from the fact that, according to (4.5) and (4.8), $g(L_c, \gamma_c|0) = g(L_c, \gamma_c) \geqslant g(0, \gamma_c) > g(0, \gamma_d)$.[15] Using this inequality in (4.16), we see that it is profitable to adopt the new available technology γ_d, if nobody else does it. Thus, at least some firms will switch from central coordination to decentral communication. The question is, at which level of L_d does the relative attractiveness of the new type of organization vanish because of the fact that network organization is difficult if the work force includes people with low interactive abilities.

If more and more firms switch to γ_d, they have to employ also workers with lower interactive abilities. This raises the non-production requirements. Now two cases must be distinguished: i) If L_{PR}^{*} is low compared to the threshold L_T defined by condition (4.8) i.e., if $L_{PR}^{*} \leqslant L_T$, then it is clearly attractive for all firms to switch from γ_c to γ_d. This case is called *dominating reorganization technology*. ii) If $L_{PR}^{*} > L_T$, then both total and partial reorganization can arise in equilibrium. This case will be called *non-dominating reorganization technology*.

---

[14] Firms charge the same price and have equal market shares. In equilibrium, capacities are fully utilized. Thus, the production capacity $\bar{x}_d = \frac{\bar{l}_d}{A} = \frac{\bar{L}_d^x/n_d}{A}$ of a reorganized firm is equal to the capacity $\bar{x}_c = \frac{\bar{l}_c}{A} = \frac{\bar{L}_c^x/n_c}{A}$ of a non-reorganized firm. This implies $n_c/n_d = \bar{L}_c^x/\bar{L}_d^x$.

[15] $g(0, \gamma)$ is to be read as $\lim_{\epsilon \to 0^+} g(\epsilon, \gamma)$.

4.4.1 Equilibrium with dominating reorganization technology

According to (4.6) and (4.8), $g(L_c, \gamma_c | L_d) > g(L_c + L_d, \gamma_c) > g(L_c + L_d, \gamma_d)$, for all $0 < L_c, 0 < L_d$ and $L_c + L_d \leqslant L^*_{PR} \leqslant L_T$. Thus, even if almost all firms have reorganized work so that $L_c = L^*_{PR} - L_d = \epsilon$, the remaining firms have an incentive to switch to the new form of organization, according to (4.16). This means, we have total reorganization with $L^*_d = L^*_{PR}$ and $L^*_c = 0$.

Whereas the equilibrium structure of employment (L^*_d, L^*_c) is determined by (4.16) - (4.18), the level of aggregate equilibrium employment is determined by (4.19) or (4.20). If there is no firm of type γ_c, (4.19) is the relevant condition and the mechanism determining $L^*_d = L^*_{PR}$ is exactly the same as analyzed in chapter 2. Firms expand employment until $\mu - 1 = g(L_d, \gamma_d)$, or full-employment is reached. Thus, we have the following total reorganization equilibrium

$$L^*_c = 0 \quad \text{and} \quad L^*_d = L^*_{PR} = \min\{L_0(\gamma_d, \mu), 1\} \tag{4.23}$$

where $L_0(\gamma_d, \mu)$ is defined by the condition $\mu - 1 = g(L_0, \gamma_d)$.

Figure 4.6, based on the non-production input functions shown in the figures 4.1 and 4.5, illustrates this equilibrium for the case that the competitive situation (μ) and the organization technology (γ_d) imply that full employment is not profitable for the firms i.e. if $L^*_{PR} = L_0(\gamma_d, \mu) < 1$. Before the new organization technology is available to firms, the equilibrium level of employment is L^*_{AR} determined by the intersection point C of the old organization technology $g(L, \gamma_c)$ with $\mu - 1$. When firms have got the choice between central coordination and decentralized communication, the relevant non-production input functions are $g(L, \gamma_d)$ and $\widetilde{g}(L, L_d)$.

At any point L to the left of L_T the conditional non-production-input function $g(L_c, \gamma_c | L_d) = \widetilde{g}(L, L_d)$ for $L_c = L - L_d$ lies certainly above the $g(L, \gamma_d)$-curve, whatever is the value of L_d. (The reason is that for $L \leqslant L_T$ even the unconditional function $g(L, \gamma_c)$ is not lower than $g(L, \gamma_d)$.) Thus, if $\mu - 1$ is not higher than $g(L_T, \gamma_d)$, then γ_d-type firms don't wish to expand employment further than $L^*_{PR} \leq L_T$, where L^*_{PR} is determined in the same way as equilibrium employment in figure 2.4. Expanding employment by hiring in γ_c-firms the workers left over by γ_d-type firms would cost much more non-production input than expanding employment in the γ_d-firms (See point B compared with point D) and is thus certainly not profitable in view of $\mu - 1$. Formally, $\mu - 1 < g(L_c, \gamma_c | L^*_{PR})$ for $L_c = L - L^*_{PR} > 0$ and thus $d\pi^n_c / d\bar{l} < 0$, according to (4.20).

Alternatively, expansion of L_d could be stopped by the full-employment constraint $L \leqslant 1$. In sum, we have a dominating reorganization technology leading to the total reorganization equilibrium characterized by (4.23) if

$$\mu - 1 \leqslant g(L_T, \gamma_d) \quad \text{or} \quad 1 \leqslant L_T\,. \tag{4.24}$$

More interesting is of course the case that the interactive abilities of the labor force are not sufficiently high such that the decentralized communication

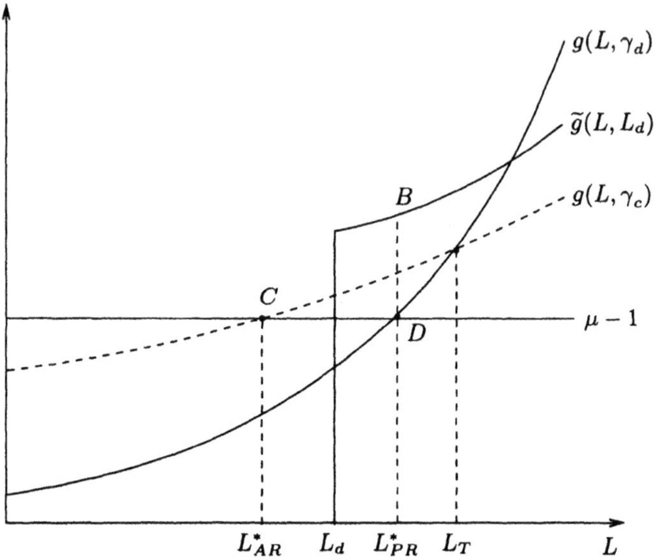

Fig. 4.6. Total reorganization with dominating reorganization technology ($L^*_{PR} < L_T$).

technology would be definitely superior to traditional forms of organization. Let us therefore consider the case that (4.24) is violated. It will be seen that nonetheless total reorganization ($L^*_d = L^*_{PR}, L^*_c = 0$) may result in equilibrium. However, also partial reorganization ($0 < L^*_d < L^*_{PR}, L^*_c > 0$) is possible.

4.4.2 Equilibrium with non-dominating reorganization technology

Suppose that $L_T < L^*_{PR}$. Considering (4.8) one might be inclined to think that it is always attractive to employ some labor under the traditional organization technology γ_c in this case. However, $g(L,\gamma_c)$ is of hypothetical nature as soon as a new technology option exists. It describes the non-production input required per organized units of production work only if a firm using the old organization technology has access to the whole range of abilities $[z_0(L), \bar{z}]$. But since the more able workers go to firms organized in the new way, a firm keeping the traditional form of organization is left with the relatively less able workers. Thus, there is an incentive to switch to the new organization technology even if with access to the whole ability range the old technology would be better. Formally, according to (4.4) not $g(L,\gamma_c)$ but $g(L_c,\gamma_c\,|L_d) = \tilde{g}(L,L_d)$ ($> g(L,\gamma_c)$, according to (4.6)) describes the relevant organization costs for central coordination if L_d units of labor are employed in firms which have switched to decentralized communication. Thus, although $g(L_{PR}^*, \gamma_d) > g(L_{PR}^*, \gamma_c)$ in the case of a non-dominating reorganization technology, we may have $\tilde{g}(L_{PR}^*, L_d) > g(L_d, \gamma_d)$ for any $L_d < L_{PR}^*$. Then, according to (4.16), even the last firms, if L_d is already arbitrarily close to L_{PR}^* and $L_c = L_{PR}^* - L_d$ almost zero, switch to γ_d and we have a PR-equilibrium with total reorganization i.e.: $L_c^* = 0$, $L_d^* = L_{PR}^*$, where $L_{PR}^* = \min\{L_0(\gamma_d, \mu), 1\}$ is determined in the same way as in (4.23).

Partial reorganization results in equilibrium if there are $L_c^* > 0$ and $L_d^* > 0$ so that firms are indifferent between γ_c and γ_d.[16] According to (4.18) and (4.4), this requires:

$$\tilde{g}(L_c^* + L_d^*, L_d^*) = g(L_d^*, \gamma_d) \ . \tag{4.25}$$

Moreover, according to (4.19) and (4.20), firms expand employment until

$$\tilde{g}(L_{PR}^*, L_d^*) = g(L_d^*, \gamma_d) = \mu - 1 \tag{4.26}$$

unless they are stopped by the full employment constraint $L_{PR}^* = L_c^* + L_d^* = 1$. For the formulation of a necessary and sufficient condition for such an equilibrium with total or partial reorganization it is useful to define the following auxiliary function $\tilde{g}_0$:

$$\tilde{g}_0(L_d) \equiv \lim_{L_c \to 0^+} \tilde{g}(L_c + L_d, L_d) \ . \tag{4.27}$$

This function describes the non-production input (required for organizing a unit of production work in the traditional way) which a firm faces if it wants to switch to γ_c in an economy in which all employment is organized with the new technology ($L = L_d$).[17]

Characterization of total reorganization. Suppose $\tilde{g}_0(L_v) \geqslant g(L_v, \gamma_d)$ at the potential total reorganization equilibrium $L_v \equiv \min\{L_0(\gamma_d, \mu), 1\}$. Part a) of figure 4.7 illustrates this case for $L_v = L_0(\gamma_d, \mu)$. At employment level L_v no firm wishes to switch from γ_d to γ_c, since, even if no other firm switches, the work organization costs in a γ_c-firm are $\tilde{g}_0(L_v)$ and thus higher than in the γ_d -firms. Moreover, no firm can expand employment if $L_v = 1$. And no firm wishes to expand if $L_v = L_0(\gamma_d, \mu) < 1$. Since in the latter case $\mu - 1 = g(L_v, \gamma_d)$, according to (4.19), expansion beyond L_v is not profitable under the γ_d-organization and even less profitable if the additional workers would be employed in a traditional firm. Only workers with relatively low abilities are left over by the reorganized firms. Formally, $\tilde{g}(L_c + L_v, L_d) > \tilde{g}_0(L_v) \geqslant g(L_v, \gamma_d) = \mu - 1$ and thus $L_c^* = 0$, according to (4.20). The following condition summarizes this argument:

[16] As stated at the beginning of this section, $L_d^* > 0$ is always guaranteed, since decentralized networks are certainly superior to centralized organization if only clever people are employed.

[17] By definition, $d\tilde{g}_0/dL_d > 0$ and $\tilde{g}_0(L_d) < \tilde{g}(L_d', L_d) < \tilde{g}_0(L_d')$ for $L_d < L_d'$, since $\partial\tilde{g}/\partial L > 0$ and $\partial\tilde{g}/\partial L_d > 0$ (see (4.4)).

$$L_c^* = 0 \text{ and } L_d^* = L_v \text{ if } \widetilde{g}_0 (L_v) \geqslant g (L_v, \gamma_d) \tag{4.28}$$

where $L_v \equiv \min \{L_0 (\gamma_d, \mu), 1\}$ is the aggregate equilibrium employment under the new mode of work organization. Part a) of figure 4.7 illustrates this equilibrium for the case of an unemployment equilibrium ($L_{PR}^* < 1$).

Part a): Total reorganization.

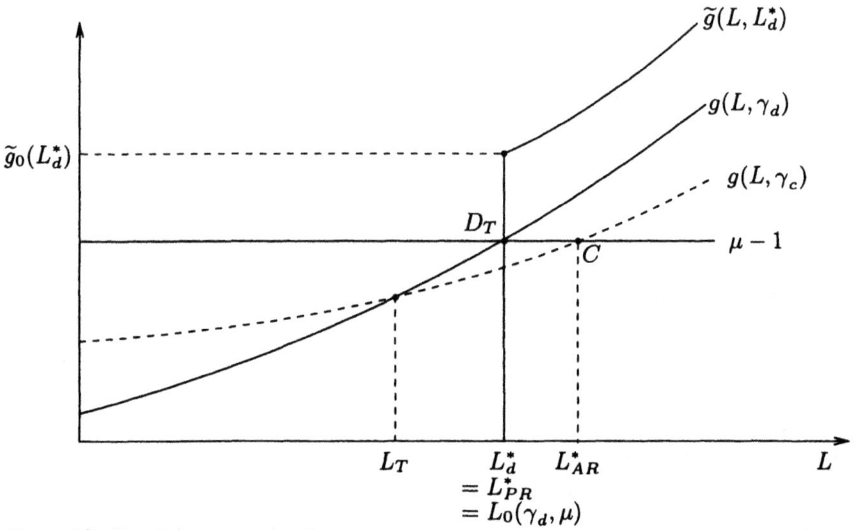

Part b): Partial reorganization.

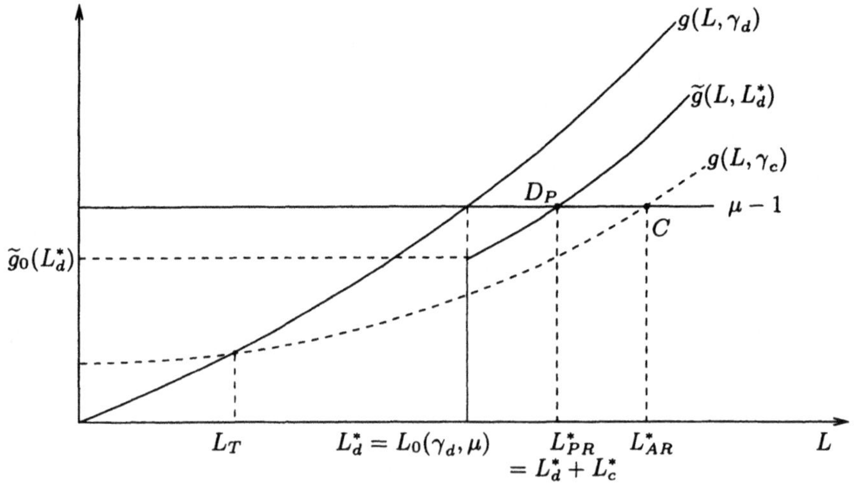

Fig. 4.7. Equilibrium with non-dominating reorganization technology ($L_T < L_{PR}^*$).

The traditional form of central coordination would be better suited to organize the whole employment level L^*_{PR} than the new mode of organization since L^*_{PR} includes workers who are not easily organized in a decentralized network. But central coordination is driven out of the market. The reason is that firms adopting the new mode of organization attract the workers with higher interactive abilities and traditional firms are left with relatively low abilities. This shifts their organization costs upwards and they switch also to the new form of organization. As a new type firm they can attract the same sample of abilities like all other new type firms. (Note that the decisions of firms are made simultaneously).

Characterization of partial reorganization. Suppose now that $\tilde{g}_0(L_v) < g(L_v, \gamma_d)$ at $L_v \equiv \min\{L_0(\gamma_d, \mu), 1\}$. We show that in this case the equilibrium is characterized by partial reorganization. Thus, condition (4.28) is also necessary for total reorganization.

If $L_v = 1$, employment cannot be expanded beyond L_v. But instead of organizing all work with γ_d it is profitable for some firms to switch to γ_c, since $\tilde{g}_0(1) < g(1, \gamma_d)$ in this case. Thus, $L^*_c > 0$ and $L^*_d < 1$. Equation (4.18) together with the full employment condition $L^*_c + L^*_d = 1$ determine the equilibrium mix of employment in the different forms of organization.

If $L_v = L_0(\gamma_d, \mu) < 1$, then employment can be expanded. The situation is illustrated in part b) of figure 4.7. For γ_d-firms it is not profitable to expand employment beyond L_v, since $g(L_v, \gamma_d) = \mu - 1$ in this case. Thus, $L^*_d = L_0(\gamma_d, \mu) < 1$. But since $\tilde{g}_0(L^*_d) < g(L^*_d, \gamma_d) = \mu - 1$, we have $g(L_c, \gamma_c | L^*_d) = \tilde{g}(L_c + L^*_d, L^*_d) \leq \mu - 1$ as long as $L_c \leq L_c(\gamma_c, \gamma_d, \mu)$, where $L_c(\gamma_c, \gamma_d, \mu)$ is given by the intersection point D_P of $\tilde{g}(L, L^*_d)$ with $\mu - 1$. Formally, it is implicitly defined by the condition

$$\tilde{g}(L_c + L_0(\gamma_d, \mu), \; L_0(\gamma_d, \mu)) = \mu - 1 \,. \tag{4.29}$$

Thus, according to (4.20), employment under γ_c-type organization is expanded up to the $L^*_c = \min\{L_c(\gamma_c, \gamma_d, \mu), 1 - L_v\}$. Summarizing this argument, we have

$$\begin{aligned} L^*_d &= L_0(\gamma_d, \mu) < 1, \text{ and} \\ L^*_{PR} &= L^*_d + L^*_c = \min\{L^*_d + L_c(\gamma_c, \gamma_d, \mu), 1\} \,, \end{aligned} \tag{4.30}$$

where $L_c(\gamma_c, \gamma_d, \mu)$ is defined by (4.29).

Part b) of figure 4.7 illustrates this equilibrium for the case of $L^*_{PR} < 1$.

In a decentralized communication network only workers whose interactive abilities are not lower than $z_0(L^*_d)$ can be profitably organized. But at least some of the workers who find no employment in a reorganized firm can be profitably organized under central coordination. Does this diversification among firms and workers worsen or improve the job situation in comparison to the macroeconomic equilibrium that had prevailed before the new organization techniques became available? The answer is given in the next section.

4.5 Job creation, job destruction and lean management

At the firm level the analyzed equilibrium reorganization of work is successful quasi by definition: The profit-maximizing i.e. the best available form of organization is adopted by firms. But how well does the new macroeconomic equilibrium compared to the old one? This section compares first the aggregate equilibrium employment L^*_{PR} with L^*_{AR} and then the equilibrium ratio of non-production to production work before and after reorganization. After all the firm's will to bring this ratio down is the driving motive behind the process of reorganization. Finally, it will be discussed how the analysis applies to employment problems implied by current trends of shareholder orientation and globalization.

4.5.1 Is reorganization harmful for employment?

For an assessment of the job situation many dimensions like job satisfaction or stress are relevant. Here the only aspect which is considered is the aggregate level of employment. Combining the analysis of section 2.4 with the results in 4.4, we can easily rank L^*_{PR} and L^*_{AR}. The comparison concentrates on cases in which at least in one of the two situations there is unemployment in equilibrium. Otherwise the situation would be trivially alike with respect to the criterion aggregate employment. Consider first the case of a dominating reorganization technology. The employment equilibrium after reorganization is given by $L^*_d = L^*_{PR} = \min\{L_0(\gamma_d, \mu), 1\}$, according to (4.23). In contrast to this, the equilibrium before reorganization was $L^*_{AR} = \min\{L_0(\gamma_c, \mu), 1\}$, according to (2.37). In figure 4.6, the employment equilibrium L^*_{PR} is determined by intersection point D, whereas L^*_{AR} is given by intersection point C, provided that unemployment prevails in both equilibria. It can be seen immediately that $L^*_{AR} < L^*_{PR}$ in this case. This ranking holds also if we have unemployment only in one of the two equilibria. Obviously, L^*_{AR} is the unemployment equilibrium in this case, since $L^*_{AR} = 1$ would imply $L^*_{PR} = 1$.

Thus, the reorganization of work with a dominating reorganization technology leads to more jobs indeed. The advantages of the new organization technology are so high and the interactive abilities of the workers are good enough that more employment can be profitable organized than under the traditional mode of organization with central coordination of specialized workers.

Is this positive employment effect of work reorganization robust? Is it to be expected also if the reorganization technology is not dominating? The answer is clearly no. With a non-dominating reorganization technology the employment equilibrium L^*_{AR} under the old organization technology is, for the case of an unemployment in the equilibrium, again given by the intersection point C in figure 4.7, part a) and part b), respectively. If full employment prevails ($L^*_{AR} = 1$), the equilibrium is to the left of point C. In contrast to this, aggregate employment L^*_{PR} in the equilibrium resulting when the new organization technology becomes available to the firms is determined by intersection point D_T in the case of total reorganization (part a) of figure 4.7) and by D_P in the case of partial reorganization (part b) of figure 4.7)), respectively. ($L^S = 1$ to the left of D would imply $L^*_{PR} = L^*_{AR} = 1$ which was excluded from this comparison, since with full employment in both regimes, a comparison of employment levels is meaningless.) The comparison shows that $L^*_{PR} < L^*_{AR}$ regardless of whether total or partial reorganization results in equilibrium. That means, the reorganization of work destroys employment opportunities in the organized economy. At least some workers with low interactive abilities who had a job before are no longer employed, neither in a decentralized firm nor in a traditionally organized firm. If the economy switches totally to the new mode of work organization, workers lose their jobs since they do not have the abilities required for profitable employment in a decentralized communication-based network. In an equilibrium with partial reorganization there are workers who remain employed in firms which organize work in the old way, but some people with relatively low abilities loose their job since the old firms have lost the employees with relatively high interactive abilities to the reorganized firms. The coordination and supervision costs per work place increase if the best qualified workers leave the firm. This is compensated by cutting down employment of those workers who are more difficult to organize.

4.5.2 Is reorganization successful in bringing down the ratio of non-production to production work?

One of the forces behind modern trends of reorganizing work is the idea of lean management. By switching from strict labor division between specialists in centrally organized firms to decentralized interaction in a network-like organizational structure one cuts hierarchies and hopes that the extent of non-production employment can be downsized. It is exactly this calculation on which the adoption behavior of firms was based in section 4.3. According to (4.16) and (4.17), each single firm chooses that organization technology which implies a lower ratio of non-production to production work. The question is if in the macroeconomic equilibrium the wish to bring this ratio down is fulfilled for the firms.

Denote by g^*_{AR} and g^*_{PR} the equilibrium ratio of non-production labor to production labor before and after the reorganization technology is available, respectively. According to (2.39), the equilibrium ratio which was relevant before the reorganization process started is given by the equation

$$g^*_{AR} = g\left(L^*_{AR}, \gamma_c\right) . \tag{4.31}$$

In the equilibrium resulting after the new organization technology γ_d has become available to firms, the ratio of non-production labor to production labor in reorganized firms is $g\left(L^*_d, \gamma_d\right)$, according to (4.11). And, according to (4.10), the equilibrium ratio in the non-reorganized part of the economy is $g(L_c^*, \gamma_c | L_d^*) = \tilde{g}(L_{PR}^*, L_d^*)$, provided that there is such a part i.e., if $L_c^* > 0$.[18] But if $L_c^* > 0$, then $\tilde{g}(L_{PR}^*, L_d^*)$ must be equal to $g(L_d^*, \gamma_d)$, since otherwise firms would not be indifferent between the two organization technologies (see (4.18) and (4.25)). Hence,

$$g_{PR}^* = g(L_d^*, \gamma_d) \ . \tag{4.32}$$

For a comparison of (4.32) and (4.31), we must distinguish the case that unemployment arises in both equilibria from the case that we have full employment at least in one equilibrium ($L_{AR}^* = 1$ or $L_{PR}^* = 1$).[19] If $L_{AR}^* < 1$ and $L_{PR}^* < 1$, then, according to (2.38), $g(L_{AR}^*, \gamma_c) = \mu - 1$, and according to (4.26) and (4.30), $g(L_d^*, \gamma_d) = \mu - 1$. Thus,

$$g_{AR}^* = g_{PR}^* \quad \text{if} \quad L_{AR}^* < 1 \quad \text{and} \ L_{PR}^* < 1 \ . \tag{4.33}$$

When firms are not constrained by labor supply the equilibrium ratio of non-production to production work is determined by the competitive situation in the goods market. If the market bears high non-production costs, firms expand employment until net profits (after deduction of overhead costs) are driven down to zero. If organizational change, ceteris paribus, changes non-production requirements, competition induces firms to adjust employment so that the ratio of non-production to production costs is again consistent with the equilibrium condition implied by the degree of monopoly in the goods market. This conclusion would only be altered if the equilibrium would be affected by additional market distortions, e.g. if the zero profit condition would be hurt due to rents for the firm owners. As discussed in 3.3, such a rent would decrease the relevant μ to $\tilde{\mu} = \mu(1 - R) < \mu$ with the implication that not only equilibrium employment decreases to some level $\tilde{L}^* < L^*$ (see (3.18)) but also the equilibrium ratio $g^*\left(\tilde{L}^*, \gamma\right) = \tilde{\mu} - 1 < \mu - 1 = g(L^*, \gamma)$, regardless of the organization technology (γ) in operation. The market forces, not the organization technology, determine the ratio of non-production to production labor in the macroeconomic equilibrium.

If the expansion of employment by firms is stopped by the full employment constraint $L^* = 1$ rather than by profitability considerations, then the equilibrium ratio g^* is lower then the one which would be allowed by the margin between goods price and variable cost, since $g(L^*, \gamma) < \mu - 1$ in this case. Figure 4.6 shows that with a dominating reorganization technology the ratio of non-production to production labor is indeed brought down in the reorganization equilibrium if the labor force is fully employed in this equilibrium.

18 Remember that $L_d^* > 0$ is always guaranteed.

19 Strictly speaking, we must distinguish between an equilibrium constrained by labor supply and an equilibrium which is not constrained. The case that $L^* = L_0 = 1$, which means that we have full employment but the equilibrium is not constrained by labor supply since firms don't wish to increase employment, is to be treated as an unemployment case.

With full employment L^*_{PR} is to the left compared to point D, and we have $g(L^*_{AR}, \gamma_c) > g(1, \gamma_d)$. Thus, with a dominating reorganization technology:

$$g^*_{PR} < g^*_{AR} \text{ if } L^*_{PR} = 1 \,. \tag{4.34}$$

However, if the reorganization technology is not dominating, the opposite is true. Suppose that $L^*_{AR} = 1$ in figure 4.7 so that a point to the left of C is realized in the equilibrium before reorganization. In any such point, we have $g^*_{AR} = g(1, \gamma_c) < \mu - 1$ but also $g(1, \gamma_c) < g(1, \gamma_d)$. Thus, with a non-dominating reorganization technology:

$$g^*_{AR} < g^*_{PR} \text{ if } L^*_{AR} = 1 \,. \tag{4.35}$$

In sum, the reorganization is only successful in bringing down the equilibrium ratio of non-production to production work if the reorganization technology is dominating and leads to full employment. If it is non-dominating and creates unemployment in an economy in which labor was fully employed before reorganization, the ratio is even biased in favor of non-production labor. In all other cases it is not affected at all by the availability of a new organization technology. This underlines again: In the general equilibrium, the reorganization process produces effects which are different from what the partial view of individual firm management suggests. What is true from the perspective of individual firms is not nearly true at the macroeconomic level.

4.5.3 Some remarks on the role of shareholder orientation and globalization for the reorganization of work

The presented analysis characterized the possible macroeconomic equilibria in an economy in which exogenous technical progress, for instance, the availability of powerful information and communication technologies, makes it possible for firms to organize work in a new way. The following remarks try to combine the results with two other recent trends to which firm management is exposed, namely, the increasing weight of the interests of firm owners and the more global sphere of action. It should be made clear that, apart from technological changes and changes in the skills endowment of the labor force, these trends have an important impact on the extent to which new methods of work organization are adopted by firms and on the implied macroeconomic equilibrium.

Reorganization of work and shareholder power. Shareholder orientation means that the management of a firm puts more weight on the interests of the owners of the firm when deciding about firm policy. In the basic model considered so far there is no role for non-wage incomes, since labor is the only input in both the production- and organization technology. So the proper income for firm owners cannot be analyzed in this framework. But, whatever is the input provided by the owners of the firms, in a perfect market economy they should be paid according to their marginal product. Thus, the reorientation of firm management towards the interest of the owners of the firms can only mean two things: Either in the past the owners have not been paid according to the marginal product of the inputs provided by them, or they require a rent. In any case their power must have been strengthened for some reason.

As discussed in section 3.3, a change in the power of firm owners can be captured in the presented framework by a change in the parameter R which denotes the amount of income (in real terms) that firms have to pay to their owners per unit of capacity. According to (3.18), for given R, the equilibrium employment level resulting under a technology γ is $\widetilde{L}^* = \min\{L_0(\gamma, \widetilde{\mu}), 1\}$, where $\widetilde{\mu} = \mu(1-R)$. A change in R can have far-reaching consequences for the extent to which firms adopt new methods of organizing work. In particular, it is possible that a non-dominating reorganization technology becomes dominating if firm-owner claims are getting stronger. This is shown in figure 4.8 which combines the reorganization equilibria analyzed in figure 4.6 and 4.7.

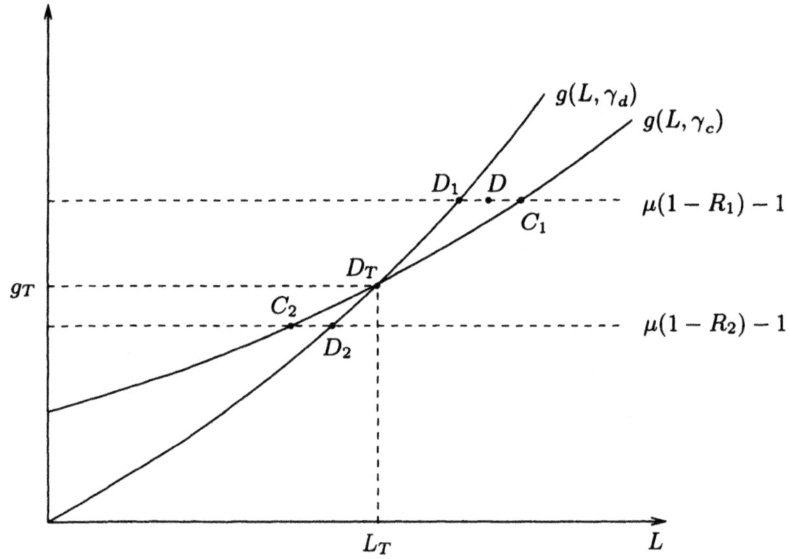

Fig. 4.8. Impact of firm-owner power on employment and reorganization of work ($R_2 > R_1$).

At a low level R_1 of the payment required by firm owners the amount $\widetilde{\mu}_1 = \mu(1-R_1)$ of the profit margin μ remains for financing non-production labor for the organization of production work. This allows a relatively high level of employment. In figure 4.8 a situation is shown, in which the corresponding equilibrium level of aggregate employment lies to the right of the threshold L_T.[20] At $\widetilde{\mu}_1 = \mu(1 - R_1)$, the equilibrium ratio g^* of non-production to production labor is higher than g_T. If employment is not constrained by labor supply, the employment equilibrium is given by a point D at the line $\widetilde{\mu}_1 - 1$. According to the analysis in 4.4, the equilibrium lies at the intersection point D_1 (i.e. D coincides with D_1) in case of total reorganization (see part a) of figure 4.7)) or somewhere between D_1 and intersection point C_1 in case of partial reorganization (part b) of figure 4.7). If the position of the owners of firms is strengthened so that they can require $R_2 > R_1$, aggregate equilibrium employment is reduced for any given organization technology. This negative effect on employment was discussed in section 3.3. Figure 4.8 shows a situation, in which the negative employment effect leads to an equilibrium to the left of threshold L_T. In this case, organizing work in form of decentralized communication (γ_d) becomes the dominating technology. The new equilibrium is point D_2 at the line $\mu(1 - R_2) - 1$. At D_2 we have total reorganization of work and a lower equilibrium ratio ($g^* < g_T$) of non-production to production labor than at equilibrium point D (where $g^* > g_T$).

This shows that shareholder orientation, which puts more weight on the interests of firms owners, induces the managers of the firms to adopt the new modes of work organization to a larger extent. In this sense shareholder orientation reinforces the process of reorganizing work which has become feasible by new organization techniques. From the normative point of view of employment policy the reorganization of work is welcome if the increase of the shareholder power is accepted as *fait accompli.* For R_2, aggregate employment after total reorganization is higher than without reorganization (point D_2 is to the right of C_2 in figure 4.8). However, reducing the claims of firm owners to R_1 would be better for employment, and at R_1 the reorganization of work is in conflict with employment policy unless there is full employment. (Point D lies to the left of C_1).

In sum, the fact that the reorganization of work becomes attractive at least for some firms is not the consequence of shareholder orientation but depends on the availability of new technological possibilities. However, the shareholder orientation of management increases the pressure towards reorganization and depresses the level of equilibrium employment.

Globalization. The switch to network-like forms of organization described in section 4.2 is not only a consequence of new management trends emphasizing flat hierarchies, team- and customer orientation or multi- instead of single tasking. Also the extension of the firms' radius of action to an international or global level increases the need for complex interactions and direct communication between workers in different subunits at different locations. The multi-nationalization of enterprises is a dominant feature of current economic developments. The international organization of production is not confined to

[20] It is assumed that $L_T < 1$.

multinational corporations. It includes contractual relationships[21] with outside firms. Recent contribution to the trade literature have emphasized that the integration of trade is accompanied by "disintegration of production".[22] That is, production processes are vertically fragmented with upstream production in one country and downstream production in another country, or there is horizontal fragmentation with the same type of activity being undertaken at different locations (see e.g. Venables [65]).

The basis for this international organization of economic activities are changing technical possibilities. Falling production costs as well as modern information and communication technologies make it possible to organize production globally. But at the same time the global organization of production requires from workers relatively higher interactive abilities. Trivial examples are the handling of electronic communication tools or the mastery of foreign languages. Also workers who are equally efficient as specialists for certain tasks differ with respect to the required interactive skills. As long as only few firms operate at a global level, they can pick that part of the work force which has no difficulties with international interaction. But when globalization is the common trend, then all firms need the same interactive abilities and we have exactly the situation analyzed in this study. The range of available abilities depends on the aggregate employment levels. And if there are two types of firms - traditionally organized firms requiring relatively little interactive abilities on the one hand and globally organized networks with high interactive requirements on the other hand -, we are in the situation analyzed in this chapter. Firms have to choose between the traditional and the global mode of organizing production. When making their choice they take the macroeconomic conditions as given. These macroeconomic conditions however are the result of the simultaneous decisions of the individual firms. Thus, the results obtained in 4.4 also apply to employment problems implied by global organization of economic activities.

A concrete example of non-production resources required to organize internationally disintegrated production are business services providing the coordination and communication infrastructure or creating a corporate culture. Firms may produce them internally or purchase the services from outside[23]. The essential point is that the provision of these services requires labor that is both endowed with high interactive abilities *and* high-skilled in the conventional sense of formal training. In the following chapter, we keep the framework of symmetric firms which employ non-production resources in a first stage to organize production and competition taking place at stage 2. But apart from heterogeneous interactive abilities labor is supplied in two qualities, skilled and unskilled. With this extension of the presented model it

[21] In contrast to anonymous exchange in polypolistic markets.

[22] See Feenstra [27] for a general discussion of this phenomenon.

[23] Burda and Dluhosch [14, 15], for instance, present a model in which a distinct competitive sector provides the business services for the global organization of disintegrated production.

will be possible to address the question of the skill structure of unemployed workers in a more differentiated way.

5. Skilled and unskilled labor

In the approach of this study, people's abilities are characterized by two dimensions: the skills which are relevant for individual productivity in a specific task, and the abilities which determine the costs of organizing the interaction of individuals. So far the analysis has been focused on heterogeneity of workers with respect to their interactive abilities. In particular, it was assumed that there is only one type of labor which can be used in non-production as well as production work. In the presented model non-production work comprises all activities which are necessary to transform individual labor inputs supplied in the labor market into earnings in the product market. In modern business, these activities require high knowledge, for instance, of legal and financial matters, of marketing and management methods, or of training, developing and supervising manpower. It is thus unrealistic to assume that each worker can be employed more or less efficiently in both production and non-production. This chapter accounts for this fact by extending the analysis to *two types of labor*. The labor market is assumed to be segmented into workers with high formal education (*skilled* or *high-skilled labor*) and workers with no higher education (*unskilled* or *low-skilled labor*). Whereas skilled labor can be employed in production as well as in non-production activities, unskilled labor can only be used in production.

The education system affects on the one hand the interactive abilities of workers. On the other hand, it changes the skill structure of the labor force. In the last century, in particular in the second half of the century, the supply of high-skilled labor rose sharply. The purpose of this chapter is to analyze the impact of the skill structure on the macroeconomic equilibrium, in particular on the equilibrium level of organized work places and on the wage gap between skilled and unskilled workers. In the standard equilibrium model with skilled and unskilled labor as inputs employed in a neoclassical production function, a growing number of high-skilled workers lowers their relative wage and induces firms to produce with higher skill intensity. The theory developed in this study points to another role of skilled labor, namely, as an input in the organization technology. An increase in the supply of high-skilled labor does not only allow to use more skilled labor in production but also means that, ceteris paribus, more resources are available to provide the non-production services which are necessary for organizing production work.

The literature on skill-biased technological change discussed in the introduction argues that labor demand has been shifted by technical progress in favor of high-skilled labor. This can explain why in many countries during the last decades despite the increased supply of skilled labor the wage of high-skilled workers was rising rather than falling relative to the wage of low-skilled workers. There are two principal reasons for the increased demand of skilled labor: First, technical progress may induce firms to choose a higher skill intensity in production. This is suggested by the prevailing theoretical models of skill-biased technological change. Second, the non-production input of skilled labor required for organizing production may rise relative to the labor used in the production process itself. This is pointed out by empirical studies (see the references in section 1.4). Since the framework developed in this book explicitly considers the *organization* of work, as opposed to *production*, the different aspects of the macroeconomic relationship between skill structure and technological change can be analyzed in a natural way. In particular, it is possible to analyze the impacts of an increase in the supply of skilled labor and of technological change on the equilibrium ratio of non-production to production employment.

Employment is the main concern of this study. The interesting question with two types of labor is if the aggregate employment levels of high-skilled and low-skilled workers move in the same direction or if employment of one skill group is raised at the cost of higher unemployment of the other group. Actually, many people seem to fear that the increased supply of skilled labor makes low-skilled workers jobless. A theoretical justification for such a rivalry would be that firms are filling their vacancies with high-skilled rather than low-skilled workers if more high-skilled workers are available. "When the proportion of skilled workers in the labor force is higher, the unskilled employability deteriorates because the skilled are more easily found" (Saint-Paul [57], p. 13. See also Saint-Paul [58]). In the model presented here there is a complementarity between the supply of skilled labor and the number of jobs for unskilled labor. A larger skilled labor force means that more resources are available for organizing production work places at which also low-skilled workers can be employed. In section 5.1 this basic complementarity is illustrated for the extreme case of a limitational relationship between skilled and unskilled labor. Then the relationship is analyzed in an equilibrium of an economy with internal organization of work. As long as all wages are flexible, the skilled labor force will always be fully employed either in the organization of production or in the production process itself. However, low-skilled workers, who can only be employed in production, may be unemployed if not enough production work places are created in equilibrium. If wages are rigid, unemployment arises according to standard arguments. In particular, also high-skilled workers may be unemployed if their wage is too high relative to the wage of low-skilled workers.[1] In a standard framework firms simply substitute skilled labor by unskilled labor if the price for skilled labor is too high. The following analysis will show a new aspect which arises from the fact that skilled labor is not only an input in production but is also required for the organization of production. High wages of non-production workers push up the costs of organizing production work. Thus, any power of high-skilled non-production workers like managers and their staffs to require a rent has negative effects on production labor, in particular negative employment effects on unskilled labor.

5.1 Skilled labor as a limiting factor

Before turning to the general analysis of the interaction between skilled and unskilled labor in the two-stage model of an economy with organized work, a much more simple framework is considered to illustrate why employment of unskilled labor may be limited by skilled labor supply. In this simple framework zero non-production requirements have to be provided at stage 1 and firms produce with a limitational production technology. Thus, the organization of work is not separated from production. There is no stage 1 at which the capacity to organize production work has to be arranged by employing non-production labor. Only production workers are employed and the more capable among them coordinate and supervise work parallel to their production activities. One may think of skilled foremen or heads of teams who have a look at less skilled coworkers.

Formally, let N_H, N_L be the endowment of the economy with skilled and unskilled labor, respectively. For the moment, it is assumed that labor is homogeneous within each skill group with respect to both individual productivity and interactive abilities. (This assumption will be dropped in the general analysis of the following sections.) There is monopolistic competition between n firms as in the basic model described in chapter 2. However, there is no separate organization technology. The production technology is given by a linear production function with labor coefficient A. The two types of labor are assumed to be perfect substitutes in production. But unskilled workers must be guided or supervised by skilled workers whose supervision capacity is limited. If h_i units of skilled labor are employed in firm i, they produce h_i/A units of output and, in addition to their production work, can coordinate and supervise

$$l_i \leq \bar{l}_i = h_i/\chi \tag{5.1}$$

units of unskilled labor, where χ is an exogenously given constant reflecting both the complexity of production and the quality of the work force. Employ-

[1] Unemployment of high-skilled workers means that they don't find employment in a job for skilled labor. Of course, they could occupy the work place of a low-skilled worker if they accepted the wage paid for unskilled labor.

ment of unskilled labor without guidance and supervision is unproductive. In sum, the production possibilities of a firm are:

$$x_i = \begin{cases} (h_i + l_i)/A & , \text{if } \ l_i < h_i/\chi \\ (1 + 1/\chi)\, h_i/A & , \text{if } \ l_i \geq h_i/\chi \, . \end{cases} \tag{5.2}$$

Figure 5.1 shows the corresponding isoquants. The maximally feasible output of the economy is $\bar{X}$. With endowment point $B = (N_L, N_H)$, aggregate employment of low-skilled workers is limited to $\bar{L} = N_H/\chi$, since there is not enough skilled labor to coordinate and supervise the whole unskilled work force. At endowment point B' full employment of unskilled labor is feasible.

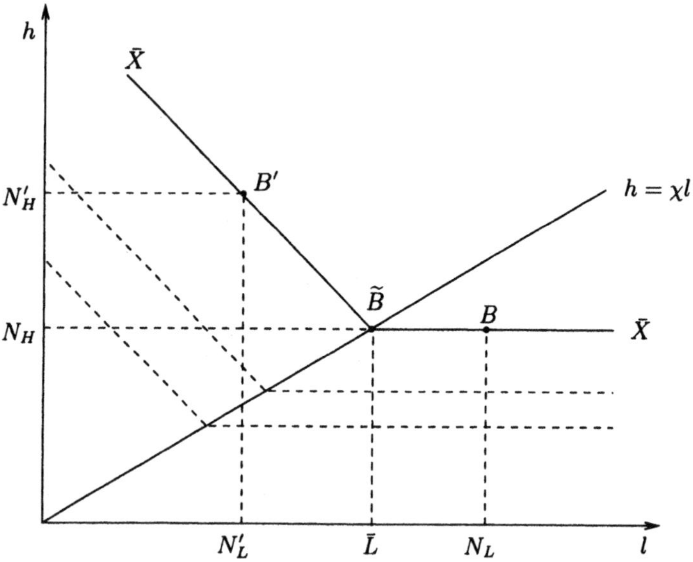

Fig. 5.1. Isoquants with supervision of low-skilled production workers by high-skilled production workers.

Facing these isoquants and the wage rates w_L, w_H for unskilled and skilled labor, respectively, firms choose the cost-minimizing skill-combination. Let $\omega \equiv w_H/w_L$ be the relative wage of skilled labor. Then, $l_i = 0$ if $\omega < 1$ and $h_i/l_i = \chi$ if $\omega > 1$. For $\omega = 1$, firms are indifferent between skill-intensity χ and any intensity higher than χ. The cost of one unit of output is thus given by[2]

[2] The A units of labor which are necessary for producing one unit of output are provided only by high-skilled workers if $\omega < 1$. For $\omega \geq 1$, they are provided by $\frac{A}{1+\chi}$ low-skilled workers and $\chi\frac{A}{1+\chi}$ high-skilled workers, since optimal skill-intensity is $h_i/l_i = \chi$.

$$c = \begin{cases} w_H A, & \text{if } \omega < 1 \\ wA, & \text{if } w_H = w_L = w \\ \frac{w_L + w_H \chi}{1+\chi} A, & \text{if } \omega > 1 \,. \end{cases} \tag{5.3}$$

Under monopolistic competition firms set their price by charging a mark-up on these costs. In view of demand function (2.9), we obtain

$$p_i = p = \mu c\,, \quad \mu = \frac{\sigma}{1-\sigma}, \tag{5.4}$$

and

$$x_i = x = \frac{Y}{n\mu c} \tag{5.5}$$

in the goods market equilibrium.

According to (5.2) and (5.3), this implies for aggregate demand $H^D \equiv \sum_i h_i$, $L^D \equiv \sum_i l_i$ of skilled and unskilled labor, respectively:

$$H^D = \frac{Y}{\mu w_H}\,, \quad L^D = 0 \tag{5.6}$$

if $\omega < 1$, and[3]

$$H^D = \frac{Y}{\mu\,(w_L + w_H \chi)}\chi\,, \quad L^D = \frac{H^D}{\chi} \tag{5.7}$$

if $\omega > 1$.

According to (5.6), all low-skilled workers would be unemployed if they required a wage which is higher than the wage paid for skilled labor. If they accept a wage which is lower than w_H, their employment depends on the level of employment of skilled labor.

Under flexible wages the wage rate w_H will go down until skilled labor is fully employed, and we have

$$H^* = N_H \tag{5.8}$$

for aggregate equilibrium employment of skilled labor. Then, according to (5.7), $L^D = N_H/\chi$ as long as $w_L < w_H$. If $L^D = N_H/\chi > N_L$ (as it is the case if labor endowment is given by point B' in figure 5.1), this demand for unskilled labor cannot be satisfied so that competition drives up the wage rate w_L. As soon as $w_L = w_H$ is reached, firms are indifferent between employing skilled or unskilled labor so that $L^D = N_L$ and $H^D = N_H$ in equilibrium. (The equilibrium coincides with the endowment B'). However, if $N_H/\chi < N_L$ (as with endowment point B in figure 5.1), the equilibrium employment level L^* of unskilled labor is $L^D = \bar{L} = N_H/\chi$ (see point $\widetilde{B}$). There is no way to raise labor demand L^D by lowering the wage w_L, since employment L is limited by the organizational capacity $\bar{L} = N_H/\chi$ of high-skilled workers. In sum, we have

$$L^* = \min\{N_L, N_H/\chi\}\ . \tag{5.9}$$

[3] For $\omega > 1$, we have $h_i/l_i = \chi$ and thus, according to (5.2), $H^D = \frac{A\chi}{1+\chi}\sum_i x_i$.

This shows that low-skilled workers may remain jobless even if they accept any wage below w_H. The reason is that the capacity to organize work is limited by the availability of skilled labor. More specifically, unemployment of low-skilled workers arises in equilibrium if $\chi > N_H/N_L$.[4] According to (5.1), parameter χ reflects the supervision intensity implied by the complexity of the used technology and the quality of the economy's work force. If this intensity is high compared to the supplied skill structure (N_H/N_L) of the labor force, some unskilled labor remains unemployed.

The limitational relationship between skilled and unskilled labor leading to production technology (5.2) is of course a drastical simplification. But the idea that skilled labor is an important resource for organizing work - not only a production input - is quite robust. The further analysis works out the idea in a generalized version of the basic model presented in chapter 2.

5.2 Extension of the basic model to two types of labor

The model outlined in the last section in which skilled production workers organize work parallel to their production activities, without any separate non-production work preceding production, may be adequate for certain traditional ways of production or some special sectors of a modern economy. But it cannot be considered as typical of modern organization of economic activity. As argued in the introduction, firms are characterized by their capacity to organize the interaction of individual subjects. This organizational capacity is provided by non-production inputs. Formally, this means that an adequate model must comprise an explicit representation of the organization technology, in addition to the usual technology of production. This section takes the model developed in chapter 2 and introduces the double role of skilled labor as an input in both the organization and the production technology.[5] With this extension the relationship between the employment of skilled and the employment of unskilled labor and the impacts of a changing supply of skilled labor or of technological change on this relationship can be analyzed in a differentiated way.

5.2.1 Endowment and technology

Aggregate supply of skilled and unskilled labor is given by N_H and N_L, respectively. Within each group workers may be heterogeneous as far as their interactive abilities are concerned. At stage 2, firms produce their output

[4] A social planner who maximizes aggregate output is indifferent between $\bar{L} = N_H/\chi$ and any employment level $L > \bar{L}$. (As figure 5.1 shows, with labor force $B = (N_L, N_H)$ any employment combination $(L, N_H), L \in [\bar{L}, N_L]$ produces the maximal output $\bar{X}$.) Thus, full employment is an efficient solution.

[5] A first version of this extension was presented in Falkinger and Grossmann [25].

x_i by employing h_i skilled production workers and l_i unskilled production workers under a concave linear-homogeneous production function F:

$$x_i = l_i f(\chi_i) \equiv F(h_i, l_i), \tag{5.10}$$

where $\chi_i \equiv h_i/l_i$ denotes skill-intensity in production.[6] The production function is differentiable with $f'(\chi) > 0$ and $f''(\chi) < 0$.

However, production workers can only be employed within the range of the organized capacity of work places, i.e. $h_i \leq \bar{h}_i$ and $l_i \leq \bar{l}_i$, where $\bar{h}_i$, $\bar{l}_i$ denote the work place capacity arranged at stage 1 for skilled and unskilled labor, respectively. To provide the capacity of organizing the production work of $\bar{h}_i$ units of skilled and $\bar{l}_i$ units of unskilled labor, a firm has to employ m_i units of skilled labor according to the following organization technology:

$$m_i = \bar{l}_i g(\bar{\chi}_i, H, L) \equiv G(\bar{h}_i, \bar{l}_i, H, L), \tag{5.11}$$

where $\bar{\chi}_i \equiv \bar{h}_i/\bar{l}_i$ and, for all H, L, the function $G(.,.,H,L)$ is non-decreasing and linear-homogeneous in $\bar{l}$ and $\bar{h}$. This guarantees that there are constant economies of scale ex ante and the number of firms plays no role for the macroeconomic equilibrium. L is the aggregate employment level of unskilled labor, which is used in production only. H denotes the aggregate level of employment of skilled labor. It is composed of aggregate employment in production, denoted by H^x, and aggregate employment in non-production M. The aggregate employment levels H and L are taken as given by the individual firms. They determine the range of interactive abilities which are available to the firms in the respective skill groups.[7]

What are reasonable properties of the organization technology? Two types of assumption are made. The first assumption concerns the reaction of non-production requirements to a firm's own decisions. The other assumptions deal with the impact of the aggregate employment levels which determine the range of abilities available to a firm.

First, it will be assumed that the marginal input of non-production labor required for providing the capacity to organize an additional unit of skilled production labor is not too high. Formally, $\partial G/\partial \bar{h} < \mu - 1$ or, equivalently,

$$0 \leq \frac{\partial g}{\partial \bar{\chi}} < \mu - 1, \tag{5.12}$$

where $\mu - 1$ is the price-cost margin achieved in monopolistic competition at stage 2. With respect to the impact of $\bar{l}$ on G only non-negativity is assumed.

Function $g(\bar{\chi}, H, L)$ describes the amount of skilled-non-production labor required per organized unit of unskilled labor, given that the skill structure

6 In contrast to section 5.1, skill-intensity χ is now not an exogenous technological parameter but an endogenously adjusted variable.

7 By analogy with (2.1), the relevant ranges are $[z_0^H(H), \bar{z}^H]$ and $[z_0^L(L), \bar{z}^L]$, respectively.

of jobs is $\bar{\chi}$ and the firm has access to the range of abilities determined by the aggregate employment situation. Assumption (5.12) guarantees that the non-production input for organizing the interaction of workers does not rise sharply when firms choose a higher skill intensity. This is plausible if one accepts that skilled labor has also good interactive abilities. One might object that skill-intensive production is more complex and requires thus relatively more non-production resources. This would be a misunderstanding. Assumption (5.12) concerns the effect of a change in skill-intensity for a given technology. In contrast to this, the argument about the complexity of skill-intensive production refers to shifts in the methods of production. The effects of changes in the production or organization technology will be discussed in section 5.4, in particular also the effects of skill-biased technological change.

As discussed in chapter 2, a higher level of aggregate employment implies that also less able workers must be employed. This raises the non-production resources required for organizing production work. Thus, an analogous assumption to (2.2) is:

$$\frac{\partial g}{\partial H} \geq 0 \text{ and } \frac{\partial g}{\partial L} \geq 0 \tag{5.13}$$

with strict equality holding if workers are homogeneous within the relevant skill group.

The next assumption is related to the productivity of skilled labor. It is natural to assume that employment of additional skilled labor is always productive. That means, for all $H \leq N_H$, the maximal feasible output of the economy is an increasing function of H. For formulating this assumption in a proper way we consider first which output is feasible if labor resources are used efficiently. Efficiency requires that all firms produce with the same skill intensity and that all arranged work places are occupied so that $\chi_i = \bar{\chi}_i = \bar{\chi} = H^x/L$. Now, by definition, $H^x = H - M$, where $M = Lg(\bar{\chi}, H, L)$ according to (5.11). Thus, $\bar{\chi}$, H and L are related by the condition

$$\bar{\chi} = H/L - g(\bar{\chi}, H, L) \ . \tag{5.14}$$

Condition (5.14) defines the efficient skill-intensity in production as an implicit function $\bar{\chi} = \chi(H, L)$ of the aggregate employment levels. Thus, according to production technology (5.10), the maximal aggregate output which can be produced with employment levels H and L is given by $X = Lf(\chi(H, L))$, and the property that X increases with H is equivalent to the assumption:

$$\frac{\partial \chi(H, L)}{\partial H} > 0 \, , \tag{5.15}$$

for all $H \leq N_H$ and $L \leq N_L$.[8] In words, a higher level of aggregate employment H may imply that skilled workers with relatively lower interactive

[8] Using (5.14), one obtains $\frac{\partial \chi}{\partial H} = -\frac{\partial g/\partial H - 1/L}{1 + \partial g/\partial \bar{\chi}}$. Thus, (5.15) is equivalent to $L\partial g/\partial H < 1$. Since $M = Lg(\bar{\chi}, H, L)$, according to (5.11), the condition $L\partial g/\partial H < 1$ means that a marginal increase of one unit of high-skilled la-

abilities enter the production process and more non-production resources for the organization of production work are necessary, if skilled labor is heterogeneous at all (see (5.13)). But this effect can never be so strong that an increase in the employment of skilled labor is totally absorbed in non-production. There remains always a positive effect on skilled labor in production H^x, and thus on the skill intensity.

In the characterization of the macroeconomic equilibrium and its comparative-static properties a further assumption is used which comprises both organization technology g and production technology f. The elasticity of the non-production input function $g(\bar{\chi}, H, L)$ with respect to changes in skill intensity $\bar{\chi}$ must be lower than the elasticity of the marginal product function $f'(\bar{\chi})$.

$$\frac{\partial g}{\partial \bar{\chi}} \frac{\bar{\chi}}{g} < -\frac{f'' \bar{\chi}}{f'} . \tag{5.16}$$

The condition has a clear economic interpretation if one uses the later shown fact that in equilibrium, where all work places are occupied and firms are symmetric ($\chi_i = \bar{\chi}_i = \bar{\chi}$), the marginal product $f'(\bar{\chi})$ is proportional to the real wage rate w_H/p of skilled labor. The right-hand side of inequality (5.16) is thus the relative decline in this wage rate implied by a rise in the skill intensity, whereas the left side expresses the relative increase in skilled non-production labor input g. In sum, condition (5.16) guarantees that the real non-production labor costs gw_H/p, which are required per unit of unskilled labor, decrease if skill intensity in production is raised. Note that here the impact of skill intensity on equilibrium wages is also taken into account, whereas in the discussion of assumption (5.12) only the amount of the physical non-production input was relevant. Obviously, condition (5.16) is fulfilled for any production function if the interaction of skilled non-production workers requires no extra organizational input of non-production labor so that $\partial g/\partial \bar{\chi} = 0$. But in general, additional information about f is needed to determine the equilibrium effects on the non-production costs. (5.16) is sufficient for getting unambiguous results.

5.2.2 Monopolistic competition at stage 2

Firms enter monopolistic competition at stage 2 with the organizational capacity provided at stage 1. Suppose that each firm has arranged capacities for $\bar{h} \leq N_H/n$ and $\bar{l} \leq N_L/n$ work places of skilled and unskilled labor, respectively. ($\bar{h}$, $\bar{l}$ are determined at stage 1 in anticipation of the profit situation resulting at stage 2. See the next section. Clearly, firms don't provide more places than can be filled with the existing labor force.)

---

bor H raises aggregate non-production requirements M by less than one unit. Also note that $\partial \chi/\partial L < 0$ is implied by the assumptions (5.12) and (5.13), since $\frac{\partial \chi}{\partial L} = -\frac{H/L^2 + \partial g/\partial L}{1 + \partial g/\partial \bar{\chi}}$, according to (5.14).

All firms are confronted with the same wage rates w_H and w_L for skilled and unskilled production work. They choose the same cost-minimizing skill-intensity $\chi = h_i/l_i$, $h_i \leq \bar{h}$, $l_i \leq \bar{l}$. It is determined by the rule

$$MRS\,(\chi) = \omega \tag{5.17}$$

where $\omega \equiv w_H/w_L$ is the relative wage of skilled labor and MRS is the marginal rate of substitution between the two types of labor. According to production technology (5.10), we have

$$\begin{aligned} MRS\,(\chi) &= \frac{\partial F/\partial h}{\partial F/\partial l} \\ &= \frac{f'(\chi)}{f(\chi)-\chi f'(\chi)}\,. \end{aligned} \tag{5.18}$$

This establishes a monotonously decreasing relationship

$$\chi\,(\omega)\;, \qquad \chi'\,(\omega) < 0 \tag{5.19}$$

between the skill-intensity chosen by the firms and the prevailing relative wage.

Moreover, firms have identical constant marginal production costs. By employing $h_i = \chi l_i$ and l_i units of production work, a firm can produce $x_i = l_i f\,(\chi)$ units of output and has production costs $C\,(x_i) = w_H h_i + w_L l_i$. Thus, the costs per unit of output are given by the equation

$$c = \frac{w_h \chi + w_L}{f\,(\chi)}\,. \tag{5.20}$$

As discussed in detail in chapter 2, flexible wage adjustment leads to wages at which the firms' labor demand at stage 2 is exactly equal to the work places provided at stage 2.[9] Thus, $h_i = \bar{h}$, $l_i = \bar{l}$ and

$$p_i = p = \mu c\,, \quad with \;\; \mu = \frac{\sigma}{\sigma - 1} \tag{5.21}$$

in the symmetric monopolistic competition equilibrium (see chapter 2 for a detailed presentation of the price-setting process under monopolistic competition. The only difference is that here the firms' marginal production costs are c, as given by (5.20), instead of wA in the basic model). As a result, the real profit achieved per unit of output in the monopolistic competition equilibrium at stage 2 is given by the equation

$$\frac{p - c}{p} = 1 - \frac{1}{\mu}\,. \tag{5.22}$$

[9] As long as there is an unoccupied work place, unemployed workers underbid wages so that they get the free place. If there is still unemployment after all places have been occupied, the unemployed cannot underbid wages successfully. There is no place for them even if they were willing to work at zero wages. They are unemployable, given the firms' decisions at stage 1.

5.2.3 The firms' provision of work places at stage 1

When deciding about the organizational capacity firms anticipate the profit which can be achieved by their business in the monopolistic competition equilibrium at stage 2. And they assume that the macroeconomic situation is not influenced by the behavior of a single firm. The question is thus which work place capacities $\bar{h}$ and $\bar{l}$ are optimal for an individual firm that takes wage rates, aggregate employment levels and the profit situation of stage 2 as given. (In the equilibrium, the macroeconomic variables on which the individual decisions are based must have the values implied by the simultaneous decisions of the individual firms. This equilibrium will be determined in section 5.3.) By assumption, $H \leq N_H$ and $L \leq N_L$. Obviously, a firm doesn't want to expand its work place capacity for skilled or unskilled labor if the respective labor force is already fully employed.[10] Moreover, the firm will choose the skill structure in production $\bar{\chi} = \bar{h}/\bar{l}$ in such a way that it is consistent with cost-minimization at stage 2, i.e. $\bar{\chi} = \chi(\omega)$. For $H < N_H$ and $L < N_L$, each firm can expect that its capacity will be fully used at stage 2, since unemployed labor will underbid wages until all work places are occupied. So a firm providing the capacity to organize $\bar{h} = \bar{l}\bar{\chi}$ units of skilled and $\bar{l}$ units of unskilled labor knows that its sold output is given by

$$x = F\left(\bar{h}, \bar{l}\right) = \bar{l} f\left(\bar{\chi}\right) . \tag{5.23}$$

The firm also knows that the real profit to be expected per unit of sold output is $1 - 1/\mu$, according to (5.22). Combining this with organization technology (5.11), a firm which maximizes expected real net profits $\tilde{\pi}^n \equiv \pi^n/p = \left[(p-c)\,x - w_H G\right]/p$ is confronted with the decision problem: $\max_{\bar{h},\bar{l}} \left\{(1-1/\mu)\, F\left(\bar{h},\bar{l}\right) - (w_H/p)\, G\left(\bar{h},\bar{l},H,L\right)\right\}$ where $\bar{h} = \bar{l}\bar{\chi} \leq N_H/n$ and $\bar{l} \leq N_L/n$. This can be rewritten in the form:

$$\max_{\bar{l}} \ \tilde{\pi}^n = \left(1 - \frac{1}{\mu}\right) \bar{l} f\left(\bar{\chi}\right) - \frac{w_H}{p} \bar{l} g\left(\bar{\chi}, H, L\right) . \tag{5.24}$$

The first term of the expression to be maximized represents expected real gross profit. The second term describes the real costs of skilled non-production labor required for achieving this profit. For any given $\bar{\chi}$, both the expected real gross profit and the real costs are linear with respect to $\bar{l}$. Thus,

$$\frac{\partial \tilde{\pi}^n}{\partial \bar{l}} >,=,< 0 \ \text{ if } \ \left(1 - \frac{1}{\mu}\right) f\left(\bar{\chi}\right) >,=,< \frac{w_H}{p} g\left(\bar{\chi}, H, L\right) . \tag{5.25}$$

Firms expand $\bar{l}$ as long as the expected gross profit of a low-skilled worker is higher than the non-production costs of organizing the work of low-skilled labor.

[10] Either it could not fill these work places or it had to overbid the wages paid by the competing firms which would push up its price.

5.2.4 Aggregate employment and wages implied by the behavior of firms

If each firm arranges work place capacities $\bar{h}$ and $\bar{l}$ and flexible wages guarantee that all places are occupied, aggregate employment in production is $H^x = n\bar{h}$ and $L = n\bar{l}$. Total employment of skilled labor is given by $H = M + H^x = Lg(\bar{\chi}, H, L) + H^x$, where $\bar{\chi} = \bar{h}/\bar{l}$ is the skill structure of the provided production jobs. Since $\bar{\chi}$ is identical in all firms, it must be equal to the average skill-intensity H^x/L of the economy which is a function $\chi(H, L)$ of aggregate employment levels, implicitly defined by equation (5.14). Thus, we have on the one hand:

$$\bar{\chi} = \chi(H, L) \quad \text{with} \quad \frac{\partial \chi}{\partial H} > 0, \quad \frac{\partial \chi}{\partial L} < 0 . \tag{5.26}$$

($\partial\chi/\partial H > 0$, according to (5.15), and $\partial\chi/\partial L < 0$ is implied by (5.12) and (5.13).) On the other hand, wages are adjusted so that the skill-intensity of actual employment at stage 2, which is given by (5.19), is equal to the skill structure of the arranged production work places. Thus, at the equilibrium wage rate ω^* ($= w_H^*/w_L^*$), the following equation holds:

$$\bar{\chi} = \chi(\omega^*) \quad \text{with} \quad \chi'(\omega) < 0 . \tag{5.27}$$

(To save notation the same function symbol χ was used for the cost-minimizing skill intensity as a function of ω and average skill intensity as a function of H, L. The arguments make clear which function is meant.)

Combining (5.27) with (5.26), we obtain:

$$\chi(\omega^*) = \chi(H, L) . \tag{5.28}$$

Condition (5.28) determines ω^* as a function of the employment levels implied by the firms' decision about the organization of work places at stage 1.

Nominal prices and wages are determined by the condition that aggregate money income Y (given by the exogenous money supply) must be equal to aggregate nominal supply $pX = pLf(\bar{\chi})$. Since $p = \mu w_L(\omega\bar{\chi} + 1)/f(\bar{\chi})$, according to (5.20) and (5.21), the condition $Y = pLf(\bar{\chi})$ implies

$$w_L^* = \frac{Y}{\mu(\omega^*\bar{\chi} + 1) L} , \tag{5.29}$$

where $\bar{\chi}$ and ω^* depend on H and L, as determined by the equations (5.26) and (5.28). Obviously, with w_L^*, ω^* and $\bar{\chi}$ all other nominal variables w_H^*, c^* and p^* are determined as functions of H and L). And the real wage rates are[11]

[11] Use $p = \mu w_L(\omega\chi + 1)/f(\chi)$ to get $\frac{w_L}{p} = \frac{f(\chi)}{\mu(\omega\chi+1)}$. Then substitute ω determined by (5.17) and (5.18) into this expression.

$$\frac{w_L^*}{p^*} = \frac{f(\bar{\chi}) - \bar{\chi} f'(\bar{\chi})}{\mu} \tag{5.30}$$

and[12]

$$\frac{w_H^*}{p^*} = \frac{f'(\bar{\chi})}{\mu}, \tag{5.31}$$

respectively.

5.3 Employment and skill structure of jobs in the macroeconomic equilibrium

In a macroeconomic equilibrium the levels of aggregate employment and wages implied by the job-creation behavior of the single firms must be consistent with the wage level and the values of H and L on which the firms have based their decisions about the organization of work places. Moreover, the aggregate employment levels are restricted by the supply constraints $H \leq N_H$ and $L \leq N_L$.

The profit-maximizing choice of work place provision by firms was analyzed in section 5.2.3. It depends on the expected relative wage ω which determines the cost-minimizing skill structure $\bar{\chi}$ of production work places. But according to the analysis in 5.2.4, in an equilibrium with flexible wages the relative wage in turn depends on the realized aggregate employment levels. Thus, multiple equilibria are possible under rational expectations [13]. In the further analysis we focus on the equilibrium in which skilled labor is fully employed and constitutes a limiting factor for the employment of low-skilled workers. Hence,

$$H^* = N_L \,. \tag{5.32}$$

(Superscript $*$ is used to denote the equilibrium value of the respective variable.) What about aggregate employment of unskilled labor?

Firms expand or reduce the provision of work places for unskilled labor according to condition (5.25), depending on which inequality holds in the given macroeconomic situation. If equality holds, firms don't change the level of unskilled employment. Thus, in the macroeconomic equilibrium, we have full employment and $\partial \tilde{\pi}^n / \partial \bar{l} \geq 0$, or condition (5.25) must hold with equality. The left side of condition (5.25) describes the real gross profit per work place of low-skilled labor. Denote this profit by APL like average profit per low-skilled worker. In an equilibrium with aggregate employment levels $H^* = N_H$ and L to be determined, APL is given by

$$APL(N_H, L) = \left(1 - \frac{1}{\mu}\right) f(\chi(N_H, L)), \tag{5.33}$$

[12] Use $w_H^* = \omega^* w_L^*$ and (5.17), (5.18).

[13] See Falkinger and Grossmann [26] for a careful analysis of the possible equilibria. Moreover, they extend the analysis to dual labor markets.

since $\bar{\chi} = \chi(N_H, L)$ according to (5.26). Using $f' > 0$ and $\partial\chi/\partial L < 0$[14], we conclude: The average profit per work place arranged for low-skilled workers is a strictly decreasing function of L.

The right side of condition (5.25) represents the real non-production costs per work place arranged for unskilled labor. Denote this costs by ACL like average costs of a work place for low-skilled workers. In an equilibrium with aggregate employment levels $H^* = N_H$ and L, ACL is given by

$$ACL(N_H, L) = \frac{f'(\chi(N_H, L))}{\mu} g(\chi(N_H, L), N_H, L) , \tag{5.34}$$

since $w_H/p = f'(\chi(N_H, L))/\mu$, according to (5.31). Using $f'' < 0$, $\partial\chi/\partial L < 0$ and assumption (5.16), we conclude that ACL is a strictly increasing function of L.[15] The reason is that organizing a higher employment level of unskilled labor implies a rise in the wage of skilled labor which increases non-production costs as long as production and organization technology fulfill assumption (5.16).

Equating APL, which is strictly decreasing in L, with ACL, which is strictly increasing in L, we obtain a function $L_0(N_H)$ implicitly defined by the condition

$$APL(N_H, L_0) = ACL(N_H, L_0) . \tag{5.35}$$

If $L_0(N_H) \leq N_L$, aggregate equilibrium employment L^* of unskilled labor is equal to $L_0(N_H)$, since according to (5.25) firms don't find it profitable to expand employment of unskilled workers further. (Nor do they wish to reduce employment.) If $L_0(N_H) > N_L$ the expansion stops at the full-employment constraint $L^* = N_L$. Hence, we have

$$L^* = \min\{L_0(N_H), N_L\} \tag{5.36}$$

in the macroeconomic equilibrium. Figure 5.2 illustrates this equilibrium for the case of $L_0(N_H) < N_L$.

The picture shows the costs and returns of a work place for unskilled labor as functions of aggregate employment of unskilled labor. For a fixed level of high-skilled work force N_H, the return (APL) on arranging a work place for unskilled labor declines, since an increase in employment of low-skilled workers implies a low skill-intensity in production and thus a lower productivity of unskilled labor. At the same time, the costs (ACL) of arranging a work place rise because a lower skill intensity in production implies a higher

---

[14] Remember that $\chi(H, L)$ is implicitly defined by equation (5.14) and that $\frac{\partial\chi}{\partial L} = -\frac{H/L^2 + \partial g/\partial L}{1 + \partial g/\partial\bar{\chi}} < 0$ because of (5.12) and (5.13).

[15] $\frac{\partial ACL}{\partial L} > 0$ is equivalent to the inequality $f'\frac{dg}{dL} > -f''\frac{\partial\chi}{\partial L}g$. Using $\frac{dg}{dL} = \frac{\partial g}{\partial\bar{\chi}}\frac{\partial\chi}{\partial L} + \frac{\partial g}{\partial L}$ and rewriting the inequality we get the condition $\frac{\partial g}{\partial\bar{\chi}}\frac{1}{g} < -\frac{f''}{f'} - \frac{\partial g}{\partial L}\frac{1}{g\partial\chi/\partial L}$ (Recall $\partial\chi/\partial L < 0$). This condition is fulfilled because of assumption (5.16), $\partial\chi/\partial L < 0$ and $\partial g/\partial L \geq 0$.

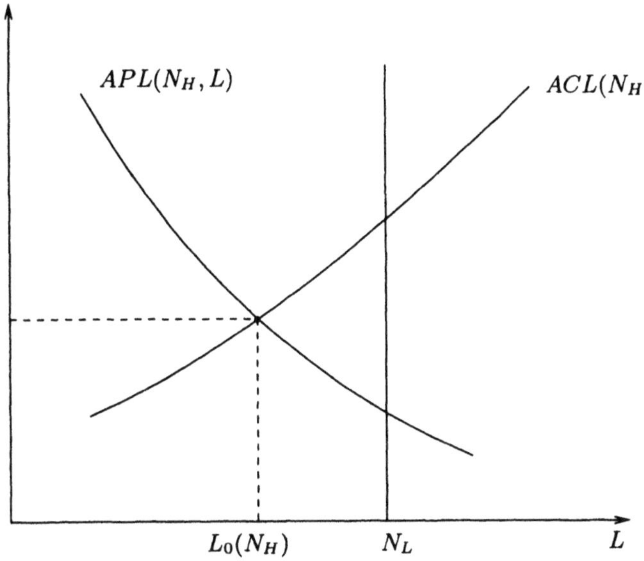

Fig. 5.2. Equilibrium with unemployment of unskilled labor.

wage of skilled labor including non-production labor. This is true regardless of whether interactive abilities vary within the group of low-skilled workers. It should be noticed that the argument was derived by using (5.13) which includes the case of homogeneous labor within the skill groups.

This defines for each level of supply of skilled labor N_H a unique limit L_0 for profitable employment of unskilled labor. If the unskilled labor force is larger than this level of profitable employment some low-skilled workers will find no job no matter how low their wage. The next section discusses how the level of this unemployment is affected by the supply of skilled labor. Moreover, the possible impacts of technological change on the (un-)employment equilibrium are analyzed.

5.4 The role of skill supply and technological change for the employment of unskilled labor

Skilled labor is always fully employed in the considered equilibrium resulting under flexible wages, but there may be unemployment of unskilled workers. Is it good or bad for the employment of low-skilled workers if the supply of skilled labor increases? First, the question will be answered without paying attention to where the additional skilled labor comes from. But if the increase in the supply of skilled labor results from an upgrading of unskilled labor, there is at the same time a change in the low-skilled labor force. Its size is necessarily reduced but also its quality may decline if the relatively more able unskilled workers switch to the skilled labor force. This indirect effect affects the non-production requirements of organizing production with unskilled labor. So it works like a change in the organization technology in the present model. Such effects of changes in the organization technology as well as the effects of the usually considered skill-biased change in the production technology are analyzed in a second step.

5.4.1 Supply of skilled labor and (un-)employment of unskilled labor

According to (5.36), the equilibrium level of aggregate employment of unskilled labor is a function of the aggregate level of available skilled labor if we are in an unemployment equilibrium. The following analysis concentrates on this case, i.e. $L^* = L_0(N_H)$.

To see the effects of an exogenous change in N_H on L_0 consider first the impact of N_H on the APL-curve defined by (5.33). Since $f' > 0$ and $\partial\chi/\partial H > 0$, according to (5.15), this curve is shifted upwards by an increase in N_H. The reason is that a larger skilled labor force allows to produce with higher skill-intensity and thus increases the productivity of unskilled labor. But N_H affects also the ACL-curve which is defined by (5.34). $f'' < 0$ and $\partial\chi/\partial H > 0$ imply that the real wage of skilled labor goes down if more skilled labor is supplied. This is a standard effect. It induces firms to produce with a higher skill-intensity. In the present framework it implies a cost-dampening effect not only on the costs of skilled labor in production but also on the costs of skilled non-production labor. This shifts the ACL-curve downwards. However, there is also a cost-increasing effect, since the quantity of required non-production labor rises with employment H.[16] According to (5.16) this cost-increasing effect is limited. If the additional skilled labor has the same interactive abilities as the least able skilled worker had before the increase of N_H, i.e. if $\partial g/\partial N_H = 0$, then condition (5.16) guarantees $\partial ACL/\partial N_H < 0$.[17] Otherwise, assumption (5.16) would have to be strengthened to account for the additional effect on non-production costs resulting from declining

16 The total impact of H on $g(\chi(H,L), H, L)$ is given by $\frac{dg}{dH} = \frac{\partial g}{\partial \bar{\chi}}\frac{\partial \chi}{\partial H} + \frac{\partial g}{\partial H} \geq 0$ (recall (5.12), (5.13) and (5.15)). Only if the organization of the interaction of skilled production workers requires no non-production resources (i.e. $\partial g/\partial \bar{\chi} = \partial G/\partial \bar{h} = 0$) and skilled labor is homogeneous (i.e. $\partial g/\partial H = 0$), this impact is zero.

17 $\frac{\partial ACL}{\partial N_H} < 0$ is equivalent to $f''\frac{\partial \chi}{\partial H}g + f'\left[\frac{\partial g}{\partial \bar{\chi}}\frac{\partial \chi}{\partial H} + \frac{\partial g}{\partial H}\right] < 0$ at $H = N_H$. Rearranging this inequality, we get the equivalent condition $\frac{\partial g}{\partial \bar{\chi}}\frac{1}{g} + \frac{\partial g}{\partial H}\frac{1}{g\partial\chi/\partial H} < -\frac{f''}{f'}$. (Recall $\partial g/\partial H \geq 0$ and $\partial\chi/\partial H > 0$.) For $\partial g/\partial H = 0$, the condition is equivalent to (5.16), but if $\partial g/\partial H > 0$ a stronger condition is needed to guarantee $\partial ACL/\partial N_H < 0$. (That is, if $\partial g/\partial N_H > 0$, the decrease in real non-production labor costs gw_H/p per unit of unskilled labor has to be sufficiently large if N_H shifts up.)

interactive abilities of new skilled labor. In the following discussion of the impact of N_H such additional effects are ignored and $\partial g/N_H = 0$ is assumed. ($\frac{\partial g}{\partial N_H}$ is used as short cut for $\frac{\partial g}{\partial H}|_{H=N_H}$.) Obviously, $\partial g/\partial N_H = 0$ is not a necessary condition for the derived comparative static result.

In sum, an exogenous increase of skilled labor supply N_H shifts the APL-curve upwards and the ACL-curve downwards. This implies

$$\frac{dL_0}{dN_H} > 0\,. \tag{5.37}$$

The result is illustrated in figure 5.3.

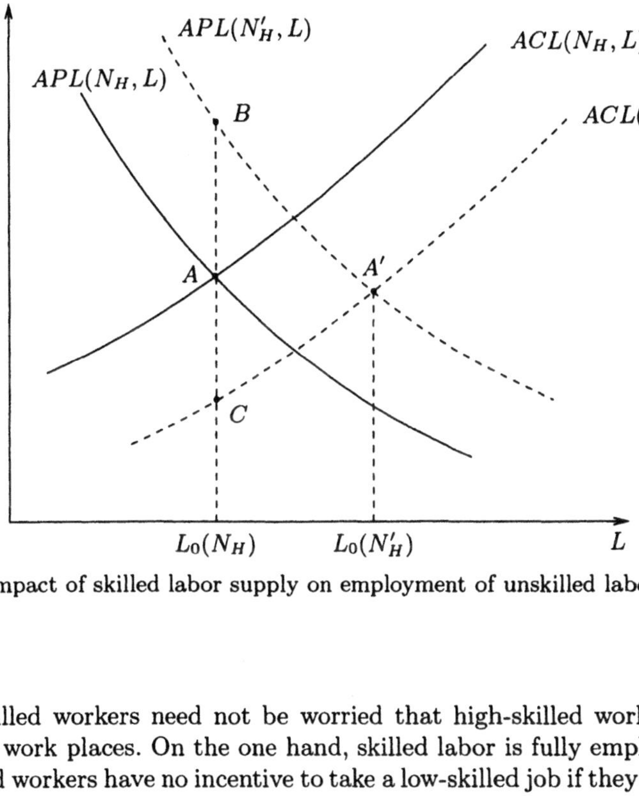

Fig. 5.3. Impact of skilled labor supply on employment of unskilled labor ($N'_H > N_H$).

Low-skilled workers need not be worried that high-skilled workers take away their work places. On the one hand, skilled labor is fully employed. So high-skilled workers have no incentive to take a low-skilled job if they can have a qualified place.[18] On the other hand, more work places for unskilled labor can be profitably organized by the firms if they have more skilled labor at their disposal. Of course, the conclusion depends on the assumption that wages are flexible and firms earn zero profits in equilibrium. When N_H increases to N'_H, say by immigration of skilled labor, profits become positive at the initial level

[18] With rigidities leading to unemployment of skilled labor this conclusion is no longer true.

of employment (see BC in figure 5.3). With power of firm owners the profit span may be absorbed by rents instead of being invested in the provision of more work places for unskilled labor (see the discussion in chapter 3). In an analogous way, the gains arising from the expansion of the skilled labor resource may be absorbed by rents for skilled labor if high-skilled workers have market power. The effects of a distorted wage structure will be analyzed in section 5.5.

Apart from the positive employment effect, figure 5.3 shows also that the effect of an increase in the supply of skilled labor on the equilibrium average costs of arranging work places for low-skilled workers is ambiguous. Although these costs decrease for every given level of employment L, they may rise in equilibrium, since at the same time the aggregate level of employment of unskilled labor is increased from $L_0(N_H)$ to $L_0(N'_H)$. This expansion raises the costs of organizing unskilled work along the ACL-curve which has strictly positive slope for the reasons discussed in the preceding section.

5.4.2 The impacts of technological change

Since there are two types of technology in the model presented - the organization and the production technology - two types of technological change must be considered. First, the non-production requirements for the organization of production work may rise or fall. Since only skilled labor is used in non-production, such changes have different impacts on skilled and unskilled labor, respectively. Secondly, there can be a skill-biased change in the production technology, as it is usually discussed in the literature.

Changes in the non-production requirements for organizing work. The non-production input of skilled labor required for organizing the work of a unit of unskilled labor is represented by the function g. Consider two different functions g_1 and g_2 with $g_1(\chi, H, L) < g_2(\chi, H, L)$ in the relevant range of employment levels.[19] A change from g_1 to g_2 may result when firms adopt organization methods which require more interactive abilities. As discussed in chapter 4, more non-production labor is necessary if workers with low abilities are to be organized under such a technology. Also without a change in the skill requirements of the used mode of work organization the non-production requirements rise if the abilities of the unskilled labor force decline. Thus, the possible indirect effect of an increase in the supply of skilled labor which was addressed at the beginning of section 5.4.1, namely, that the relatively able part of unskilled labor acquires skills and the remaining unskilled labor force has relatively low interactive abilities, is also reflected by a switch from g_1 to g_2.

[19] As we have seen in the analysis of chapter 4, firms may adopt organization technologies which have low non-production requirements at low levels of employment, whereas relatively high non-production resources are required at high levels of employment. For the comparative-static analysis, the ranking of technologies in the neighborhood of the equilibrium employment levels is relevant.

Non-production requirements g have a direct effect on the ACL-curve, according to (5.34), and an indirect effect on both APL and ACL through skill-intensity χ. According to (5.14), skill-intensity in production is reduced, if more skilled labor is needed in non-production.[20] Formally, if $g_1(\bar{\chi}, H, L) < g_2(\bar{\chi}, H, L)$, then $\chi_1(H, L) > \chi_2(H, L)$ holds for the skill intensity $\chi_i(H, L)$ defined by the condition $\chi_i(H, L) = H/L - g_i(\chi_i(H, L), H, L)$. Using this and $f' > 0$ in (5.33), we conclude that a switch form g_1 to g_2 shifts the APL-curve downwards. This effect is illustrated in figure 5.4 by APL^1 and APL^2. At the same time, the switch from $\chi_1(H, L)$ to $\chi_2(H, L) < \chi_1(H, L)$ shifts the ACL-curve upwards, since under assumption (5.16) the non-production cost ACL is inversely related to skill intensity.[21] This indirect effect through the skill-intensity enhances the direct effect of the rise in g on the costs of providing employment. In figure 5.4, a change in the non-production requirements from $g_1(\bar{\chi}, H, L)$ to $g_2(\bar{\chi}, H, L) > g_1(\chi, H, L)$ corresponds to a shift from ACL^1 to ACL^2. As a result, equilibrium employment $L_0(N_H)$ definitely declines with rising non-production requirements.

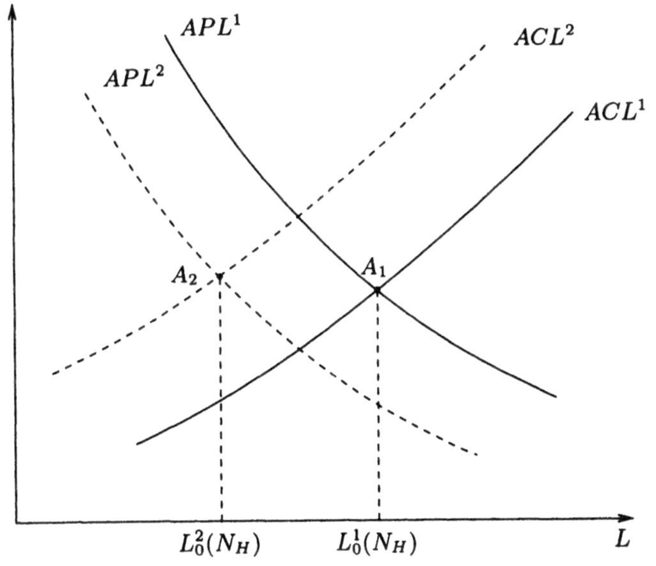

Fig. 5.4. Changing non-production requirements ($g_2(\chi, H, L) > g_1(\chi, H, L)$).

If the non-production input required for organizing work of unskilled labor rises because firms adopt organization methods with more demanding skill requirements or because only workers with relatively low interactive abilities

[20] Note that $\frac{\partial \bar{\chi}}{\partial \gamma} = -\frac{\partial \tilde{g}/\partial \gamma}{1+\partial \tilde{g}/\partial \bar{\chi}} < 0$ for $\tilde{g}(\bar{\chi}, H, L, \gamma) \equiv g_\gamma(\bar{\chi}, H, L)$ and $\partial \tilde{g}/\partial \gamma > 0$.

[21] $\frac{\partial ACL}{\partial \bar{\chi}} < 0$ if $f''g + f'\frac{\partial g}{\partial \bar{\chi}} < 0$. The latter inequality is equivalent to (5.16).

are left in the unskilled labor force, then the maximal level of profitable employment of unskilled labor declines. If there was unemployment of low-skilled workers $\left(L_0^1(N_H) < N_L\right)$, unemployment increases $\left(L_0^2(N_H) < L_0^1(N_H)\right)$. If there was full employment in the original equilibrium $\left(L_0^1(N_H) \geq N_L\right)$, unemployment may arise.

Skilled labor has nothing to fear. To the contrary, not only that it remains fully employed, it earns also a higher wage. The rising need for skilled labor in non-production decreases skill-intensity in production and drives up the real wage w_H^*/p^* given by (5.31).

Finally, figure 5.4 shows that a rise in the amount of skilled non-production labor required per unskilled production worker does not automatically lead to an increase of ACL in equilibrium. The reason is that the decrease in aggregate employment of unskilled labor implies a downward move along the upward shifted curve of average costs ACL^2 of arranging work places for low-skilled workers. In particular, if firms provide no longer work places for low-skilled workers with relatively low interactive abilities, the costs of organizing work are lowered. This may more than compensate the upward shift of these costs resulting when the level of employment is hold constant.

Skill-biased change of production technology. A change in the production technology means that firms switch from a production function f_1 to a different production function f_2, whereas the organization technology represented by g remains the same. Such a switch has no consequence for the relationship $\chi(H, L)$ between aggregate employment levels and skill-intensity in production given by equation (5.14). But both the APL-curve and the ACL-curve are affected by a change in production technology f. Denote by APL_i and ACL_i the functions defined by (5.33) and (5.34), respectively, for $f = f_i$, $i = 1, 2$. Technical progress which raises both the productivity of unskilled labor $(f_2 > f_1)$ and the real wage of skilled labor $(f_2' > f_1')$ shifts both curves upwards so that no definite conclusion can be drawn without further specifications.

Skill-biased technological change is usually specified as a change which increases the marginal return on skilled labor relative to the marginal return on unskilled labor, i.e., raises the marginal rate of substitution MRS. As a consequence, the wage of skilled labor rises relative to the wage of unskilled labor as long as average skill-intensity is fixed by the aggregate employment levels. Denote by MRS_i the marginal rate of substitution between skilled and unskilled labor corresponding to production function f_i, $i = 1, 2$. A technological change from f_1 to f_2 which increases the relative wage ω of skilled labor implies $MRS_2 > MRS_1$ and thus, according to (5.18),

$$\frac{f_1'(\chi)}{f_1(\chi)} < \frac{f_2'(\chi)}{f_2(\chi)}\,. \tag{5.38}$$

To see the effect of a change from f_1 to f_2 suppose that with production technology f_1 an equilibrium is reached at L_1^* defined by the condition

$$APL_1(N_H, L_1^*) = ACL_1(N_H, L_1^*) \ . \tag{5.39}$$

Inequality (5.38) implies that[22]

$$APL_2(N_H, L_1^*) < ACL_2(N_H, L_1^*) \tag{5.40}$$

at the original equilibrium level L_1^*. This means that firms reduce the number of work places provided for low-skilled workers until the equality between profits per work place and costs per work place is reestablished (Remember that APL is a strictly decreasing function of L and ACL is strictly increasing in L). Hence, $L_2^* < L_1^*$.

A skill-biased change of the production technology reduces the equilibrium level of employment of unskilled labor if unemployment prevailed in the original equilibrium.[23] The reason is that a rise in the relative wage of skilled labor corresponding to such a change makes the skilled non-production workers required for the organization of production more costly.

5.5 (Un)employment of skilled and unskilled labor when high-skilled workers have the power to acquire a rent

In the considered macroeconomic equilibrium only unskilled labor is concerned with the problem of joblessness. Employment in an organized economy is determined by the fact that workers are only employable if a work place is organized for them. In a market economy the decision about how much work is organized depends on the profit consideration of firms. And under flexible wages the only obstacle to full employment is that it may be not profitable to the firms to organize jobs for workers with low interactive abilities.

Wage rigidity is a possible additional source of unemployment. That wage rigidity together with a fixed money supply depresses the aggregate activity level at stage 2 and induces firms to create fewer jobs at stage 1 was already analyzed in chapter 3. But what is the impact of wage rigidity if there are two types of labor? In particular, can it explain why also high-skilled workers may be unemployed to a substantial degree like, for instance, in several Western European countries in the nineties.[24] Another question is which wages are meant by wage rigidity if there are more types of labor. Is the wage of unskilled labor rigid, the wage of skilled labor or rather the relative wage? Or are only the non-production workers protected against underbidding of

---

[22] According to (5.33) and (5.34), equation (5.39) implies $\frac{f_1'}{f_1} = \frac{\mu-1}{g}$, whereas inequality (5.40) is equivalent to $\frac{f_2'}{f_2} > \frac{\mu-1}{g}$.

[23] If $APL_1(N_H, N_L) > ACL_1(N_H, N_L)$ so that $L_1^* = N_L$ we could still have $APL_2(N_H, N_L) \geq ACL_2(N_H, N_L)$ and thus $L_2^* = N_L$, despite of (5.40).

[24] According to Nickell and Bell [49], in Western European countries the increase in unemployment was roughly of the same order for both skill groups.

their wage? Clearly, all wage costs including income equivalents of legal and other institutional arrangements of job protection are relevant for assessing the respective rigidities. The following analysis concentrates on relative wage rigidity between skilled and unskilled labor and on distortions arising from the power of non-production workers to require a premium over the wage of production workers. Whereas the real effects of rigidities in the nominal wage level of production workers can be overcome by adjusting money supply (see the discussion in section 3.2)[25], the effects of relative rigidity and rigidity of the wage of non-production labor are independent of Y. It is not intended to provide an explanation for why such rigidities arise. The purpose of the analysis is to show the role of exogenously given rigidities in an economy with organized work, in particular their impacts on the employment of skilled and unskilled labor.

5.5.1 Rigidity of the relative wage of skilled labor

Suppose that a downward rigidity constraint

$$\omega \geq \bar{\omega} > \omega^* \tag{5.41}$$

is imposed on the relative wage rate $\omega = w_H/w_L$ for some exogenously given $\bar{\omega}$, whereas the nominal wage level can be adjusted freely. This reflects the view that the observed wage differentials between skilled and unskilled labor, and in particular between staff workers and unskilled production workers, are not determined by their relative marginal productivities but by the power position of high-skilled workers. The power may come from market imperfections or through the political process. If one accepts the view that workers have the power to earn rents (i.e. income which is not generated by the marginal contribution to economic output), it is quite natural in an approach which focuses on the role of organized interactions, to assume that the power is on the side of skilled labor. After all they have the relatively higher interactive abilities, and interactive abilities are not only relevant for the organization of work but also for market power or organization of political pressure. Obviously, this argument is in contrast to the usual assumption that the power is on the side of unskilled labor whose wages are pushed up by trade unions so that $\omega < \omega^*$.

What are the macroeconomic consequences of relative wage rigidity wherever it comes from? In particular, can rigidity constraint (5.41) explain unemployment of skilled labor, or do the unskilled workers bear all the costs of the distortion in form of higher unemployment despite lower wages?

[25] According to (5.29), the nominal wage level w_L^* resulting in equilibrium is proportional to Y. By varying Y it can be adjusted to any exogenously given level $\bar{w}_L$ without any change in the equilibrium values ω, χ and L. In an analogous way, $w_H^* = \frac{Y}{\mu(\bar{\chi}+1/\omega^*)L}$ can by adjusted to any exogenous $\bar{w}_H$.

Restriction (5.41) implies that $\bar{\omega}$ instead of ω^* is the equilibrium ratio of relative wage rates, since wages are prevented from being adjusted to the values consistent with the equilibrium $H^* = N_H$ and $L^* = \min\{L_0(N_H), N_L\}$ derived in section 5.3. $\bar{\omega}$ is exogenous. That means, according to (5.19), skill-intensity in the distorted equilibrium is fixed at the value

$$\widetilde{\chi} = \chi(\bar{\omega}) \ . \tag{5.42}$$

($\sim$ is used to denote equilibrium values in the distorted equilibrium.)

Of course, $\widetilde{\chi} < \chi^*$ with $\chi^* \equiv \chi(H^*, L^*)$ since $\bar{\omega} > \omega^*$. According to (5.30) and (5.31), this implies that the real wage rate of unskilled labor declines compared to the equilibrium with no rigidity whereas the real wage of skilled labor rises. Thus, in terms of real wages the burden of the rigidity is borne by unskilled while skilled labor gains. Is this also true with respect to employment?

Using (5.42) in (5.25) and (5.31), we obtain as relevant criterion for the decisions of firms about the profit-maximizing level of work places for unskilled labor the condition

$$APL(\bar{\omega}) >,=,< \quad ACL(\bar{\omega}, H, L) \tag{5.43}$$

where

$$APL(\bar{\omega}) \equiv \left(1 - \frac{1}{\mu}\right) f(\chi(\bar{\omega})) \ , \tag{5.44}$$

$$ACL(\bar{\omega}, H, L) \equiv \frac{f'(\chi(\bar{\omega}))}{\mu} g(\chi(\bar{\omega}), H, L) \ . \tag{5.45}$$

Since $\chi' < 0$ and $f' > 0$, APL is a decreasing function of $\bar{\omega}$, whereas ACL is increasing in $\bar{\omega}$, since ACL is decreasing in $\widetilde{\chi}$, according to (5.16). Moreover, ACL is non-decreasing in H and L, according to (5.13).

Firms wish to expand their work-place capacity as long as the left side in (5.43), representing the average profit of a work place for unskilled labor, is greater than the right side, which represents the average cost of a work place. If the opposite inequality holds, firms reduce work places. Equality means they have no incentive to change the employment situation.

Condition (5.43) differs from the corresponding condition (5.35) in two respects: On the one hand, there is no indirect effect of aggregate employment through ω and $\widetilde{\chi}$, since $\widetilde{\chi}$ is given by the exogenous $\bar{\omega}$.[26] Thus, the left side of condition (5.43) is independent of aggregate employment. Also the real wage rate of skilled non-production labor $(f'(\widetilde{\chi})/\mu)$ is fixed by $\widetilde{\chi}$, i.e. by $\bar{\omega}$. On the other hand, total employment of skilled labor H is not necessarily equal

[26] From the missing impact of aggregate employment on χ one implication follows immediately. If labor is homogeneous within each group of labor so that equality holds in (5.13), both the left and the right side of condition (5.43) are constant. Thus, it is either profitable to expand employment until the labor supply constraint is reached or to produce nothing at all.

to full-employment N_H, but simultaneously determined with employment of unskilled labor L.

Combining (5.26) with (5.42), we see that aggregate employment levels are restricted by the condition $\widetilde{\chi} = \chi(\bar{\omega}) = \chi(H, L)$. This condition defines a unique relationship[27]

$$H(L, \bar{\omega}) \quad \text{with} \quad \frac{\partial H}{\partial L} > 0, \; \frac{\partial H}{\partial \bar{\omega}} < 0 \tag{5.46}$$

between those values of L and H which are compatible with the skill-intensity implied by the exogenous $\bar{\omega}$. For the intuitive understanding of relationship $H(L, \bar{\omega})$ one should remember that $\chi(H, L)$ was defined by the condition that the ratio H/L of total skilled labor to unskilled labor must be equal to the sum of skill-intensity in production, χ, and skilled non-production labor g per unit of unskilled labor i.e.: $H/L = \chi + g(\chi, H, L)$. From this it is clear that H must increase with L to hold χ fixed at $\widetilde{\chi}$. And if $\widetilde{\chi}$ declines because of a rise of $\bar{\omega}$, H must also decline to lower the ratio H/L for a given L.

Condition (5.43) and (5.46) together with the full-employment constraints $H \leq N_H, L \leq N_L$ define for any $\bar{\omega} > \omega^*$ and thus $\widetilde{\chi} = \chi(\bar{\omega}) < \chi^*$ the implied aggregate equilibrium values $\widetilde{H}$, $\widetilde{L}$. The first fact to notice is that, almost always, at least one type of labor will be unemployed in an equilibrium. This follows from the fixed relationship between total skilled and unskilled labor, which is defined by (5.46) and is a consequence of the fixed skill-intensity in production $\widetilde{\chi}$ implied by the rigid relative wage $\bar{\omega}$. If the given structure of skill supply N_H, N_L doesn't coincide with this fixed relationship by chance, we have either unemployment of skilled as well as unskilled labor,or employment of one type of labor is restricted by the respective full-employment constraint whereas part of the other type of labor remains unemployed. In the latter case the equilibrium level of the type of labor whose supply constraint is not binding is given by $\widetilde{H} = H(N_L, \bar{\omega})$ if $\widetilde{L} = N_L$ and by $N_H = H\left(\widetilde{L}, \bar{\omega}\right)$ if $\widetilde{H} = N_H$, respectively. From (5.46) follows immediately that $\partial\widetilde{H}/\partial\bar{\omega} < 0$ in an equilibrium with full employment of unskilled labor and $\partial\widetilde{L}/\partial\bar{\omega} > 0$ in an equilibrium with full employment of skilled labor.[28] Thus, as long as skilled labor is fully employed, the power of high-skilled workers to acquire a rent is bad for the low-skilled workers in terms of their real wage, but good in terms of aggregate employment. Is this a robust result? The further analysis considers the comparative-static properties of an equilibrium with unemployment of skilled as well as unskilled workers.

An equilibrium in which one of the supply constraints $L \leq N_L$ or $H \leq N_H$ is binding implies that employment is not restricted by the borderline of prof-

---

[27] Use $\partial\chi/\partial H > 0$, $\partial\chi/\partial L < 0$ and $\chi'(\omega) < 0$.

[28] Moreover, $\partial\widetilde{H}/\partial N_L > 0$ and $\partial\widetilde{L}/\partial N_H > 0$ in the respective situations. An increase of the fully employed factor is always good for the other factor. For instance, if unskilled labor is fully employed, skilled labor benefits from immigration of low-skilled workers.

itable provision of work places defined by the criterion (5.43). That means $APL \geq ACL$ at the equilibrium values. Otherwise firms would have stopped the provision of work places before one of the supply constraint restricts the expansion of employment. According to (5.44) and (5.45), $APL \geq ACL$ for all L and H, if $\partial g/\partial H = 0$ and $\partial g/\partial L = 0$.[29] Thus, for an equilibrium with unemployment of both types of labor, at least one of the two skill groups must be heterogeneous so that strict inequality $\partial g/\partial H > 0$ or $\partial g/\partial L > 0$ holds in (5.13). (In the following analysis heterogeneity of both types of labor is assumed. The cases that either only $\partial g/\partial L > 0$ or only $\partial g/\partial H > 0$ are treated in footnotes. These borderline cases do not lead to essentially different conclusions.) If aggregate employment is not restricted by the supply constraints, profit-maximizing provision of work places implies that aggregate employment expands until condition (5.43) holds with equality. Then the equilibrium values $\widetilde{H}, \widetilde{L}$ are determined by the following two conditions: On the one hand, $\widetilde{H}$ and $\widetilde{L}$ must be consistent with the skill intensity implied by $\bar{\omega}$. This means, they must fulfill the relationship

$$\widetilde{H} = H\left(\widetilde{L}, \bar{\omega}\right) , \qquad (5.47)$$

defined by (5.46). On the other hand, $\widetilde{H}$ and $\widetilde{L}$ must fulfill the condition $APL(\bar{\omega}) = ACL(\bar{\omega}, H, L)$ implied by the profit-maximizing provision of work places for unskilled labor. For $\partial g/\partial L > 0$ and $\partial g/\partial H > 0$, this condition defines a function $L(H, \bar{\omega})$.[30] Hence[31],

$$\widetilde{L} = L\left(\widetilde{H}, \bar{\omega}\right) \quad \text{with} \quad \frac{\partial L}{\partial H} < 0, \quad \frac{\partial L}{\partial \bar{\omega}} < 0 . \qquad (5.48)$$

The equilibrium $\widetilde{L}$, $\widetilde{H}$, defined by (5.47) and (5.48), is illustrated in figure 5.5.

The upward sloping $H(L, \bar{\omega})$-curve is the locus of all employment combinations which are consistent with the cost-minimizing expansion path implied by the exogenous relative wage $\bar{\omega}$.[32] The decreasing line $L(H, \bar{\omega})$ defines the locus of employment levels for which $APL = ACL$.[33] In the region to the

[29] For $L = 0$, $APL > ACL$. Otherwise the economy would not be viable.

[30] If $\partial g/\partial H = 0$ and $\partial g/\partial L > 0$, the aggregate employment level of unskilled labor resulting from the profit-maximizing condition (5.43) is independent of H. Denote this level by $L(\bar{\omega})$, where $dL/d\bar{\omega} < 0$. If $\partial g/\partial H > 0$ and $\partial g/\partial L = 0$, only the employment level of skilled labor is fixed by (5.43). Let this level be denoted by $H(\bar{\omega})$, where $dH/d\bar{\omega} < 0$.

[31] ACL is increasing in $\bar{\omega}$, H and L, whereas APL is decreasing in $\bar{\omega}$.

[32] Note that $H(L, \bar{\omega})$ is not the expansion path ($H^x = \widetilde{\chi}L$) in production alone but includes non-production labor.

[33] In the case that labor is homogenous within a group, we have a vertical line at $L(\bar{\omega})$, if $\partial g/\partial H = 0$ and $\partial g/\partial L > 0$, and a horizontal line at $H(\bar{\omega})$, if $\partial g/\partial H > 0$ and $\partial g/\partial L = 0$. If both $\partial g/\partial H = 0$ and $\partial g/\partial L = 0$, there is no borderline $L(H, \bar{\omega})$ and the intersection point of the $H(L, \bar{\omega})$-curve with the supply constraint $N_H B N_L$ defines the equilibrium. As noted earlier, at least one of the two inequalities in (5.13) must hold strictly in an interior equilibrium.

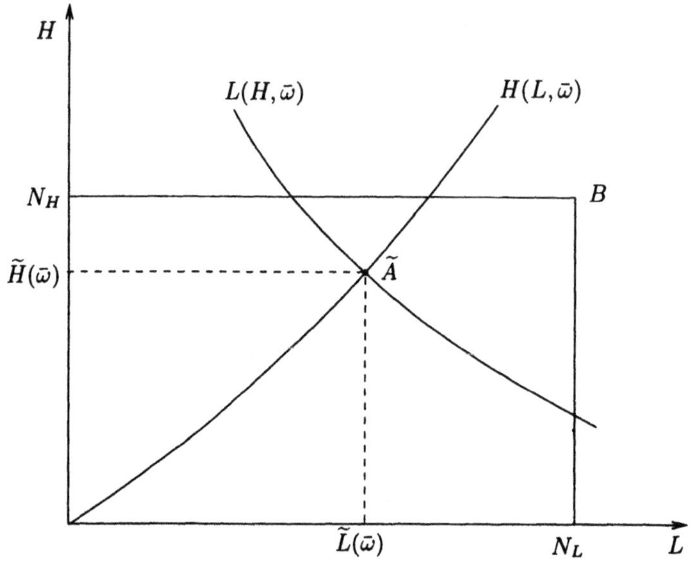

Fig. 5.5. Employment equilibrium under relative wage rigidity.

Northeast of the line we have $APL < ACL$, since ACL is increasing in L and in H. Thus, firms are reducing work places. In the region to the Southwest of $L(H, \bar{\omega})$, we have $APL > ACL$ and firms provide more work places. The provision of work places by the profit-maximizing firms expands along $H(L, \bar{\omega})$ and is stopped by the borderline $L(H, \bar{\omega})$ or by the labor supply constraints. If the intersection point of the two curves lies within the feasible set $N_H B N_L$, we have unemployment of both skilled labor and unskilled labor.

An increase in $\bar{\omega}$ shifts the $H(L, \bar{\omega})$-curve downwards, according to (5.46), while the $L(H, \bar{\omega})$-curve is shifted inwards, according to (5.48). As a consequence, aggregate employment of skilled labor decreases, whereas aggregate employment of unskilled labor may rise or fall. Figure 5.6 illustrates the employment effects of relative wage rigidity by comparing an equilibrium $\tilde{A}$ resulting under rigidity to a flexible wage equilibrium A^* with fully employed skilled labor and unemployment of unskilled labor.

If ω is increased from ω^* to $\bar{\omega} > w^*$, skill-intensity in production and thus the ratio of total skilled labor to unskilled labor is reduced. This downward shift of the $H(L, \bar{\omega})$-curve has a negative effect on employment of skilled labor and a positive effect on employment of unskilled labor (see point C). However, production with a lower ratio of skilled to unskilled labor makes work places for low-skilled workers less productive and their provision more costly. This is reflected by the inward shift of the $L(H, \bar{\omega})$-curve. It has a negative effect on employment of both skilled and unskilled labor. The total effect on employment of skilled labor is clearly negative, whereas the net

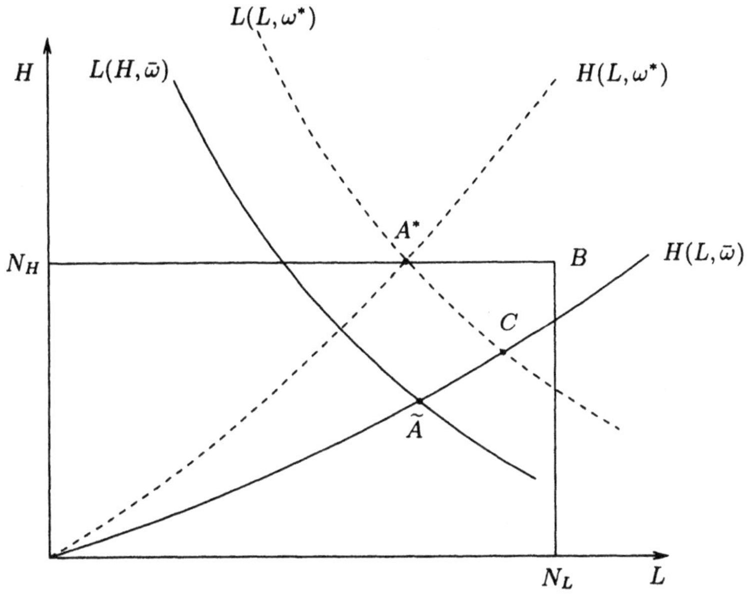

Fig. 5.6. The impact of rents for skilled labor on employment of skilled and unskilled labor ($\bar{\omega} > \omega^*$).

effect on employment of unskilled labor is ambiguous (see $\widetilde{A}$). The surprising point is that also the employment level of unskilled labor may be reduced despite the falling real wage implied by the rise of the relative wage to $\bar{\omega}$.[34] The reason is that the costs of skilled non-production labor are rising with $\bar{\omega}$, and unskilled labor becomes less productive since less skilled labor is used in production per unit of unskilled labor.

In sum, three important conclusions about the consequences of relative wage rigidity follow from this analysis: First, under relative wage rigidity it is possible that both skilled and unskilled labor are unemployed in equilibrium. Second, skilled labor earns a higher real wage but suffers a loss in employment. Third, unskilled labor looses getting a lower real wage. And in addition, it may loose in terms of employment too.

5.5.2 Rents of non-production workers

In an economy with internally organized interactions one should expect that skilled labor which is endowed with relatively high abilities is relatively powerful, if power of workers plays a role anyway. The effects of the relative wage rigidity arising from such power were analyzed in the preceding subsection. Thinking out the idea that organization is crucial for economic life, one

[34] This is, for instance, definitely the case if $\partial g/\partial H = 0$ and $\partial g/\partial L > 0$ so that we have a leftward shifting vertical line $L(\bar{\omega})$ instead of the $L(H, \bar{\omega})$-curve.

should attribute the most powerful position to those who own the units in which the internal organization of economic activity takes place, i.e., to the owners of the firms. The macroeconomic consequences of the power of firm owners to require a rent have already been analyzed and discussed in chapter 3. But next to the firm owners are the agents who manage the owners' business. In the abstract framework of this study there is no separate group of managers but all labor employed for providing the prerequisites of organized production work are summarized to the group of non-production workers. If this subgroup of skilled labor, not skilled labor in general, has the power to acquire a rent, the macroeconomic consequences are similar to the effects of firm-owner rents. This is shown in the following analysis.

Suppose that non-production workers can require a premium φ over the wage w_H of skilled production labor so that the wage of non-production workers, denoted by w_M, is given by the relationship

$$w_M = (1+\varphi)\, w_H\,, \quad \varphi \geq 0\,. \tag{5.49}$$

No other rigidities and distortions are considered. Thus, for $\varphi = 0$, we have an economy with flexibility of all wages and the equilibrium analyzed in section 5.3. What are the consequences if φ is raised above zero?

Restriction (5.49) changes the costs of the non-production labor required for organizing work. Since the real wage rate w_M/p of non-production workers is now $(1+\varphi)\, f'(\bar{\chi})/\mu$ in equilibrium, instead of $f'(\bar{\chi})/\mu$, the average costs per work place for low-skilled workers is

$$\widetilde{ACL}\,(N_H, L) = (1+\varphi)\, ACL\,(N_H, L)\ , \tag{5.50}$$

where $ACL(N_H, L)$ is the average cost function if $w_M = w_H$, defined by (5.34). Thus, a rent φ has the effect to shift the ACL-curve upwards in figure 5.2 (The shift is shown in figure 5.7 following later.) We see that an existing unemployment problem is aggravated by an increase in rent φ for non-production workers. Formally,

$$\frac{\partial L_0}{\partial \varphi} < 0\,. \tag{5.51}$$

Since skilled labor remains fully employed as long as the wages of both skilled and unskilled production workers are flexible, a lower aggregate level of employment of unskilled labor implies an increase of total skill-intensity H/L but also an increase of the skill-intensity in production χ.[35] Using this in (5.30) and (5.31), we see that the real wage of unskilled workers increases, whereas the real wage of skilled production workers declines. Thus, the analysis brings to light a very interesting conflict. The power of skilled non-production workers to require a premium over skilled production workers has negative distortionary effects. On the one hand, the burden of these negative

[35] According to (5.12) - (5.14), $\partial\chi/\partial L < 0$.

effects is borne by unskilled labor in terms of a decline in employment. But on the other hand, also the skilled production workers have to bear a burden in terms of lower real wages.

Combining this insight with the results about the role of rents for firm owners, we see that there is a certain coincidence of interests of firm owners and skilled non-production workers on the one side and production workers on the other side. Suppose that, in addition to the premium $\varphi > 0$ of non-production labor, the firm owners have the power to acquire a rent R as analyzed in chapter 3. It was assumed that R is the real fee levied by firm owners per unit of capacity created at stage 1. Thus, in the extended model, the real fee to be paid by a firm with capacity $\bar{x} = \bar{l} f(\bar{\chi})$ is equal to the amount $R\bar{l}f(\bar{\chi})$. Ex post, at stage 2, capacities and thus the payment $R\bar{l}f(\bar{\chi})$ are fixed. Using this in (5.24) and (5.33), we see that R changes the real return per organized work place for low-skilled workers from $APL(N_H, L)$ to

$$\widetilde{APL}(N_H, L) = \left(1 - \frac{1}{\mu} - R\right) f(\chi(N_H, L)) . \tag{5.52}$$

Everything else is unaffected. In particular, the price equilibrium is still given by (5.21), since non-production costs and thus the fee levied by the owners of a firm are fixed at stage 2 and cannot be passed on to the price in monopolistic competition.

As a result, the APL-curve in figure 5.2 is shifted downwards and aggregate employment of unskilled labor declines provided that we start in an unemployment equilibrium (more precisely, provided that $L_0(N_H) \leq N_L$ so that equilibrium employment is given by $L_0(N_H)$):

$$\frac{\partial L_0}{\partial R} < 0 . \tag{5.53}$$

The employment effect of both the premium φ for non-production workers and the rent R for firm owners is illustrated in figure 5.7.

The decrease of L_0 by rent R implies in the same way as the reduction of L_0 by φ an increase in skill intensity χ and thus a decrease of the relative wage ω of skilled production labor to unskilled labor. What happens if skilled production workers are not going to put up with this decline? The answer can quickly be found by going to the analysis of relative wage rigidity. In an equilibrium with full employment of skilled labor the equilibrium level of employment of unskilled labor L is determined by the condition $N_H = H\left(\widetilde{L}, \bar{\omega}\right)$ and we have $\partial\widetilde{L}/\partial\bar{\omega} > 0$, according to (5.46). Thus, in terms of employment[36], it is good for unskilled labor if skilled production workers oppose the decline of the relative wage rate implied by firm-owner rents or premia for non-production workers. However, in an interior equilibrium with

[36] The real wage rate of unskilled labor declines ceteris paribus, if the relative wage is kept up.

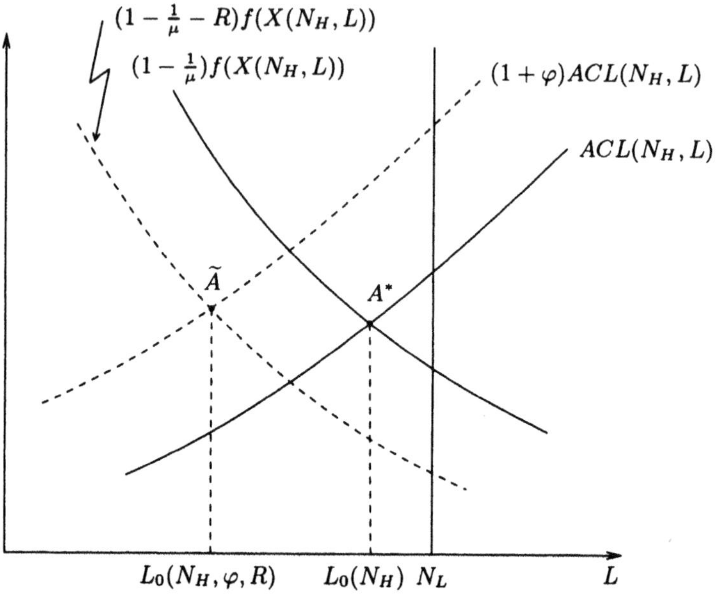

Fig. 5.7. The impact of rents for firm owners ($R > 0$) and skilled staff workers ($\varphi > 0$) on employment of low-skilled workers.

no supply constraint being binding the aggregate employment levels are determined by the intersection of $H(L,\bar{\omega})$ with the curve $L(H,\bar{\omega})$ defined by the zero-profit condition $APL(\bar{\omega}) = ACL(\bar{\omega},H,L)$. (Figure 5.5 showed the two curves and the resulting equilibrium.) With rents φ and R this condition changes to

$$\widetilde{APL}(\bar{\omega}) = \widetilde{ACL}(\bar{\omega},H,L) \ , \tag{5.54}$$

where

$$\widetilde{APL}(\bar{\omega}) = \left(1 - \frac{1}{\mu} - R\right) f(\chi(\bar{\omega})) \ , \tag{5.55}$$

and

$$\widetilde{ACL}(\bar{\omega},H,L) = (1+\varphi)\, ACL(\bar{\omega},H,L) \tag{5.56}$$

instead of (5.44) and (5.45), respectively.

Thus, the curve $L(H,\bar{\omega},\varphi,R)$ defined by the zero-profit(after rents) condition (5.54) is shifted inwards if R or φ is increased.[37] In contrast to this, the curve $H(L,\bar{\omega})$ is not affected by R or φ. Only technological conditions

[37] Remember that $\partial g/\partial L > 0$ or $\partial g/\partial H > 0$ in an interior equilibrium. And ACL increases with L, if $\partial g/\partial L > 0$, and increases with H, if $\partial g/\partial H > 0$. The curve $L(H,\bar{\omega},\varphi,R)$ is only defined if $\partial g/\partial L > 0$. In this case, ACL increases with L. If $\partial g/\partial L = 0$ and $\partial g/\partial H > 0$, then only H is defined by (5.54). In this case, we have a horizontal line instead of $L(H,\bar{\omega},\varphi,R)$. Since ACL increases with H, this line is shifted downwards, if φ or R rises.

are relevant for the locus of aggregate employment levels which are consistent with the skill intensity $\chi(\bar{\omega})$ implied by the fixed relative wage $\bar{\omega}$. Figure 5.8 shows the impact of φ and R on the employment equilibrium.

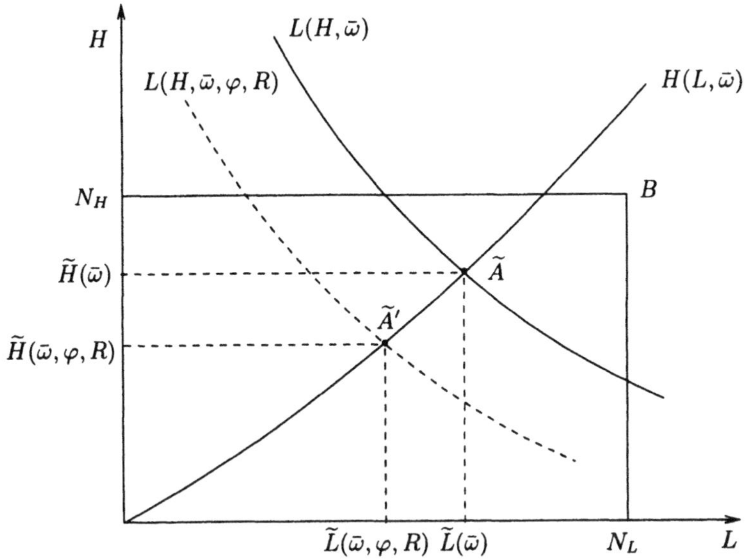

Fig. 5.8. The employment effects of rents for firm owners ($R > 0$) or skilled staff workers ($\varphi > 0$) when relative wages of production workers are rigid.

If the relative wage rate is fixed, rents of firms owners ($R > 0$) or of non-production workers ($\varphi > 0$) aggravate any existing unemployment of both unskilled or skilled labor. Thus, if skilled production workers oppose the decline of their real wage rate, they bear a burden imposed by the rent of firm owners or skilled non-production workers in the form of a loss of work places.

In sum, in an economy, in which the wages of all production workers are flexible, whereas firm owners earn rents and the agents who are organizing their business get salaries which are higher than what can be explained by the free adjustment of supply and demand, one has to expect a lower real wage of skilled production labor[38] and a loss of organized work places for low-skilled workers. In an economy, in which the skilled production workers successfully oppose the declining real wage, they too may suffer a loss of organized employment.

[38] Of course, if skilled production workers have shares in the firms, their total income may rise despite the decline of the wage earned as a production factor.

6. Capital and the provision of work places

This study has the aim to work out the determinants of organized employment in a macroeconomic equilibrium framework. Starting point of this project was the view that modern economic production requires internal organization of the interaction of individual workers. To analyze this idea and its macroeconomic implications in a rigorous and systematic way, a model was developed whose central innovative feature is that firms have to employ non-production resources for organizing work according to an organization technology. So far the analysis has been concentrated on labor as the only input in both the organization and the production technology. The purpose of this chapter is to work out the role of capital in an economy with internal organization of work. In particular, the equilibrium allocation of capital and its effect on the aggregate level of organized employment are determined.

In a standard model, capital is a factor of production which is used in combination with labor for producing output according to a given production function. The capital endowment of an economy together with its marginal productivity determines the rate of return on capital. Moreover, it determines the capital-intensity of production and affects thus the marginal productivity of labor and the firms' demand for labor. With flexible wage adjustment this establishes a relationship between capital allocation and wages while the labor force is always fully employed.[1] In contrast to this role of capital as an input in the production function, the focus of the following analysis is the role of capital as an input for the provision of the organizational infrastructure which is necessary for making business possible in a modern world, i.e., for transforming the efforts of individual workers into a marketable good or service. Formally, capital as an input in the organization technology rather than in the production technology is considered.

[1] With labor market imperfection there are additional effects. For instance, the bargaining power of workers may be influenced by the supply of capital. So Rodrik [54, 55] pointed out that international capital flows weaken the position of workers. In a dynamic context, there are also additional effects on labor, since the supply of capital affects the interest rate and thus, for instance, the costs of education. That interest rates are an important determinant of labor market outcomes was recently emphasized by Phelps and Zoega [52]. See also Atkinson [4].

Organizing the interaction of workers in a firm may require more or less non-production resources depending on the used technology of organization and the interactive abilities of the employed workers. The analysis of chapter 2 showed how the non-production requirements determine the macroeconomic equilibrium, in particular the equilibrium level of work places provided by firms. Chapter 4 analyzed the equilibrium consequences of current trends of reorganizing work. New organizational methods may drastically change the structure of firms from centrally coordinated hierarchies to decentralized communication networks. This process of reorganization does not imply that in the equilibrium of a reorganized economy the non-production resources vanish. To the contrary, the empirical literature on skill-biased technological change (see section 1.4) underlines the importance of non-production labor. And capital seems to be an even more important prerequisite for participating in modern competition. To think that capital plays no role for a typical modern corporation is obviously naive. Capital is an important prerequisite for a modern firm's capacity to combine individual work to a profitable output. One think of the provision of the information and communication technology, the logistic infrastructure, the distribution networks and marketing capacities. To analyze this role of capital as an input for the provision of a firm's infrastructure for production work, the next section extends the basic model of chapter 2. Essentially, the organization technology is generalized so that the provision of the capacity to organize production work is a function of non-production labor as well as capital. By this generalization the employment level resulting in the macroeconomic equilibrium is determined as a function of the aggregate capital stock of the economy. This expresses in a rigorous way the idea that the provision of work places depends on the supply of capital. The return on capital is determined by its productivity in the creation of work places. While first capital endowment is exogenous, later the consequences of elastic capital supply and, in particular, of international capital allocation are considered. This will contribute to the understanding of the fundamental determinants of capital flows and addresses a central issue in the current globalization debate, namely, how international capital mobility affects the provision of jobs.

6.1 Introducing capital into the basic model

Labor supply, production technology and demand are as described in section 2.1. In addition to the labor endowment, the economy is endowed with an exogenously supplied aggregate capital stock K^S. Capital is used by the firms for providing their capacity to organize production work. This means, the infrastructure – which is required for employing, coordinating, supervising and training workers in a firm, supporting their information processing and enabling them to communicate, designing, managing, financing and marketing their work and their product – is provided by employing capital in addition to non-production labor. Formally, organization technology (2.2) is modified as follows: For the capacity to organize $\bar{l}_i$ units of production labor, a firm i has to provide

$$y_i = g(L, \gamma)\, \bar{l}_i \tag{6.1}$$

units of non-production services, where $g(0, \gamma) > 0$ and $\partial g / \partial L \geq 0$.[2] In contrast to (2.2), non-production services y_i are not only delivered by the firm's non-production labor input m_i but also by its capital input k_i. It is assumed that y_i is produced according to a strictly increasing concave linear-homogeneous function Q

$$y_i = m_i q(\kappa_i) \equiv Q(k_i, m_i), \tag{6.2}$$

where $\kappa_i \equiv k_i / m_i$ denotes capital intensity in the provision of work places. Differentiability with $q'(\kappa) > 0$, $q''(\kappa) < 0$ is assumed.

At stage 2, firms produce output, according to the linear technology (2.3), where the employment of labor in production, l_i, is limited by the work place capacity $\bar{l}_i$ determined by their choice of k_i and m_i at stage 1. Thus, like in the basic model output, x_i is given by

$$x_i = l_i / A, \qquad l_i \leq \bar{l}_i. \tag{6.3}$$

(A is constant.)

Since demand and production technology are the same as in the basic model, also the symmetric equilibrium resulting in monopolistic competition at stage 2 is identical to the one derived in chapter 2. Wages go down until all provided work places are occupied and firms set their price p_i by charging a mark-up on marginal production costs, i.e., on the wage costs wA of a unit of output.[3] In equilibrium,

$$p_i = p = \mu w A, \tag{6.4}$$

with $\mu = \frac{\sigma}{\sigma - 1}$, where σ is the price elasticity of the demand curve (2.9).

At stage 1, firms decide about the work place capacity $\bar{l}_i$ which they want to arrange by employing non-production labor m_i and capital k_i. Obviously, whatever is the optimal level of $\bar{l}_i$, a profit-maximizing firm chooses the input combination $\kappa_i = k_i / m_i$ such that the costs $C(k_i, m_i)$ of providing $\bar{l}_i$ is minimized. All firms are confronted with the same factor price of capital (i.e. interest rate), denoted by r, and the same wage rate w.[4] In view of (6.1) and (6.2), firm i's cost-minimization problem is

---

[2] Remember that non-production requirements depend on the quality of the employed work force, which varies with aggregate employment if workers are heterogenous with respect to their interactive abilities. If they are homogeneous, $\partial g / \partial L = 0$.

[3] All firms choose the same capacity at stage 1, since they are confronted with the same demand and supply situation.

[4] Like in the basic model of chapter 2 it is assumed that, as far as differences in individualized productivity are concerned, labor is homogeneous. All remaining

$$\min C(k_i, m_i) = rk_i + wm_i \tag{6.5}$$

subject to

$$g(L,\gamma)\bar{l}_i = Q(k_i, m_i), \tag{6.6}$$

where $g(L,\gamma)$ is external to the individual firm. This gives us the first-order condition $r/w = \frac{\partial Q/\partial k_i}{\partial Q/\partial m_i}$. Denoting by $\rho \equiv r/w$ the relative factor price of capital and using $Q(k_i, m_i) = m_i q(\kappa_i)$, we can rewrite this condition in the form

$$\rho = MRS(\kappa_i) \equiv \frac{q'(\kappa_i)}{q(\kappa_i) - \kappa_i q'(\kappa_i)}, \tag{6.7}$$

where the marginal rate of substitution MRS decreases with κ.[5]

Equation (6.7) defines the cost-minimizing capital intensity as a function $\kappa_i = \kappa(\rho)$, $\kappa' < 0$, of the relative factor price of capital. Since factor prices are the same for all firms, the optimal capital intensity is identical too.

Firms know that under flexible wages the capacity they organize at stage 1 is fully used at stage 2, provided that the organized capacity is not larger than full employment allows. As long as not all work places are occupied, unemployed workers underbid wages to get a free work place. Thus, a firm organizing production work for $\bar{l}$ units of labor can expect to sell $\bar{x} = \bar{l}/A$ units of output in the symmetric equilibrium at stage 2. Since the equilibrium price is $p = \mu w A$, according to (6.4), this implies for the gross profit $\pi = (p - wA)\bar{x}$ achieved in the equilibrium at stage 2:

$$\pi = (\mu - 1) w\bar{l}. \tag{6.8}$$

According to the organization technology given by (6.1) and (6.2), the volume of non-production labor required for organizing $\bar{l}$ units of production work amounts to

$$m = \frac{g(L,\gamma)}{q(\kappa)}\bar{l}, \tag{6.9}$$

where κ is the cost-minimizing capital intensity determined by condition (6.7). Combining this with (6.5), we obtain the following cost function for the provision of work places:

$$\begin{aligned} C &= (\rho\kappa + 1) wm \\ &= \tfrac{\rho\kappa+1}{q(\kappa)} g(L,\gamma) w\bar{l}. \end{aligned} \tag{6.10}$$

Thus, a firm's net profit $\pi^n = \pi - C$, which is achieved by organizing $\bar{l}$ units of work, is given by

heterogeneities concern interactive abilities which cannot be internalized by wage differentials. To assume that non-production workers are a separate group which get higher wages, would add a dampening effect on aggregate employment, as shown by the analysis in chapter 5.

[5] Use $q'' < 0$.

$$\pi^n = [(\mu - 1) - AC(\kappa, L, \gamma)]\, w\bar{l}, \tag{6.11}$$

where[6]

$$AC(\kappa, L, \gamma) = \frac{g(L, \gamma)}{q(\kappa) - \kappa q'(\kappa)} \tag{6.12}$$

are average non-production costs (in terms of money wage w) of providing a work place. This gives us the following criterion for the profit-maximizing choice of work-place capacity $\bar{l}$:

$$\frac{d\pi^n}{d\bar{l}} >,=,< 0 \text{ if } \mu - 1 >,=,< AC. \tag{6.13}$$

For a given relative factor price $\rho = r/w$, each firm chooses the cost-minimizing combination of capital and non-production labor κ, as determined by (6.7). This implies for each firm the same non-production costs per organized work place, AC. According to (6.12), these costs also are a function of the aggregate level of employment L, which influences the range of abilities available to the firms. Both ρ and L are taken as given by the individual firm when it decides about the provision of work places. $\mu - 1$ is the profit per work place (in terms of money wage w), which can be earned at stage 2. As long as this profit is higher than the cost AC of providing a work place, firms wish to expand their capacity. If AC is higher than the profit $\mu - 1$, they provide fewer work places, and if $\mu - 1$ is equal to AC they don't change the volume of organized work. Hence, either $\mu - 1 = AC$ in the macroeconomic equilibrium or the expansion is stopped by the full-employment constraint and $\mu - 1 > AC$.

6.2 Employment and interest rate in the macroeconomic equilibrium

The preceding section described how profit-maximizing firms decide about the employment of non-production labor and capital for the organization of production work when the relative factor price is ρ and aggregate employment is L. While ρ and L are exogenously given from the point of view of the individual firms, they are endogenously determined in the general equilibrium of the economy. What are the equilibrium values implied by the exogenous factor supply L^S and K^S on the one hand and the derived behavior of firms on the other hand?

By definition, total employment L is the sum of aggregate non-production labor $M = \sum_i m_i = nm$ and aggregate production labor $L^x = \sum_i l_i = n\bar{l}$.[7]

[6] Use (6.7) to calculate $\rho\kappa + 1 = \frac{q}{q - \kappa q'}$. Substituting this in (6.10), one gets (6.12) for $AC = \frac{C}{w\bar{l}}$.

[7] Under flexible wages all provided work places are occupied in equilibrium and all firms provide the same work place capacity so that $l_i = \bar{l}$.

Since $L^x = Mq(\kappa)/g(L,\gamma)$, according to (6.9), the equation $L = M + L^x$ implies

$$M = \frac{L}{1 + q(\kappa)/g(L,\gamma)}. \tag{6.14}$$

Also by definition, aggregate demand for capital $K^D = \sum k_i = \sum \kappa_i m_i$. Since cost-minimization implies $\kappa_i = \kappa$, we have $K^D = \kappa M$. Substituting M from (6.14) into $K^D = \kappa M$, we obtain

$$K^D = K^D(\kappa, L, \gamma) \equiv \frac{\kappa L}{1 + q(\kappa)/g(L,\gamma)} \tag{6.15}$$

with

$$\partial K^D/\partial\kappa > 0 \text{ and } \partial K^D/\partial L > 0 \tag{6.16}$$

because of $\partial Q/\partial m > 0$ and $\partial g/\partial L \geq 0$.[8] In the capital-market equilibrium demand K^D must be equal to supply K^S, i.e.

$$K^D(\kappa, L, \gamma) = K^S. \tag{6.17}$$

According to (6.13), firms expand employment until it is stopped by the full-employment constraint $L \leq L^S$ or until the profit of a work place is equal the cost of creating it. Thus, in the labor market equilibrium we have

$$\begin{aligned} &\text{a)} \quad L = L^S \quad \text{or} \\ &\text{b)}\ \mu - 1 = AC(\kappa, L, \gamma), \end{aligned} \tag{6.18}$$

where $AC(\kappa, L, \gamma)$ is given by (6.12) with

$$\frac{\partial AC}{\partial\kappa} < 0 \text{ and } \frac{\partial AC}{\partial L} \geq 0 \tag{6.19}$$

because of $q'' < 0$ and $\partial g/\partial L \geq 0$.

Finally, capital intensity κ and relative factor price ρ are related by the cost-minimizing condition

$$\rho = MRS(\kappa), \tag{6.20}$$

where the marginal rate of substitution between capital and non-production labor is given by (6.7). It decreases with κ.

The two conditions (6.17) and (6.18) define the macroeconomic equilibrium values L^* and κ^* as functions of the exogenous supply of capital K^S, the mark-up parameter μ, and parameter γ representing the organization technology (and of L^S if a) holds in (6.18)). With κ^* also the equilibrium ratio of factor prices ρ^* is determined by equation (6.20).

If $\mu - 1 \geq AC(\kappa, L^S, \gamma)$, it is profitable for the firms, to provide work places for the whole labor force so that $L^* = L^S$ in the macroeconomic

[8] $\partial g/\partial L \geq 0$ implies $\partial K^D/\partial L > 0$. And $\partial K^D/\partial\kappa > 0$ is equivalent to $L\left(1 + \frac{q-\kappa q'}{g(L,\gamma)}\right) > 0$. The latter inequality holds because of $q - \kappa q' = \partial Q/\partial m > 0$.

equilibrium. The equilibrium capital-intensity κ^* is then defined by equation (6.17) evaluated at $L = L^S$. Figure 6.1 illustrates this full-employment equilibrium by plotting equilibrium condition (6.17) in the (L, κ)-space. Since demand for capital K^D increases with capital intensity κ and is non-decreasing in L, according to (6.16), the locus of (L, κ)-pairs which is consistent with a capital market equilibrium defined by condition (6.17) is a downward-sloping curve KK, the position of which depends on capital supply K^S and technology parameter γ.[9] The intersection of capital-market equilibrium curve KK with the vertical full-employment condition $L^* = L^S$ determines equilibrium capital intensity κ^*.

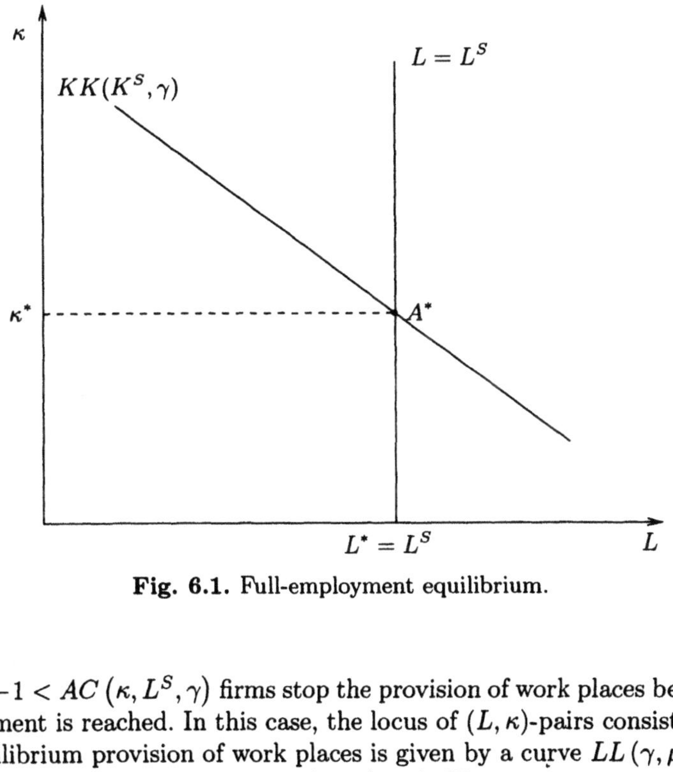

Fig. 6.1. Full-employment equilibrium.

If $\mu - 1 < AC(\kappa, L^S, \gamma)$ firms stop the provision of work places before full-employment is reached. In this case, the locus of (L, κ)-pairs consistent with the equilibrium provision of work places is given by a curve $LL(\gamma, \mu)$, which is implicitly defined by condition b) in (6.18). The curve is upward sloping if the labor force is heterogeneous (i.e. $\partial g/\partial L > 0$) and a horizontal line if labor is homogeneous so that $\partial g/\partial L = 0$.[10] The LL-curve is shown in figure 6.2. It describes the volume of labor which is employable at an organized work place if capital intensity in non-production is κ and firms organize work

[9] Implicit differentiation of (6.17) gives us $\frac{\partial \kappa}{\partial L}\Big|_{K^D=K^S} = -\frac{\partial K^D/\partial L}{\partial K^D/\partial \kappa} < 0$.

[10] In view of (6.19), $\frac{\partial \kappa}{\partial L}\Big|_{\mu-1=AC(\kappa,L,\gamma)} = -\frac{\partial AC/\partial L}{\partial AC/\partial \kappa} \geq 0$ with equality holding if $\partial g/\partial L = 0$.

with the organization technology represented by γ. Since profit-maximizing firms decide about the provision of work places, the volume of organized employment also depends on the competitive situation in the goods market reflected in μ (Remember the detailed discussion of the role of μ in chapter 2 and chapter 3.) The equilibrium level of employment L^* is simultaneously determined with equilibrium-capital intensity κ^* by the intersection point A^* between the LL-curve and the capital-market equilibrium curve KK. For $\partial g/\partial L = 0$, the LL-curve is a flat line at the value κ_0 determined for $g(L,\gamma) = g(0,\gamma)$ by (6.18), case b), and the equilibrium point is A'.

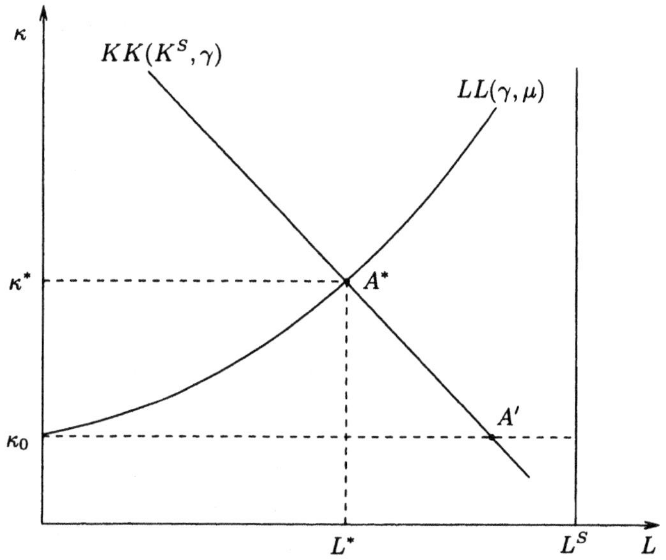

Fig. 6.2. Unemployment equilibrium.

In sum, the level of total employment realized in the macroeconomic equilibrium is characterized by

$$L^* = \min\{L_0, L^S\}, \tag{6.21}$$

where L_0 is the aggregate employment level determined by the equations (6.17) and (6.18), case b).

The equilibrium ratio ρ^* of the factor price of capital r to the wage rate w is determined by the equation $\rho^* = MRS(\kappa^*)$. By definition, $r/p = \rho w/p$. Denote by $\hat{r} = r^*/p^*$ the real equilibrium rate of interest. Since the real equilibrium wage rate is equal to $\frac{1}{\mu A}$, according to (6.4), we have for the real interest rate

$$\hat{r} = \frac{MRS(\kappa^*)}{\mu A}, \tag{6.22}$$

where $dMRS/d\kappa^* < 0$, according to (6.7). The next section analyses how the macroeconomic equilibrium, in particular the equilibrium level of employment, L^*, and the real interest rate in equilibrium, $\hat{r}$, react to changes in capital and labor supply and in the organization technology.

6.3 Comparative-static analysis of the macroeconomic equilibrium

The exogenous determinants of the equilibrium defined by (6.17), (6.18) and (6.20) are μ, K^S, L^S and γ. The effect of μ was extensively discussed in chapter 2 and chapter 3 and is not further considered here.[11] The comparative-static analysis concentrates first on the effects of capital endowment K^S and organization technology γ on an unemployment and a full-employment equilibrium, respectively. Later changes in L^S are discussed.

Formally, we consider the function $L_0\left(K^S,\gamma\right)$ defined by the equations (6.17) and (6.18), case b). According to (6.21), this function characterizes the employment equilibrium if $L_0\left(K^S,\gamma\right) \leq L^S$. Otherwise, $L^* = L^S$. Thus, equation (6.21) can be rewritten in the form:

$$L^* = \begin{cases} L_0\left(K^S,\gamma\right), & \text{if } K^S \leq \hat{K}\left(L^S,\gamma\right), \\ L^S, & \text{if } K^S \geq \hat{K}\left(L^S,\gamma\right), \end{cases} \tag{6.23}$$

where $\hat{K}\left(L^S,\gamma\right)$ is defined by the condition

$$L_0\left(\hat{K},\gamma\right) = L^S. \tag{6.24}$$

Furthermore, also equilibrium capital intensity, κ^*, and real equilibrium return on capital, $\hat{r}$, are considered as functions of capital supply K^S and of parameter γ. According to (6.22), $\hat{r}\left(K^S,\gamma\right)$ is a monotonously decreasing transformation of function $\kappa^*\left(K^S,\gamma\right)$. For $K^S \leq \hat{K}\left(L^S,\gamma\right)$, this function is determined by (6.17) and (6.18), case b), simultaneously with $L_0\left(K^S,\gamma\right)$. For $K^S \geq \hat{K}\left(L^S,\gamma\right)$, the function is determined by substituting $L^* = L^S$ into equation (6.17).

The comparative-static results are derived by using the graphical representation in figure 6.1 and figure 6.2. An analytical derivation can be found in Appendix B.

[11] The impact of μ works through the zero-profit condition $\mu - 1 = AC$. A rise in μ shifts the LL-curve in figure 6.2 downwards and A^* to the right. The positive employment effect results from the fact that in a zero-profit equilibrium a higher profit margin implies that firms incur higher non-production costs for creating work places. On the other hand, according to (6.4), a rise in μ depresses the real wage rate.

6.3.1 Equilibrium employment and interest rate as functions of capital supply

An increase in the amount of supplied capital K^S shifts the KK-curve, representing the capital market equilibrium defined by condition (6.17), upwards in figure 6.1 and figure 6.2.[12] Thus,

$$\partial L^* / \partial K^S > 0, \tag{6.25}$$

if $L^* < L^S$. (For $L^* = L^S$, an increase in K^S has no effect on employment, because of the full-employment constraint.) Moreover, $\partial \kappa^* / \partial K^S \geq 0$ and consequently, according to (6.22), $\partial \hat{r} / \partial K^S \leq 0$ (with equality holding if $L^* < L^S$ and $\partial g / \partial L = 0$ so that the LL-curve is flat in figure 6.2). The effect of K^S on κ^* and thus $\hat{r}$ is smaller in the case presented in figure 6.2 than in the full-employment case of figure 6.1. If $L^* = L^S$, an upward shift of the KK-curve is fully absorbed by an increase in capital intensity κ^*. If $L^* < L^S$, a larger capital stock is only partly absorbed by higher capital intensity in non-production, since it is also used to expand employment. In the case of a horizontal LL-curve there is only an employment effect, whereas capital intensity remains constant at the level κ_0, and the real interest rate is constant at $\hat{r}_0 \equiv MRS(\kappa_0) / (\mu A)$. Figure 6.3 summarizes the effect of K^S on the real equilibrium interest $\hat{r}$.

The curve $\hat{r}(K^S, \gamma)$ represents the real return on capital in the equilibrium of an economy whose organization technology is represented by γ. As shown in the above comparative-static analysis, the effect of K^S on $\hat{r}$ is zero if $L^* < L^S$ and $\partial g / \partial L = 0$ and negative otherwise. It is ceteris paribus stronger if $L^* = L^S$ than if $L^* < L^S$. Thus, the $\hat{r}$-curve has a kink at capital volume $\hat{K}(L^S, \gamma)$ at which full employment is reached according to (6.23).[13]

6.3.2 The effects of a change in the non-production requirements of organizing work

According to (6.1), $g(L, \gamma)$ represents the amount of non-production services required per production work place. It depends on the used method of organization and on the interactive abilities of the employed work force. For a given distribution of abilities, the range of abilities to which a firm has access is determined by the aggregate level of employment. This is the reason why g varies with L if labor is heterogeneous. For a given level of L, the costs (in terms of non-production inputs) of organizing work vary if the abilities endowment of the labor force changes or if firms adopt new forms of work organization. Such changes are represented by variations of parameter γ.

[12] Implicit differentiation of equation (6.17) gives us $\frac{\partial \kappa}{\partial K^S}\big|_{K^D = K^S} = -\frac{-1}{\partial K^D / \partial \kappa}$ which is strictly positive, since $\partial K^D / \partial \kappa > 0$, according to (6.16).

[13] Formally, $0 \geq \lim_{K \to -\hat{K}} \frac{\partial \hat{r}}{\partial K} > \frac{\partial \hat{r}}{\partial K}\big|_{K = \hat{K}}$. See Appendix B for a formal derivation of this property of the $\hat{r}$-curve.

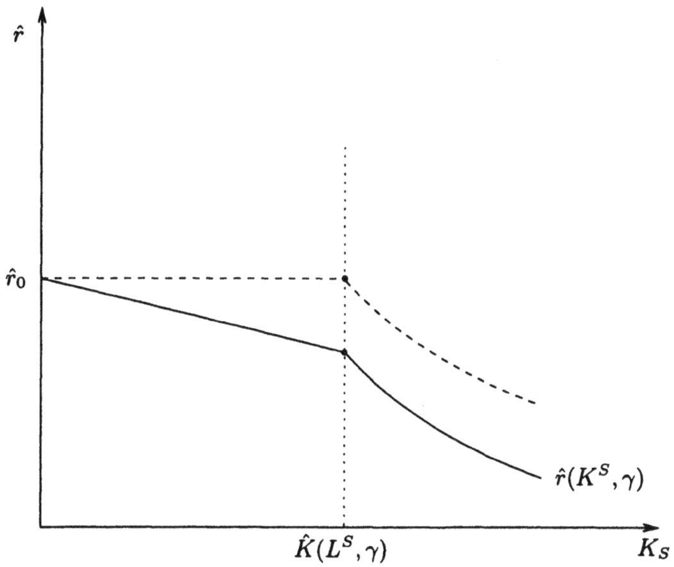

Fig. 6.3. The real equilibrium return on capital (broken line valid if labor is homogeneous).

For the comparative-static analysis of the effects of changes in the non-production requirements two situations, represented by γ_1 and γ_2, respectively, are considered. It is assumed that $\gamma_1 < \gamma_2$ and

$$\frac{\partial g\left(L,\gamma\right)}{\partial \gamma} > 0, \tag{6.26}$$

for all $L\epsilon\left\{L^*\left(K^S,\gamma\right)|\gamma\epsilon\left[\gamma_1,\gamma_2\right]\right\}$. This convention means, an increase in γ from γ_1 to γ_2 represents a switch to a world in which, ceteris paribus, the provision of work places requires relatively more non-production resources in the range of employment levels which are relevant for the macroeconomic equilibrium. (As shown in chapter 4, the non-production costs implied by a certain organization technology may be low for low employment levels so that firms have an incentive to adopt this technology. Nonetheless, in the range of employment levels in which the macroeconomic equilibrium lies, they may be higher than the non-production costs implied by the abandoned technology.)

Assumption (6.26) implies

$$\frac{\partial AC}{\partial \gamma} > 0, \ \frac{\partial K^D}{\partial \gamma} > 0, \tag{6.27}$$

according to (6.12) and (6.15). Thus, the KK-curve, which is defined by condition (6.17), is shifted downwards in figure 6.1 and figure 6.2.[14] The reason

[14] $\left.\frac{\partial \kappa}{\partial \gamma}\right|_{K^D=K^S} = -\frac{\partial K^D/\partial \gamma}{\partial K^D/\partial \kappa} < 0$, because of (6.16) and (6.27).

is that for a given level of employment L and with a given stock of capital K^S the increased amount of non-production services, $g(L,\gamma_2) > g(L,\gamma_1)$, can only be provided if technology (6.2) is operated with a lower capital-intensity. In contrast to the KK-curve, the LL-curve in figure 6.2, defined by (6.18), case b), is shifted upwards.[15] The intuition behind this upward shift is that, in view of the higher non-production requirements per production work place, a given level of aggregate employment L is only profitable if firms produce the non-production services with a relatively higher capital intensity. (Put the other way round, less employment can be profitably organized if the increased non-production requirements are provided with a given capital intensity.) Figure 6.4 shows the consequences of these shifts for the macroeconomic equilibrium. Since the consequences aren't the same in a full employment equilibrium as in an unemployment equilibrium, the equilibrium and its change are represented for three different levels K_L^S, K_M^S, K_H^S of capital endowment where $K_L^S < K_M^S < K_H^S$. Recall from the analysis of section 6.3.1 that an increase in K^S shifts the KK-curve outwards. (The broken parts of the KK- and LL-curves are not feasible because of the full employment constrained $L \leq L^S$.)

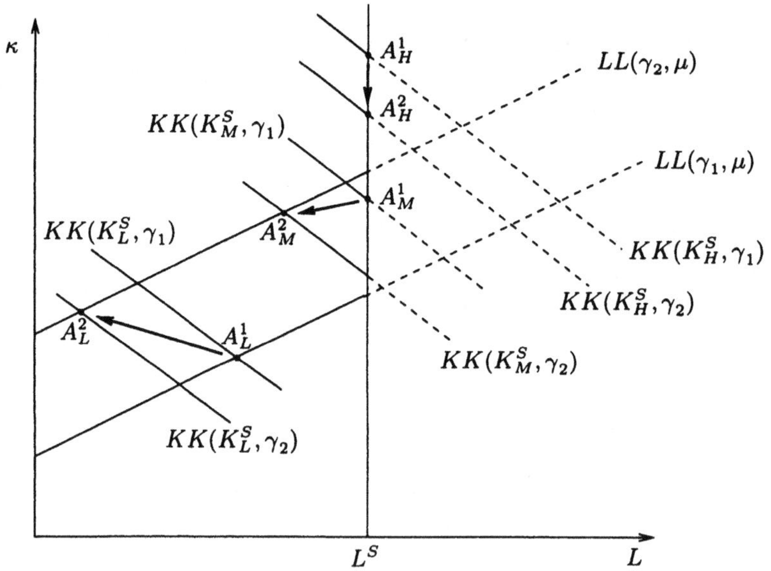

Fig. 6.4. The effects of rising non-production requirements ($g(L,\gamma_1) < g(L,\gamma_2)$) on full-employment and unemployment equilibria.

---

15 $\left.\frac{\partial\kappa}{\partial\gamma}\right|_{\mu-1=AC} = -\frac{\partial AC/\partial\gamma}{\partial AC/\partial\kappa} > 0$, because of (6.19) and (6.27).

Consider first the case of relatively high capital endowment K_H^S. If the organization technology is represented by γ_1 the equilibrium is $A_H^1 = (L^S, \kappa^*(K_H^S, \gamma_1))$. A switch to γ_2, representing higher non-production requirements, shifts the equilibrium to $A_H^2 = (L^S, \kappa^*(K_H^S, \gamma_2))$ with $\kappa^*(K_H^S, \gamma_2) < \kappa^*(K_H^S, \gamma_1)$. Capital intensity declines since with a given stock of capital the higher level of non-production services can only be provided if they are produced in a less capital intensive way. As a consequence, the share of non-production workers M in total employment L^Sincreases.[16] Nonetheless, capital supply is high enough so that it remains profitable for the firms to employ the whole labor force.

Consider next the case of a low level of capital supply K_L^S. In this case we have unemployment in both situations. Under γ_1 the equilibrium is given by $A_L^1 = (L^*(K_L^S, \gamma_1), \kappa^*(K_L^S, \gamma_1))$. When non-production requirements rise, the equilibrium moves to $A_L^2 = (L^*(K_L^S, \gamma_2), \kappa^*(K_L^S, \gamma_2))$. As before we have for a given level of employment L a negative effect on κ reflected by a downward shift of the KK-curve. But in addition, there is now a negative employment effect with positive implications for κ. In an unemployment equilibrium firms earn zero profits. The rising non-production requirements imply that at A_L^1 the provision of work places costs more than the firms earn in production. A_L^1 lies below the $LL(\gamma_2, \mu)$-curve. This cannot be compensated by producing the non-production services less capital intensive, which makes the average costs of providing a work place even more costly (see (6.19)). In sum, there is definitely a reduction of total employment. Both the downward shift of the KK-curve and the upward shift of the LL-curve have a negative impact on L so that $L^*(K_L^S, \gamma_2) < L^*(K_L^S, \gamma_1)$. The counteracting effects on capital-intensity κ of the downward-shifting KK-curve and the upward shifting LL-curve suggest an ambiguous result as long as only the qualitative effects reflected in the graphical analysis are considered. However, the analytical derivation in Appendix B shows that the positive effect dominates and, unambiguously, $\kappa^*(K_L^S, \gamma_2) > \kappa^*(K_L^S, \gamma_1)$.

In the intermediate case of K_M^S we have a full employment equilibrium A_M^1 before and an unemployment equilibrium A_M^2 after a rise in the non-production requirements. In this case the capital intensity may indeed decline as in the case of K_H^S or rise like in the case of K_L^S.

The different cases can be characterized in a systematic way by using the threshold value $\hat{K}(L^S, \gamma)$ defined by equation (6.24). This value describes the capital endowment which guarantees a full employment equilibrium. It increases with rising non-production requirements and with the size of the labor force:[17]

[16] Note that $\frac{\partial M}{\partial \gamma} > 0$ under assumption (6.26). Moreover, $\frac{\partial M}{\partial \kappa} < 0$, according to (6.14).

[17] According to (6.23), $L_0(K^S, \gamma)$ describes the employment equilibrium L^* if the equilibrium is not restricted by the labor supply constraint. We know from (6.25) that $\partial L_0 / \partial K^S > 0$. Moreover, the above analysis showed that an increase of

$$\frac{\partial \hat{K}}{\partial \gamma} > 0 \text{ and } \frac{\partial \hat{K}}{\partial L^S} > 0. \tag{6.28}$$

By means of $\hat{K}$ the results of the above analysis can be summarized as follows:

Case 1: If $K^S \geq \hat{K}(L^S, \gamma_2)$, we have full employment $L^* = L^S$ in the equilibrium under γ_1 as well as under γ_2. Moreover

$$\frac{\partial \kappa^*}{\partial \gamma} < 0 \tag{6.29}$$

in this case.

Case 2: If $K^S < \hat{K}(L^S, \gamma_1)$, we have an unemployment equilibrium under both γ_1 and γ_2 and

$$\frac{\partial L^*}{\partial \gamma} < 0 \text{ and } \frac{\partial \kappa^*}{\partial \gamma} > 0. \tag{6.30}$$

Case 3: If $\hat{K}(L^S, \gamma_1) \leq K^S < \hat{K}(L^S, \gamma_2)$, we have a full employment equilibrium under γ_1 and an unemployment equilibrium under γ_2. Thus,

$$\frac{\partial L^*}{\partial \gamma} < 0, \tag{6.31}$$

whereas $\partial \kappa^* / \partial \gamma$ can be positive, negative or zero. With the effect of γ on $\kappa^*(K^S, \gamma)$ also the effect on the real equilibrium interest rate $\hat{r}(K^S, \gamma)$ is determined, since $\partial \hat{r} / \partial \gamma$ has the inverse sign of $\partial \hat{\kappa} / \partial \gamma$, according to (6.22). In figure 6.3 the equilibrium value of $\hat{r}$ was represented as a function of aggregate capital endowment K^S. According to (6.29) - (6.31), a change in γ affects $\hat{\kappa}$ and thus $\hat{r}$ in opposed directions depending on where K^S lies relative to $\hat{K}(L^S, \gamma)$. Moreover, the threshold $\hat{K}(L^S, \gamma)$ itself varies according to (6.28). To the left of the threshold value $\hat{K}(L^S, \gamma_1)$ the $\hat{r}$-curve is shifted downwards if γ and thus, according to (6.26), the non-production requirements rise. This follows from (6.30) and (6.22). (6.22) together with (6.29) imply that at $\hat{K}(L^S, \gamma_2)$ and to the right of $\hat{K}(L^S, \gamma_2)$ the $\hat{r}$-curve is shifted upwards by an increase in γ. These shifts are shown in figure 6.5.

For $K^S \in \left[\hat{K}(L^S, \gamma_1), \hat{K}(L^S, \gamma_2)\right[$, the value of $\hat{r}(K^S, \gamma_2)$ may be above or below or identical with $\hat{r}(K^S, \gamma_1)$. But we have also the general information of section 6.3.1 about the properties of the $\hat{r}(K^S, \gamma)$-curve. First, we know that for any γ, thus also for γ_2, $\hat{r}$ is a non-increasing function of K^S. Second, for any γ, the $\hat{r}$-curve is kinked downward at the full employment level $\hat{K}$. In sum, the $\hat{r}(K^S, \gamma_2)$-curve must have the same qualitative shape as generally shown in figure 6.3 with a kink at $\hat{K}(L^S, \gamma_2)$. Since $\hat{r}(K^S, \gamma_2) < \hat{r}(K^S, \gamma_1)$ for $K^S < \hat{K}(L^S, \gamma_1)$ and $\hat{r}(K^S, \gamma_2) > \hat{r}(K^S, \gamma_1)$

γ has a negative impact on L^* in an unemployment equilibrium A_L. Thus, $\partial L_0 / \partial \gamma < 0$. Implicit differentiation of (6.24) gives (6.28).

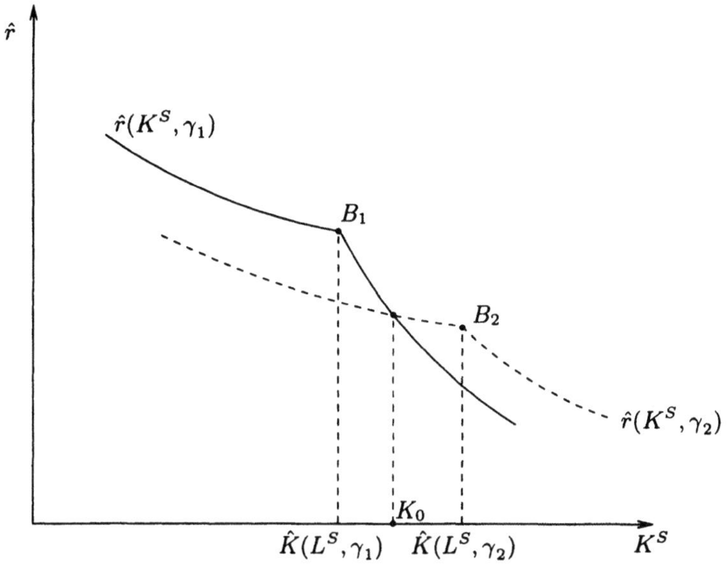

Fig. 6.5. The effects of rising non-production requirements ($g(L, \gamma_1) < g(L, \gamma_2)$) on the return on capital ($\hat{r}$).

for $K^S \geq \hat{K}\left(L^S, \gamma_2\right)$, there must be a level of capital endowment K_0 in between at which the two curves intersect. In the comparative-static analysis of section 6.5 a unique intersection point will be assumed.[18]

For the intuitive understanding of the shift from $\hat{r}\left(K^S, \gamma_1\right)$ to $\hat{r}\left(K^S, \gamma_2\right)$ in figure 6.5 it is important to call to mind that the economy is in an unemployment equilibrium as long as its capital endowment is lower than $\hat{K}\left(L^S, \gamma\right)$. If non-production requirements of organizing employment are relatively higher, the economy needs more capital to reach a full employment equilibrium. Therefore, $\hat{K}\left(L^S, \gamma_2\right) > \hat{K}\left(L^S, \gamma_1\right)$. In an unemployment equilibrium capital is scarcer than in a full employment equilibrium. This is why the return on capital is higher for $K^S < \hat{K}$ than for $K^S \geq \hat{K}$. Moreover, if more capital is supplied in an unemployment equilibrium it can be used to create new employment, whereas in a full employment equilibrium no additional workers are available. Therefore, the return on capital declines less if capital supply increases at $K^S < \hat{K}$ than at $K^S \geq \hat{K}$. If labor is homogeneous so that additional employment doesn't rise the costs of organizing production work, $\hat{r}$ doesn't decline at all as long as there are unemployed workers waiting for a job. A rise in the non-production requirements makes the creation of

[18] The intersection point is unique if at any $K^S \epsilon \left[\hat{K}\left(L^S, \gamma_1\right), \hat{K}\left(L^S, \gamma_2\right)\right]$ the curve $\hat{r}\left(K^S, \gamma_1\right)$ is steeper than $\hat{r}\left(K^S, \gamma_2\right)$. This is, for instance, guaranteed if the labor force is homogenous so that the $\hat{r}$-curves are flat for $K^S \leq \hat{K}\left(L^S, \gamma\right)$, $\gamma = \gamma_1, \gamma_2$.

work places less attractive. This depresses the return on capital resulting under γ_2 compared to the return under γ_1, as long as capital can be used for the creation of new jobs, i.e. in the region to the left of $\hat{K}\left(L^S, \gamma_1\right)$. If the creation of new jobs is no longer an investment opportunity since the whole labor force is fully employed, the fact that γ_2 requires more non-production inputs than γ_1 makes capital relatively scarce - an advantage for capital owners. This is the reason why $\hat{r}\left(K^S, \gamma_2\right) > \hat{r}\left(K^S, \gamma_1\right)$ in the region $K^S \geq \hat{K}\left(L^S, \gamma_2\right)$

6.3.3 Size of the labor force and return on capital

In a model which concentrates on the macroeconomic implications of internal organization of work the interactive abilities of the labor force are important. If labor is heterogeneous a change in the size of the labor force, say from L_1^S to $L_2^S > L_1^S$, implies also a change in interactive abilities depending on how the abilities are distributed over the range $\left]L_1^S, L_2^S\right]$ compared to the range $\left[0, L_1^S\right]$. Thus, in general, variations in the size cannot be isolated from changes in the quality of aggregate labor supply. For the comparative-static analysis this means that a change in L_1^S implies usually also a change in γ, since the quality of the labor force affects the non-production requirements for organizing work. How the macroeconomic equilibrium reacts to variations in γ was analyzed in the preceding section. This section considers the special case that an increase in aggregate labor supply L^S has no effects on γ. Formally, the function $g(L, \gamma)$, which describes the non-production requirement for organizing a unit of production work if the employed abilities are given by the range $\left[z_0(L), \bar{z}\right]$, must be identical in the economies with aggregate labor supply L_1^S and L_2^S, respectively. This is trivially guaranteed if labor is homogeneous and $g(L, \gamma) = g(0, \gamma)$ for all L. It is generally guaranteed as long as for all $L \leq L_1^S$ the interactive abilities in the economy of size L_1^S are the same as in the larger economy with labor force L_2^S. For $L \epsilon \left]L_1^S, L_2^S\right]$, we have $z_0(L) \leq z_0\left(L_1^S\right)$ with strict inequality holding if labor is heterogeneous so that $z_0'(L) < 0$. In other words, a comparative-static analysis of the effects of the size of the labor force is possible if the economy with the larger labor force L_2^S is a replication of the economy with labor force L_1^S but has more workers with relatively low interactive abilities, i.e., it is relatively rich in labor with low abilities.

An increase in the size of the labor force from L_1^S to $L_2^S > L_1^S$ which leaves everything else unchanged affects the equilibrium level of employment and the equilibrium interest rate only through one channel: More capital is needed to guarantee a full employment equilibrium. According to (6.28),

$$\hat{K}\left(L_2^S, \gamma\right) > \hat{K}\left(L_1^S, \gamma\right). \tag{6.32}$$

Regarding the aggregate level of organized employment, the switch from L_1^S to L_2^S has no effect as long as the economy starts in an unemployment equilibrium: If $K^S < \hat{K}\left(L_1^S, \gamma\right)$, then $L_1^* = L_2^* = L_0\left(K^S, \gamma\right)$. But for $K^S > \hat{K}\left(L_1^S, \gamma\right)$, the employment level will rise, since the binding labor supply constraint $L_1^* = L_1^S$ is loosened. According to (6.23), employment rises to $L_2^* = \min\left\{L_0\left(K^S, \gamma\right), L_2^S\right\}$.[19]

The consequences of (6.32) for the return on capital can be immediately seen by looking at the $\hat{r}\left(K^S, \gamma\right)$-curve in figure 6.3. Inequality (6.32) implies that the kink is shifted to the right. This means, the relatively flat part of the $\hat{r}$-curve, which is totally flat if labor is homogeneous ($\partial g/\partial L = 0$), is extended.[20] This is illustrated in figure 6.6, where $\hat{r}_1, \hat{r}_2$ denote the equilibrium interest rates in the economy of size L_1^S and L_2^S, respectively. To the left of $\hat{K}\left(L_1^S, \gamma\right)$ the two curves coincide.

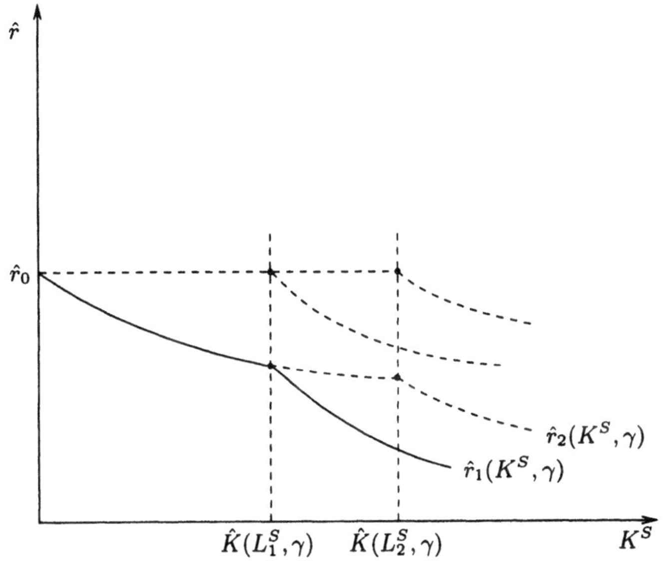

Fig. 6.6. Effects of the size of the labor force on the return on capital ($L_2^S > L_1^S$).

[19] Note $L_0\left(K^S, \gamma\right) > L_1^S$ if $K^S > \hat{K}\left(L_1^S, \gamma\right)$, since $L_0\left(\hat{K}\left(L_1^S, \gamma\right), \gamma\right) = L_1^S$ and $\partial L^*/\partial K^S > 0$ for $L^* = L_0\left(K^S, \gamma\right)$ (see (6.24) and (6.25)).

[20] Alternatively, one could say the $\hat{r}$-curve is shifted upwards in the range in which capital endowment K^S is higher than full employment of L_1^S requires. This can be seen by using the derivations of Appendix B. For $K^S > \hat{K}\left(L_1^S, \gamma\right)$, implicit differentiation of (B.1) gives us $\partial \kappa^*/\partial L^S < 0$ because of (B.2) and (B.3). Thus, $\partial \hat{r}/\partial L^S > 0$, according to (6.22). In the range of unemployment equilibria resulting for $K^S < \hat{K}\left(L_1^S, \gamma\right)$, $\hat{K}$ and thus $\hat{r}$ is determined by the system (B.9) which is independent of L^S.

If more labor is seeking employment, capital as an input for creating jobs remains scarce and yields a relatively high return even at higher levels of capital supply.

6.4 The macroeconomic equilibrium when capital supply is elastic

So far capital endowment has been given by an exogenously fixed amount K^S. Realistically, capital supply reacts to the capital return in an economy. This is clearly the case in a small open economy and in an integrated world economy with mobile capital (see section 6.5). Also in a closed economy with savings, discussed in chapter 7, the aggregate capital stock of the economy is related to the interest rate. Before the analysis turns to endogenous capital supply in capital markets or by savings, this section shortly considers the role of elastic capital supply resulting from exogenously given costs of capital without asking where these costs come from. First, the equilibrium in a perfect capital market is presented. Then, the role of capital-market imperfections for the aggregate level of job provision is discussed.

6.4.1 Equilibrium in a perfect capital market

Let $R\left(K^S\right)$ with $R' > 0$, $R'' \geq 0$ be the real cost of supplying K^S units of capital. In a perfect market capital is supplied according to the rule

$$\hat{r} = R'\left(K^S\right), \quad R'' \geq 0. \tag{6.33}$$

Capital supply increases as long as the rate of return earned in the economy is higher than the marginal cost of supplying capital. Section 6.3 determined the equilibrium interest rate $\hat{r}\left(K^S\right)$ resulting in an economy whose capital endowment is K^S.[21] Supply curve (6.33) implies for the equilibrium:

$$\hat{r}\left(K^S\right) = R'\left(K^S\right). \tag{6.34}$$

Equation (6.34) determines the equilibrium in an economy in which capital is elastically supplied in a perfect capital market. The equilibrium can be graphically analyzed by confronting the marginal cost curve $R'\left(K^S\right)$ with the $\hat{r}\left(K^S\right)$-curve of figure 6.3. This leads to a usual market diagram shown in figure 6.7. Intersection point A^* represents the real equilibrium rate of interest $\hat{r}_e$ and the equilibrium supply of capital K_e^S. With K_e^S and $\hat{r}_e$ also κ^* and L^* are determined, according to (6.22) and (6.23).

The situation shown in figure 6.7 represents an unemployment equilibrium, since $K_e^S < \hat{K}\left(L^S, \gamma\right)$. Applying the comparative-static analysis of

[21] The exogenous parameters γ and L^S, on which the $\hat{r}$-curve depends, are here omitted to save notation.

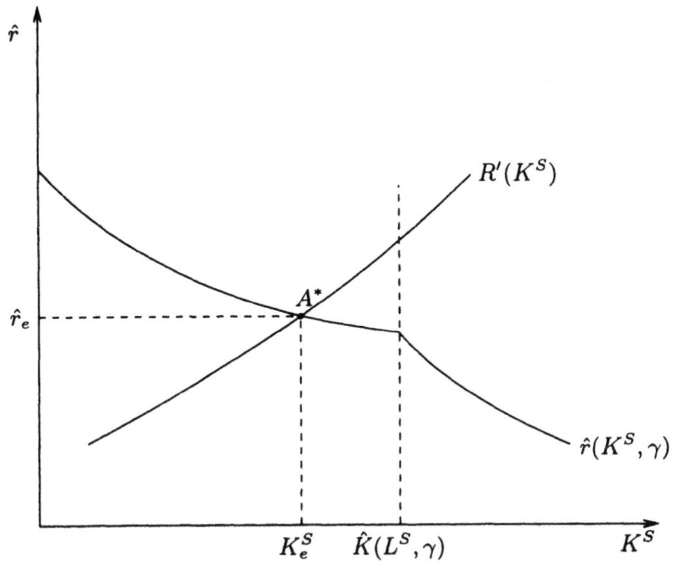

Fig. 6.7. Equilibrium in a perfect capital market.

section 6.3.2 to this equilibrium, we can conclude immediately that an increase in the non-production requirements depresses both interest rate and employment since the $\hat{r}$-curve is shifted downwards if γ rises and equilibrium supply of capital is not so high that full employment would be guaranteed. A change in the size of the labor force like discussed in section 6.3.3 has no impact on an unemployment equilibrium. Only in a full employment equilibrium it has an effect, namely, a rise in the interest rate, since the organization of more employment makes capital more scarce.

6.4.2 The impact of capital market imperfections on employment

In an imperfect capital market, capital is not supplied according to the marginal cost curve. For instance, under monopolistic or oligopolistic capital supply, investors require a mark up on marginal costs. This implies that instead of (6.33), the interest rate charged for the supply of K_S units of capital is given by

$$\hat{r} = \frac{R'\left(K^S\right)}{1-\lambda}, \tag{6.35}$$

where $\lambda < 1$ represents the market power of the investors. The equilibrium condition is then

$$\hat{r}\left(K^S\right) = \frac{R'\left(K^S\right)}{1-\lambda} \tag{6.36}$$

instead of (6.34). Market power of investors is cutting back the supply of capital in the usual way. The equilibrium is shown in figure 6.8.

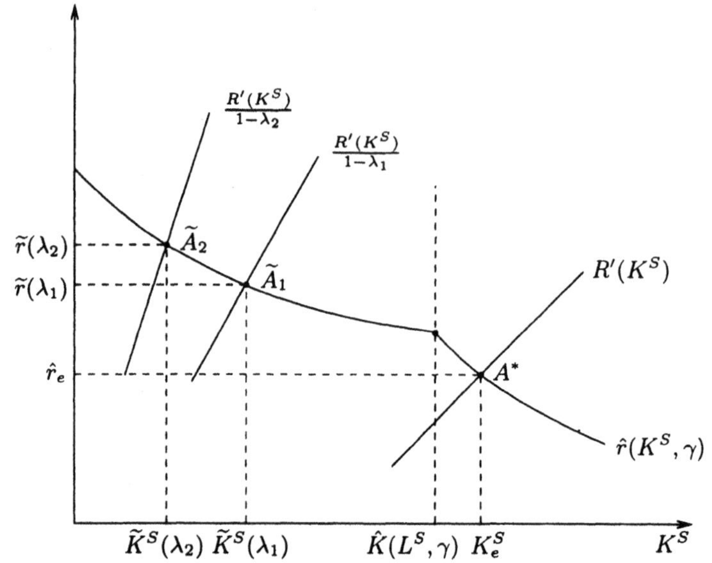

Fig. 6.8. Equilibrium under market power of investors ($\lambda_1 < \lambda_2$).

We have, for the equilibrium supply $\tilde{K}^S(\lambda)$ defined by (6.36),

$$\frac{\partial \tilde{K}^S}{\partial \lambda} < 0. \tag{6.37}$$

According to (6.23) and (6.25), the reduction of capital supply reduces also the equilibrium level of employment if the economy is in an unemployment equilibrium. Formally,

$$\frac{\partial L^*}{\partial \lambda} < 0 \text{ if } \tilde{K}^S(\lambda) < \hat{K}\left(L^S, \gamma\right). \tag{6.38}$$

A look at figure 6.8 shows that (6.38) also holds if the $\hat{r}$-curve is flat for $K^S \leq \hat{K}\left(L^S, \gamma\right)$, i.e. if labor is homogeneous. For $L^* = L^S$, the market power of investors may have no effect on employment. However, it is also possible that market power pushes the economy from a full employment equilibrium (A^*) to an unemployment equilibrium (like $\tilde{A}_1$).

In sum, this short section on capital supply backs up the conclusion of section 3.3.2 and 4.5.3, that unemployment may be caused by capital markets imperfections which allow investors to require a rent. The next section will show the effects of international capital markets.

6.5 Capital mobility and employment

In an international world capital owners invest their capital at that location which yields the highest rate of return. The amount of capital supplied to a single economy is determined by the international capital market equilibrium in which interest rates are equalized across countries. In the approach of this study, capital is used for as an input in the organization technology. As analyzed in section 6.2, its return is simultaneously determined with the level of employment that is organized by profit-maximizing firms in the macroeconomic equilibrium. According to the comparative-static analysis in section 6.3, the equilibrium level of organized employment is an increasing function of capital supply as long as the provided capacity to organize work is smaller than the size of the labor force. This reflects in a rigorous way the common view in current economic policy debates that it is important for the employment situation in a country to be an attractive location for investors. It is the purpose of this section to provide a theoretically founded analysis of the relationship between locational attractiveness and the supply of jobs when capital can move freely between different economies.

The analysis focuses exclusively on the role of capital mobility. For this purpose it is assumed that preferences and production technology are identical across the world. This guarantees that the real wage rate $\frac{w}{p} = \frac{1}{\mu A}$ (see (6.4)) is the same in all countries and labor has no incentive to migrate. Moreover, it is assumed that all economies produce the same goods, and money supply in the different economies is such that nominal price levels are equalized so that consumers are indifferent between purchasing a good at home or abroad. The economies differ only in those respects which are relevant for the return on capital, i.e., in the labor force and in the requirements of organizing work represented by the organization technology. According to the analysis of section 6.3, the real interest rate $\hat{r}$ resulting in the equilibrium of an economy is a non-increasing function of capital supply K^S. The function was shown in figure 6.3. Its shape and position depend on the non-production requirements, represented by parameter γ, and on the size of the labor force L^S. The impacts of these two exogenous determinants on the $\hat{r}\left(K^S\right)$-curve were graphically summarized in figure 6.5 and figure 6.6, respectively. The $\hat{r}\left(K^S\right)$-curve describes the attractiveness of an economy for international investors. The following analysis examines the consequences of international capital markets by comparing for a given economy the closed equilibrium with fixed national capital supply with the equilibrium resulting when capital is freely allocated according to the economy's relative attractiveness in the world. First, the case of a small open economy is considered. Then, the equilibrium of a two-country world is analyzed.

6.5.1 Equilibrium in a small open economy

In a small open economy the relevant costs of supplying capital are the foregone opportunities of investing the capital in the world capital market. These opportunities are defined by the world interest rate which is exogenously given for a small economy. Thus, the marginal cost curve of capital is in this case

$$R'\left(K^S\right) = \hat{r}^w, \tag{6.39}$$

where $\hat{r}^w$ is the world interest rate. In other words, capital supply is perfectly elastic and the supply curve corresponds to the horizontal line $\hat{r} = \hat{r}^w$. The macroeconomic equilibrium resulting in a small economy under free international capital allocation is therefore the borderline case of elastic supply analyzed in section 6.4. Figure 6.9 shows the equilibria A_1^*, A_2^*, A_3^* for three world interest rates $\hat{r}_1^w$, $\hat{r}_2^w$, $\hat{r}_3^w$, respectively, where $\hat{r}_1^w < \hat{r}_2^w < \hat{r}_3^w$.

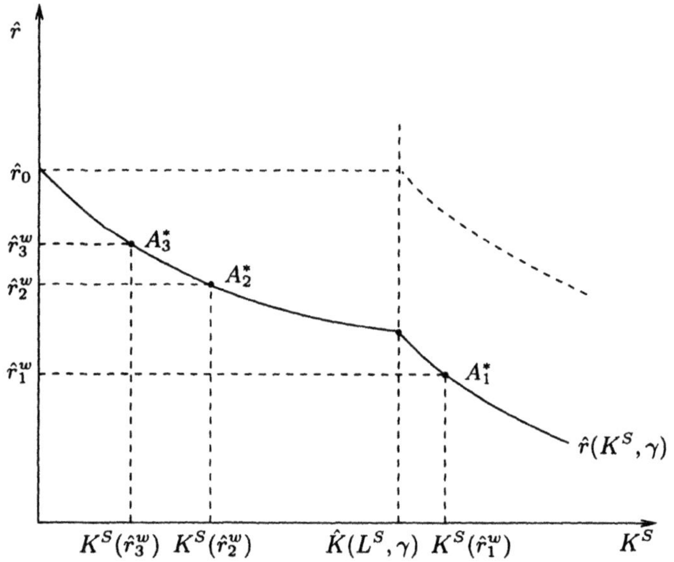

Fig. 6.9. Capital supply in a small open economy for different world interest rates.

Obviously, capital supply to the small economy declines if the world market interest rate rises:

$$\frac{\partial K^S}{\partial \hat{r}^w} < 0. \tag{6.40}$$

According to (6.23) and (6.25), this implies that also equilibrium employment declines if the economy is already in an unemployment equilibrium or at the edge of unemployment:

$$\frac{\partial L^*}{\partial \hat{r}^w} < 0 \;\text{ if }\; K^S(\hat{r}^w) \leq \hat{K}(L^S, \gamma). \tag{6.41}$$

If the economy is in a full employment equilibrium (like A_1^* in figure 6.9), a slight increase of the world interest rate has no effect on employment, but a drastical increase (like from $\hat{r}_1^w$ to $\hat{r}_2^w$) may shift the economy into an unemployment equilibrium. It should be noticed that, provided the economy can attract capital at all (i.e. $\hat{r}^w \leq \hat{r}_0$), an unemployment equilibrium never arises if labor is homogeneous so that the $\hat{r}(K^S, \gamma)$-curve is flat for $K^S \leq \hat{K}(L^S, \gamma)$ (i.e., if the broken line is relevant in figure 6.9).[22] The reason is that with homogeneous labor the average costs of organizing production work is independent of aggregate employment. Thus, also the return on capital, which is an input for the organization of work in firms, is independent of L as long as workers are available for employment. Consequently, with perfect international capital markets the economy attracts no capital at all (if $\hat{r}^w > \hat{r}_0$) or enough to create employment for the whole labor force. If labor is heterogeneous, the return on capital declines with aggregate employment L, since the organization of work becomes more costly if also less able workers have to be employed. Thus, the capital inflow may be stopped before all workers are employed. Compared to the international opportunities it is not attractive to invest capital into firms which provide the organizational capacity to integrate workers with low abilities. As a consequence, no places are organized for them in equilibrium.

An important practical implication of (6.41) is that with free international capital flows fluctuations in the world interest rate are transformed into employment fluctuations in a small economy. In particular, the jobs at the bottom of the abilities spectrum are concerned by these fluctuations.

The comparative-static analysis in section 6.3 showed that in an unemployment equilibrium the $\hat{r}$-curve is shifted downwards if the resources required for organizing work are increased in an economy (see figure 6.5 for $K^S < \hat{K}(L^S, \gamma_1)$). Combining this with figure 6.9 for world interest rates like $\hat{r}_2^w$ or $\hat{r}_3^w$, we see that capital flows off and unemployment rises if the provision of jobs becomes relatively more costly in a small economy. As discussed, the reasons for comparatively high requirements for organizing work, represented by an increase in γ, may lie in adverse technological conditions or in the quality of the work force. If the economy starts in a full-employment equilibrium like for $\hat{r}_1^w$ in figure 6.9, i.e., if a country is relatively attractive for investors compared to the world market, then an increase in γ may induce an inflow of capital, since according to figure 6.5 the $\hat{r}$-curve is shifted upwards for high levels of capital supply K^S. The reason is that in an equilibrium in which capital supply is high relative to the level required for guaranteeing full employment, a rise in the non-production requirements for organizing work makes capital more scarce. An increase in the size of the labor force as

[22] Note that this is not so if capital supply is not fully elastic and the supply curve is an increasing function ($R'' > 0$) as in figure 6.7.

considered in section 6.3.3 has the same effect. If in an economy with full employment the supply of labor increases, it is attractive to provide more work places. This attracts capital. Graphically, according to figure 6.6, the $\hat{r}$-curve is shifted upwards if the economy is in a full employment equilibrium like A_1^* in figure 6.9. As a consequence $K^S(\hat{r}_1^w)$ increases. In an unemployment equilibrium the increase of the labor force would have no effect on capital allocation as long as the quality of the labor force is not increased at the same time.[23] If the interest rate in the world market is as high as $\hat{r}_2^w$ or $\hat{r}_3^w$ it is not attractive to provide jobs for all workers in the small economy shown by figure 6.9. By expanding the labor force at the bottom of the abilities spectrum the economy doesn't become more attractive for investors. (Formally, for $K^S \leq \hat{K}(L_1^S, \gamma)$, the $\hat{r}$-curve corresponding to L_1^S and L_2^S, respectively, are the same in figure 6.6.)

6.5.2 International equilibrium with and without capital mobility

A world of two countries is considered, in which preferences as well as production technology are identical and no migration or goods trade take place between the countries. The countries may differ in factor endowment or in the organization technology. Such differences imply different returns on capital, as analyzed in section 6.3, and induce capital flows. The purpose of the analysis in this section is to characterize the patterns of capital flows and its consequences for employment. By analogy to foreign trade theory, the closed equilibrium resulting when capital is not allowed to move internationally and the international equilibrium resulting under free capital mobility are compared.

Let, for the two countries $j = a, b$, L_j^S and $\bar{K}_j$ be size of the labor force and capital endowment, respectively. Moreover, let the non-production resources required for organizing work in the two countries be represented by the organization technologies $\gamma_j, j = a, b$. Whereas in a closed equilibrium the supply constraints

$$K_j^S = \bar{K}_j, \quad j = a, b \tag{6.42}$$

hold, the international equilibrium must fulfill the world supply constraint

$$K_a^* + K_b^* = \bar{K}_a + \bar{K}_b \tag{6.43}$$

and the condition of interest-rate equalization

$$\hat{r}_a(K_a^*, \gamma_a) = \hat{r}_b(K_b^*, \gamma_b), \tag{6.44}$$

[23] In the comparative-static analysis of the effect of size L^S of the labor force it was assumed that the economy with labor force L_2^S is a replication of the economy with labor force L_1^S but has more workers with low abilities. Without this assumption changes in L^S imply in general a change in γ at the same time.

where K_a^*, K_b^* denote the equilibrium allocation of capital and $\hat{r}_j(\cdot, \gamma_j)$, $j = a, b$, are the interest rate curves derived in section 6.3 for labor force L_j^S and organization technology γ_j.

We consider first two countries which differ only in the size of their endowments while having identical organization technologies. Secondly, the case of two countries with identical endowments but different organization technologies is examined.

Capital flows induced by differences in the size of factor endowments. If the countries differ in their capital endowment while they are identical with respect to their labor force, then the direction of the capital flow is obvious. $\gamma_a = \gamma_b = \gamma$ and $L_a^S = L_b^S = L^S$ imply identical interest-rate curves $\hat{r}_a(\cdot, \gamma_a) = \hat{r}_b(\cdot, \gamma_b) = \hat{r}(\cdot, \gamma)$ as presented in figure 6.3. Thus, provided that labor is heterogeneous, condition (6.44) implies $K_a^* = K_b^*$.[24] This means capital flows from the capital rich country to the capital poor country. As a consequence, also aggregate employment levels in the two countries are equalized, according to (6.23) and (6.25). In other words, capital mobility smoothes employment disparities existing in the closed equilibria.

Let us turn now to the less trivial case of differences in the size of the labor force. It is assumed that the two countries are identical in every respect (in particular $\gamma_a = \gamma_b = \gamma$ and $\bar{K}_a = \bar{K}_b = \bar{K}$) apart from the size of their labor force. As discussed in section 6.3.3, in general it is not meaningful to order economies according to the size of their labor force if labor is heterogeneous. However, a comparative-static analysis of the implications of differences in the size of the labor force is possible if the larger economy, say b, is a replication of the smaller economy, a, to which workers with low abilities are added. In the following comparison, $L_a^S < L_b^S$ is assumed with identical abilities $z_0^a(L) = z_0^b(L) = z_0(L)$ for all employment levels $L \leq L_a^S$ and $z_0^b(L) \leq z_0(L_a^S)$ for $L \in \left]L_a^S, L_b^S\right]$. The formulation "country b is rich in low-ability labor" is used to briefly address the compared situations. Population-rich countries with a good education system which however doesn't cover the whole labor force are concrete examples. Another example would be that one of two otherwise similar economies is exposed to immigration of low-skilled labor.

According to (6.32), a larger capital stock $\hat{K}(L_b^S, \gamma) > \hat{K}(L_a^S, \gamma)$ is needed in country b than in a for guaranteeing full employment. As shown in figure 6.6 this shifts the kink of the interest-rate curve $\hat{r}_b(K^S, \gamma)$ of country b to the right compared to the interest-rate curve $\hat{r}_a(K^S, \gamma)$ relevant for country a. A convenient way to determine the international equilibrium is to compare $\hat{r}_a$ and $\hat{r}_b$ in a factor endowment box in which capital supply K_a^S in country a is measured from origin O_a to the right and capital supply K_b^s in country b is measured from origin O_b to the left. The length $\overline{O_a O_b}$ of the box is given by total factor endowment $\bar{K}_a + \bar{K}_b = 2\bar{K}$. Figure 6.10 shows this

[24] If $\bar{K}_a$, $\bar{K}_b \leq \hat{K}(L^S, \gamma)$ and labor is homogeneous so that the $\hat{r}$-curve is flat in the relevant range, there are multiple equilibria. Also in the closed equilibrium with $K_j^S = \bar{K}_j$ the equality $\hat{r}_a(\bar{K}_a, \gamma) = \hat{r}_b(\bar{K}_b, \gamma)$ would be fulfilled.

box for the case that in both the closed and the international equilibrium firms don't provide jobs for all workers, neither in country a nor in country b.

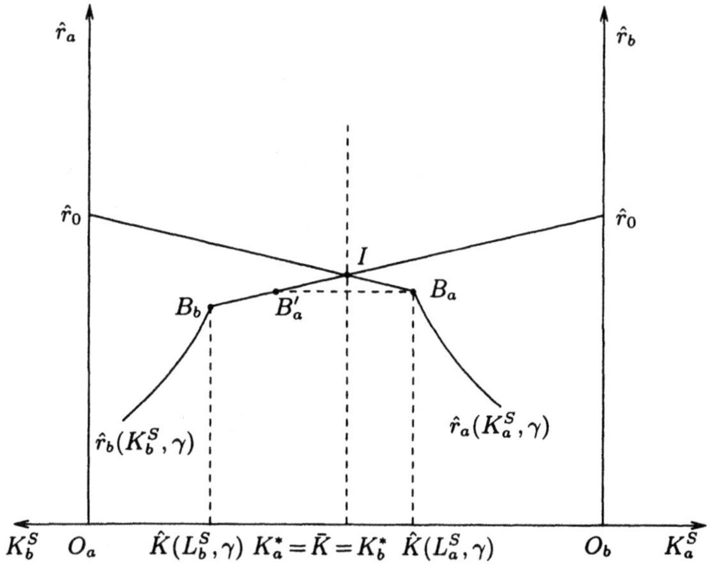

Fig. 6.10. Closed and international equilibrium with unemployment in both countries ($L_a^S < L_b^S$).

The two interest-rate curves are symmetric except that the kink of $\hat{r}_b\left(K_b^S, \gamma\right)$ of the larger country is farther away from the relevant origin O_b than the kink B_a of the $\hat{r}_a\left(K_a^S, \gamma\right)$-curve from origin O_a(Compare point B_b with B'_a). As long as $\bar{K} \leq \hat{K}\left(L_a^S, \gamma\right) < \hat{K}\left(L_b^S, \gamma\right)$, the intersection point I of the $\hat{r}_a$- and $\hat{r}_b$-curve lies at the symmetrical axis $\bar{K}$. Thus, the factor supplies $K_a^S = K_b^S = \bar{K}$ in the closed economy fulfill also condition (6.44) of interest-rate equalization. The international equilibrium coincides with the closed equilibrium. No capital flows are induced when capital markets are opened up between the two countries. The reason is that capital supply $\bar{K}$ is so scarce that even in the smaller country, a, not enough jobs are organized to employ the whole work force. As a consequence, according to (6.23), in both countries the equilibrium level of organized employment is equal to $L_a^* = L_b^* = L_0\left(\bar{K}, \gamma\right)$. Since the same labor force is employed in both locations also the return on capital is the same. The fact that country b is rich in low-ability labor has no effect on this return, since anyway the additional low-ability workers are not employed at work places organized by using capital.

The situation changes if in the closed equilibrium there is full employment in country a, i.e., if $\bar{K} > \hat{K}\left(L_a^S, \gamma\right)$. In this case the equilibrium rate of interest, $\hat{r}_a\left(\bar{K}, \gamma\right)$, in the closed economy a, lies to the right of kink B_a of the $\hat{r}_a$-curve. This equilibrium is represented by point A_a in figure 6.11.

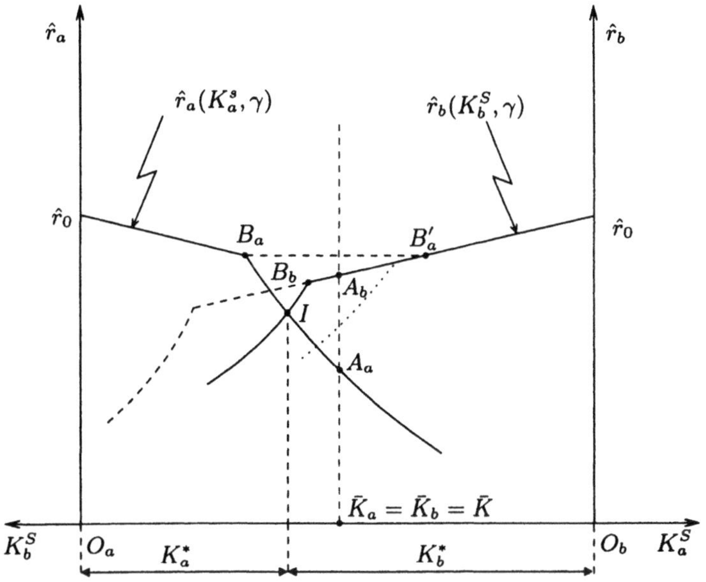

Fig. 6.11. Capital flows from fully employed country a to labor rich country b.

In economy b with the larger labor force more capital is needed to guarantee full employment. In figure 6.11, a situation is illustrated in which part of the labor force has no organized job in the closed equilibrium. The kink B_b of the interest-rate curve $\hat{r}_b\left(K_b^S, \gamma\right)$ lies to the left of the axis $K_a^S = K_b^S = \bar{K}$, i.e., $\hat{K}\left(L_b^S, \gamma\right) > \bar{K}$. In this case the closed equilibrium of economy b is given by point A_b. The dotted $\hat{r}_b$-curve shows a situation in which there is full-employment also in economy b. What is known for sure from (6.32) is that $L_b^S > L_a^S$ implies that kink B_b lies to the left of B_a' and therefore $\hat{r}_b\left(\bar{K}, \gamma\right) > \hat{r}_a\left(\bar{K}, \gamma\right)$[25]. Hence, the international equilibrium allocation of capital K_a^*, K_b^* at which condition (6.44) is fulfilled must lie to the left of the axis $\bar{K}$. That means, capital flows from country a, in which labor is fully employed to country b, in which more labor is looking for a job so that it is attractive to invest there in the organization of work. As a result, according to (6.25), employment in b increases, provided that there was unemployment in the closed economy. In the international equilibrium, represented by point

[25] Recall that, for $L_a^S = L_b^S$, $\hat{r}_a$ and $\hat{r}_b$ would be symmetric and intersect at point A_a.

I in figure 6.11 we have full employment in b since kink B_b lies to the right of intersection point I. But there could still be unemployment as shown by the broken $\hat{r}_b$-curve. In any case, intersection point I lies to the right of kink B_a. This means, despite a flow out of capital, economy a remains fully employed in the international equilibrium.

In sum, in a world of countries which differ only in the size of the labor force with low abilities, the liberalization of capital markets has no consequences as long as capital is so scarce that unemployment prevails in all countries. If capital is less scarce so that at least in the country with the relatively smaller labor force all workers have a job provided by non-production resources including capital, then the liberalization of capital markets leads to a flow of capital towards the country which is rich in low-ability labor. This capital mobility is good for employment, since it has no negative effect on employment in the source country and an employment-expanding effect in the host country with unemployed labor.

Capital flows induced by differences in the requirements of organizing work. Consider now two countries a, b with identical capital endowments $\bar{K}_a = \bar{K}_b = \bar{K}$ and identical size of the labor force $L_a^S = L_b^S = L^S$. But they differ in the non-production resources required per organized unit of production work. Without loss of generality it is assumed that job creation in country b is easier than in country a. This means, the non-production resources required per work place are lower in b than in a. Formally, with convention (6.26), $\gamma_a > \gamma_b$ and $g(L, \gamma_a) > g(L, \gamma_b)$. The economic reason for the advantage of country b can be the use of more efficient methods of work organization or a higher quality of the labor force. As far as in addition to capital other non-human resources like land or public infrastructure are important for the provision of work places, also the availability of these factors could be a source of the described locational advantage.[26]

For the analysis of the effects of free international capital allocation it is again useful to distinguish the cases that capital is relatively scarce or not so scarce, respectively. The relevant threshold value is the level of capital supply K_0 at which the interest-rate curves corresponding to γ_a and γ_b intersect according to figure 6.5. We discuss first the borderline case that $\bar{K} = K_0$. Then the case that capital endowment is relatively scarce, i.e. $\bar{K} < K_0$, and the case that capital is not so scarce, i.e. $\bar{K} > K_0$, are analyzed.

[26] Formally, suppose that factors as public infrastructure work like an output-augmenting progress in production function (6.2), i.e., $y_i = T_j Q(k_i, m_i)$, where T_j, $j = a, b$, represents the availability of public infrastructure at location j. Then, the system (6.1), (6.2) which describes the requirements for organizing work can also be written in the form $\tilde{y}_i = \tilde{g}(L, \gamma_j)\, \bar{l}_i$ and $\tilde{y}_i = Q(k_i, m_i)$ with $\tilde{g}(L, \gamma_j) \equiv g(L, \gamma)/T_j$. Thus, $\tilde{g}(L, \gamma_a) > \tilde{g}(L, \gamma_b)$ if $T_a < T_b$. Institutional or bureaucratic obstacles causing transaction costs in the provision of work places can be interpreted as a decrease of T_j.

Again, the analysis is made by comparing the interest-rate curves $\hat{r}\left(K_a^S, \gamma_a\right)$ and $\hat{r}\left(K_b^S, \gamma_b\right)$ in the capital endowment box[27]. Figures 6.12-6.14 show the $\hat{r}\left(K_b^S, \gamma_b\right)$-curve starting from the right border of the box with origin O_b. According to the analysis of section 6.3.2 summarized in figure 6.5, $\gamma_a > \gamma_b$ implies that for $K^S < K_0$ the $\hat{r}\left(K_a^S, \gamma_a\right)$-curve, starting from the left border of the box with origin O_a, is shifted downwards compared to $\hat{r}\left(K_b^S, \gamma_b\right)$. Moreover, according to (6.28), $\hat{K}\left(L^S, \gamma_a\right) > \hat{K}\left(L^S, \gamma_b\right)$, that is, more capital is required in a than in b for guaranteeing full employment. This means graphically that the kink B_a is further away from the ordinate through origin O_a than kink B_b from the ordinate through origin O_b.

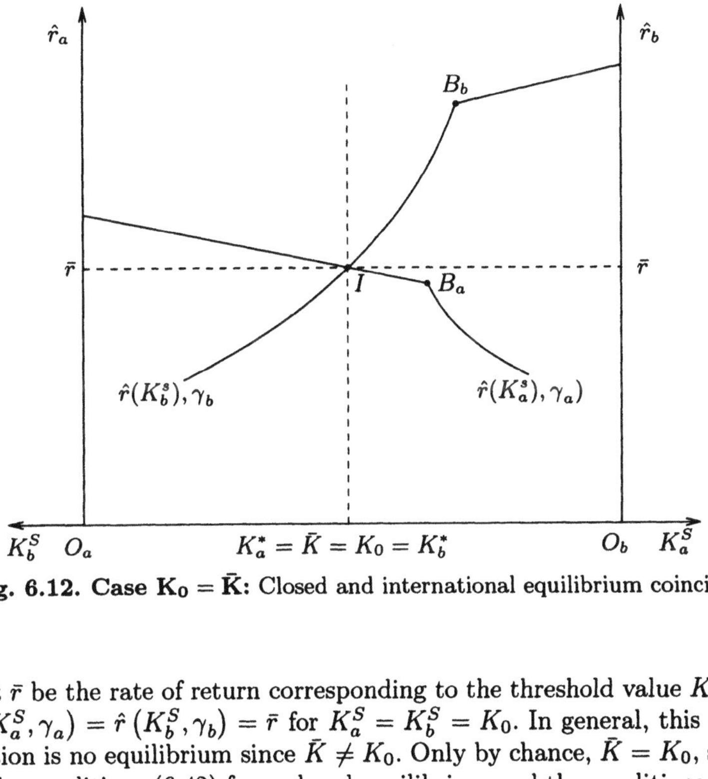

Fig. 6.12. Case $\mathbf{K_0 = \bar{K}}$: Closed and international equilibrium coincide.

Let $\bar{r}$ be the rate of return corresponding to the threshold value K_0, that is, $\hat{r}\left(K_a^S, \gamma_a\right) = \hat{r}\left(K_b^S, \gamma_b\right) = \bar{r}$ for $K_a^S = K_b^S = K_0$. In general, this capital allocation is no equilibrium since $\bar{K} \neq K_0$. Only by chance, $\bar{K} = K_0$, so that both the conditions (6.42) for a closed equilibrium and the conditions (6.43), (6.44) for an international equilibrium are fulfilled at $K_a^S = K_b^S = K_0$. In this borderline case, which is represented in figure 6.12, the international equilibrium (point I) and the closed equilibrium coincide. Opening up capital markets has no consequences in such a situation. Since $K_0 = \bar{K}$ is the symmetric axis of the box in figure 6.12, the fact that $\hat{K}\left(L^S, \gamma_a\right) > K_0 > \hat{K}\left(L^S, \gamma_b\right)$

[27] Country index $j = a, b$ is omitted in the function symbol $\hat{r}_j$ since the differences between the countries are fully reflected in parameter γ_j, $j = a, b$.

implies that both kinks B_a and B_b lie to the right of the $\bar{K}$-axis. That means there is full employment in country b in which job creation is relatively easy, whereas in country a part of the labor force remains jobless.

What happens in the case that capital is relatively scarce i.e. if $\bar{K} < K_0$?

In this case, which is represented in figure 6.13, it is still true that kink B_a must lie to the right of $K_a^S = K_0$ and kink B_b must lie to the right of $K_b^S = K_0$, since $\hat{K}(L^S, \gamma_b) < K_0 < \hat{K}(L^S, \gamma_a)$ for $\gamma_b < \gamma_a$ (see figure 6.5).[28] Moreover, for any $K^S < K_0$ we have $\hat{r}(K^S, \gamma_b) > \hat{r}(K^S, \gamma_a)$ if $\gamma_a > \gamma_b$. Hence, $\hat{r}(\bar{K}, \gamma_b) > \hat{r}(\bar{K}, \gamma_a)$ in the case of $\bar{K} < K_0$. (Compare point A_b to point A_a in figure 6.13.) As a consequence, the point of intersection I between the $\hat{r}(K_a^S, \gamma_a)$-curve and the $\hat{r}(K_b^S, \gamma_b)$-curve must lie to the left of the $\bar{K}$-axis. We conclude that free capital mobility leads to an outflow of capital from country a, in which the organization of work requires relatively high non-production resources, to country b where the creation of job is easier.

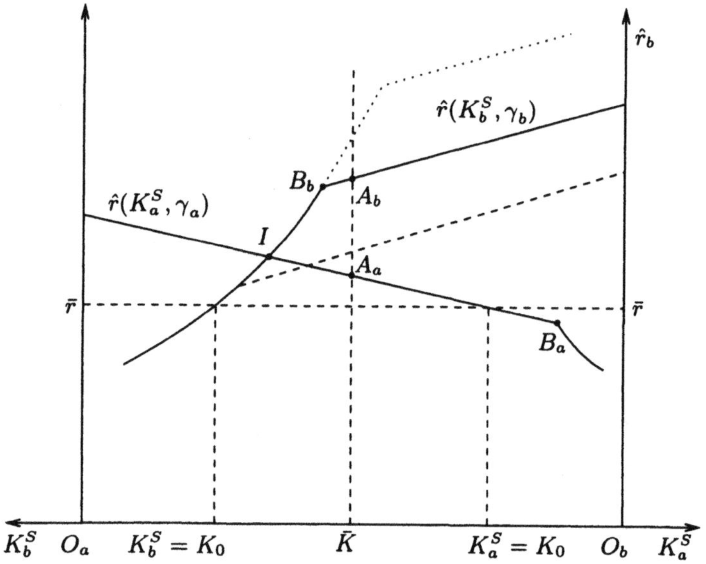

Fig. 6.13. Case $\bar{K} < K_0$: Capital flows from country a with high non-production requirements to country b with low non-production requirements.

Concerning employment, figure 6.13 shows that in the case $\bar{K} < K_0$ there is certainly unemployment in country a. Since kink B_a is to the right of $K_b^S = K_0$ we have already unemployment in the closed economy equilibrium with

[28] Note that in figure 6.12-6.14, K_b^S is measured from origin O_b at the right end of the capital box.

$K_a^S = \bar{K}$.[29] The outflow of capital in the international equilibrium aggravates this unemployment problem. Thus, to say that capital is relatively scarce if $\bar{K} < K_0$ means in economic terms that there is unemployment at least in that country which is less attractive for investors. In the more attractive country b we may have unemployment in the closed equilibrium, namely if $K_b^S = \bar{K}$ lies to the right of the kink B_b as illustrated in figure 6.13. The inflow of capital in the international equilibrium reduces this unemployment. At point I in figure 6.13 unemployment in country b is completely eliminated since I lies to the left of kink B_b. However, with a slightly different $\hat{r}\left(K_b^S, \gamma_b\right)$-curve as represented by the broken line part of b's labor force would remain without a work place despite of the inflow of capital. On the other hand, the $\hat{r}\left(K_b^S, \gamma_b\right)$-curve could also be like shown by the dotted line. Then, economy b would reach full employment already in the closed economy without capital drain from country a. Anyway, since employment decreases in a while it increases or remains constant in b, capital mobility increases employment disparities between countries in the case that capital is relatively scarce.

Finally, let us turn to the case that $\bar{K} > K_0$. We will see that in this case capital is less scarce in the sense that full employment is guaranteed at least in one of the two economies.

The investment opportunities are shown in figure 6.14. Since $\gamma_a > \gamma_b$ implies $\hat{K}\left(L^S, \gamma_b\right) < K_0 < \hat{K}\left(L^S, \gamma_a\right)$, kink B_b must lie to the right of $K_b^S = K_0$. As a consequence, we have certainly full employment in the closed equilibrium of economy b with $K_b^S = \bar{K} > K_0$. Moreover, by definition of K_0, $\hat{r}\left(K^S, \gamma_b\right) > \hat{r}\left(K^S, \gamma_a\right)$ for all $K^S < K_0$.

This together with the fact that $\hat{r}\left(K^S, \gamma\right)$ is non-increasing in K^S implies that intersection point I, at which interest rates are equalized, must lie to the left of $K_b^S = K_0$ and thus to the left of B_b. Therefore, also in the international equilibrium full employment is guaranteed in economy b.

$\gamma_a > \gamma_b$ implies further that $\hat{r}\left(K^S, \gamma_b\right) < \hat{r}\left(K^S, \gamma_a\right)$ for $K^S > K_0$. Therefore, $\hat{r}\left(\bar{K}, \gamma_b\right) < \hat{r}\left(\bar{K}, \gamma_a\right)$ in this case (Compare point A_a with point A_b). Thus, intersection point I representing the international equilibrium allocation of capital must lie to the right of the $\bar{K}$-axis. This means, when capital markets are opened up capital flows out of country b to country a, in which more resources are needed for creating jobs. The reason is that in country a capital is scarcer than in b where employment for the whole labor force can be provided with relatively low non-production requirements. For the level of employment in country a the capital inflow is positive, if unemployment prevailed in the closed equilibrium like represented by point A_a. In the shown situation with I to the right of kink B_a the inflow of capital leading to the international equilibrium eliminates unemployment completely. At point I we have full employment in both countries. However, also the broken line represents a possible $\hat{r}\left(K^S, \gamma_a\right)$-curve. In this case, some unemployment

[29] Analytically, $L_0\left(K_a^S, \gamma_a\right) < L^S$ for $K_a^S < \hat{K}\left(L^S, \gamma_a\right)$, according to (6.24) and (6.25).

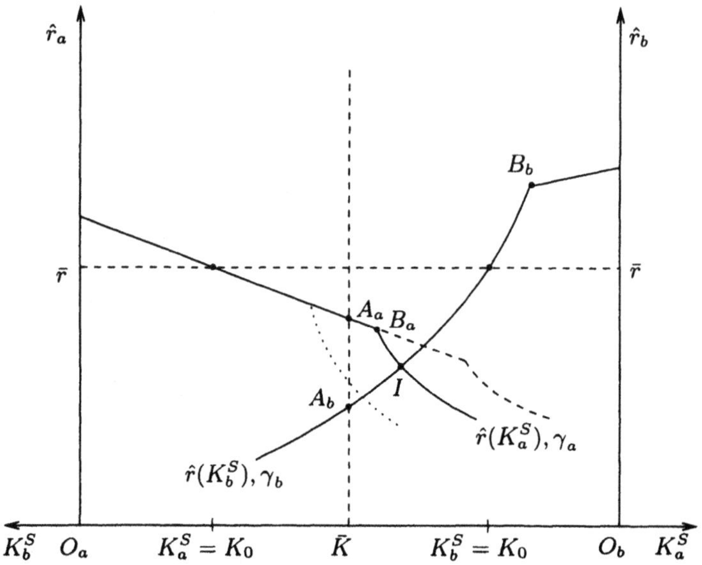

Fig. 6.14. Case $\bar{\mathbf{K}} > \mathbf{K_0}$: Capital flows from fully employed country b to country a with high non-production requirements.

remains in economy a even after the inflow of capital. On the other hand, also the dotted line is a possible $\hat{r}\left(K^S, \gamma_a\right)$-curve. In this case, world capital supply is so rich that full employment is guaranteed in both countries in the closed as well as in the international equilibrium.

In sum, if the world's capital endowment is high, then firms find it profitable to provide work places for the whole labor force at least in the country in which job creation is relatively easy, and free capital mobility leads to a flow of capital towards the economy in which job creation is more difficult. The reason is that there the need of resources for organizing work is higher and investments in the provision of work places yield a higher return. In this case, capital mobility is good for employment, since existing unemployment is reduced. However, if capital is scarce, then unemployment prevails at least in the country in which non-production requirements of organizing work are relatively high, and capital flows to the country in which job creation is easier. This aggravates the unemployment problem in the economy in which the conditions for the provision of work places are less favorable. The other economy either has no employment problem at all, since the whole labor force is fully employed even without the inflowing capital, or its employment situation is improved by the capital inflow. Thus, in this case, free international capital allocation reinforces existing employment disparities.

An immediate implication of this result is: If the differences in γ are the result of random shocks (e.g. catastrophes destroying the public infrastructure) so that situations with $\gamma_a < \gamma_b$ and $\gamma_a > \gamma_b$ alternate, free capital mobility smoothes employment fluctuations in a world with rich capital endowment. And it amplifies the employment fluctuations if capital is relatively scarce so that unemployment is surely a problem for the economy in the unfavorable state.

7. Investment and savings. Supply-side vs. demand-side macroeconomic equilibria

One of the oldest issues in the history of economic thoughts is the question whether supply determines demand or demand determines supply. The supply-side argument, known as Say's Law, is based on the idea that the motive behind supply is always the suppliers' desire to earn income for being able to satisfy their wants. Thus, supply *eo ipso* implies demand, or as it was also formulated: Supply creates its own demand. The demand-side argument, central to the theory of Kalecki and Keynes , says that not the desire to purchase (i.e. notional demand) but effective demand is relevant. Since it cannot be taken for granted that the level of effective demand is high enough to absorb any volume of supply, firms base their production and employment decisions on the level of effective demand that they expect. Thus, expected demand determines supply i.e. the level of production and employment.

At the macroeconomic level the central implication of Say's Law is that savings, i.e. the supply of non-consumed goods for accumulation, determines aggregate investment demand. By contrast, the demand-side approach argues that investment determines savings, since investment demand determines aggregate production and employment, and creates thus the income which can be saved. Ex post, when the economy has settled in an equilibrium, investment and savings must be equal. This makes it difficult to decide between the controversial views about the direction of causality empirically. However, the different views have far-reaching practical consequences: Different macroeconomic equilibria, in particular, different aggregate employment levels result if firms decide about production and employment on the basis of some state of expectations about aggregate demand, or, if they exhaust the supplied resources since they expect in accordance with Say's Law that supply always finds its demand.

The intention of this chapter is not to sum up the whole way of macroeconomic thinking from Say to Keynes and back to rational expectations. The purpose of the following analysis is to resume the discussion of chapter 3 about how the theory developed in this study is related to traditional macroeconomics. The consideration of capital as an important determinant of employment in chapter 6 allows us to complete this discussion with respect to Say's Law and the role of employment. The two-stage character of the presented model points out that two aspects of employment are important:

The provision of work places and the occupation of work places. At stage 2 the level of employment for a given capacity of organized work places is determined. With flexible wages and perfect foresight the equilibrium level of labor demand at stage 2 coincides with the capacity of work places provided by the firms' decisions at stage 1. Unemployment in the sense that firms don't hire workers for all organized work places because of a lack of effective demand is only possible in the presented framework if nominal wages are rigid or investors are pessimistic and the economy is in some kind of liquidity trap. Thus, at stage 2, the presented model reproduces the standard view of modern macroeconomics (Section 7.2 discusses the issue of supply- vs. demand-determined equilibrium at stage 2 in detail).

The new point of the presented model is that even under flexible wages and perfect foresight of firms the equilibrium provision of work places at stage 1 is not necessarily equal to full employment. Nonetheless the considered macroeconomic equilibria have been determined by the supply side. Given technological possibilities and factor supply, in particular, the supplied abilities of the labor force, firms have decided about the provision of organized jobs at stage 1 under the expectation that they can sell the capacity output at stage 2. Thus, so far the study has stuck to the supply-side approach. Section 7.3 extends the approach so that savings and accumulation can be discussed. The main purpose of this chapter is to examine the macroeconomic equilibria that result if firms base their decisions about job creation at stage 1 on pessimistic expectations about aggregate demand. In the discussion of the role of expectations within the framework of the basic model in section 3.4 it was not possible to see how employment is interrelated with investment and savings. Only the extended model with capital allows us to examine this interaction. It will be shown in section 7.4 that pessimism of firms indeed leads to an equilibrium in which employment and accumulation is lower than in the supply-determined equilibria considered so far. This is true although wages are flexible and expectations about demand are self-fulfilling in the established demand-determined equilibria. The result provides a new justification of the idea that employment is determined by effective demand. Flexible wages guarantee that employment is equal to the supplied jobs. But the equilibrium supply of jobs may be restricted by the firms' expectations about the aggregate level of effective demand. Since the equilibrium provision of work places defines also that part of the labor force which is employable under the used organization technology, one could also say: A low level of effective demand implies that more workers are considered to be unemployable.

Before the details of the differences between conventional Keynesian view, supply-determined two-stage equilibrium and demand-determined two-stage equilibrium are discussed, the next section summarizes from chapter 6 macroeconomic relationships which must hold in any equilibrium.

7.1 The relationship between investment, savings and other macroeconomic variables

For any volume of production work $\bar{L}^x = \sum_i \bar{l}_i$ that can be organized, the monopolistic competition equilibrium at stage 2 fulfills the usual macroeconomic relationships. These relationships are summarized in section 7.1.1. Then, in section 7.1.2, the macroeconomic relationships implied by a two-stage equilibrium, including the decisions about the non-production inputs for the provision of organization capacity $\bar{L}^x = \sum_i \bar{l}_i$, are presented.

7.1.1 Macroeconomic relationships in a monopolistic competition equilibrium (stage 2)

By definition, in an economy in which goods are used for consumption as well as investments, real aggregate demand X^D is the sum of real aggregate consumption C and real aggregate investment I:

$$X^D = C + I. \tag{7.1}$$

Real aggregate supply, denoted by X^S, is according to production technology (6.3) given by

$$X^S = L^x/A \le \bar{L}^x/A, \tag{7.2}$$

where $L^x \equiv \sum_i l_i$ is aggregate labor input in production and $\bar{L}^x \equiv \sum_i \bar{l}_i$ is the aggregate volume of production work that can be organized, given the firms' decisions at stage 1.[1]

In a monopolistic competition equilibrium at stage 2 we have

$$X^D = X^S = X \le \bar{X} \tag{7.3}$$

where $X = Y/p$ is the real aggregate income realized at stage 2 and $\bar{X} \equiv \bar{L}^x/A$ is the aggregate capacity output implied by the firms' decisions at stage 1.

Individual saving is a function of the interest rate and individual income. It is assumed that all individuals save the same share of their income so that the distribution of income plays no role for aggregate savings. Then, real aggregate savings, denoted by S, are given by

$$S = s(\hat{r})\, X, \qquad s' \ge 0, \tag{7.4}$$

where X is total real income and s is the propensity to save depending on the real interest rate $\hat{r}$.

[1] Consumption, investment and production are bundles of n goods. Real aggregate values are equal to the respective nominal values divided by the price index P. Since all prices are equal in equilibrium, the real aggregate values are equal to the sum of the n components of the relevant bundle. They can be measured in units of production-labor inputs: For instance, $X = \left(\sum p_i x_i\right)/P = p\left(\sum x_i\right)/p = \sum_i l_i/A$.

In any closed macroeconomic equilibrium we have

$$I = S. \tag{7.5}$$

With savings function (7.4) this equilibrium condition reduces to

$$X = \frac{I}{s(\hat{r})}. \tag{7.6}$$

Finally, equilibrium prices are

$$p_i = p = \mu w A, \tag{7.7}$$

according to (6.4). And the gross profit (before deduction of non-production costs which are fixed at stage 2) earned by a firm at stage 2 is $\pi = (p - wA)\,x$, $x \leq \bar{x}$, i.e.

$$\pi = (\mu - 1)\,wl, \qquad l \leq \bar{l}. \tag{7.8}$$

(With $n\bar{x} = \bar{X}$ and $n\bar{l} = \bar{L}^x$ in equilibrium.)

7.1.2 Relationships between macroeconomic variables in a two-stage equilibrium

In a two-stage equilibrium, in which firms at stage 1 correctly anticipate stage 2, we have further

$$X = \bar{X}, \qquad \bar{X} = \bar{L}^x/A, \tag{7.9}$$

since firms don't arrange unutilized capacities.

According to the organization technology given by (6.1) and (6.2), the aggregate volume of production work $\bar{L}^x$which can be organized is determined by the equation

$$\bar{L}^x = \frac{Mq(\kappa)}{g(\bar{L},\gamma)} = \frac{Q(K,M)}{g(\bar{L},\gamma)} \tag{7.10}$$

where

$$\kappa = \frac{K}{M} \tag{7.11}$$

and

$$\bar{L} = M + \bar{L}^x \leq L^S. \tag{7.12}$$

The equations (7.10) - (7.12) define for any values of K and γ three out of the four variables $\bar{L}$, M, $\bar{L}^x$ and κ as functions of the fourth variable. For instance, for $\bar{L} \leq L^S$ the aggregate levels of non-production labor M and organizable production labor $\bar{L}^x$, respectively, are functions of total employment $\bar{L}$ and capital stock K. We have[2]

[2] Substituting (7.10) into (7.12), we obtain $\bar{L} = M + \frac{Q(K,M)}{g(\bar{L},\gamma)}$. Implicit differentiation gives us $\partial M/\partial \bar{L} > 0$, since $\partial Q/\partial M > 0$ and $\partial g/\partial L \geq 0$. Moreover, $\partial M/\partial K < 0$, since $\partial Q/\partial K > 0$. Using this and $\bar{L}^x = \bar{L} - M$, we have $\partial \bar{L}^x/\partial K > 0$. $\bar{L}$ has in general an ambiguous impact on $\bar{L}^x$. Obviously, the derivations with respect to $\bar{L}$ are only defined for $\bar{L} < L^S$.

$$M = M\left(\bar{L}, K, \gamma\right) \quad \text{with} \quad \frac{\partial M}{\partial \bar{L}} > 0, \; \frac{\partial M}{\partial K} < 0 \tag{7.13}$$

and

$$\bar{L}^x = \bar{L}^x\left(\bar{L}, K, \gamma\right) \quad \text{with} \quad \frac{\partial \bar{L}^x}{\partial K} > 0. \tag{7.14}$$

Moreover, according to the discussion in section 3.1, as long as $\bar{L}$ has not reached the efficient level or an inefficiently high level, the capacity is increasing if additional labor is integrated into the employed work force. Thus,

$$\frac{\partial \bar{L}^x}{\partial \bar{L}} > 0 \tag{7.15}$$

(For saving notation the symbol denoting the dependent variable is also used for the function symbol.)

Equation (7.13) states that, ceteris paribus, more non-production labor is required if employment for additional labor is organized. However, for a given level of employment the volume of non-production labor declines if more capital is available for the provision of the non-production services required for organizing production work. Equation (7.14) says that more production work can be organized if more capital is available.

It should be noticed that (7.10) - (7.12) are implications of the organization technology. Thus, no behavioral assumptions regarding the firms job provision behavior at stage 1 are involved in (7.13) - (7.15). They must hold regardless of whether the equilibrium is determined by the supply side (as derived in chapter 6 and recapitulated in section 7.3) or by the demand side (as discussed in section 7.4). Finally, cost-minimizing provision of the non-production services implies

$$\hat{r} = \rho \frac{w}{p} = \frac{MRS\left(\kappa\right)}{\mu A}, \tag{7.16}$$

where $\rho = r/w$, and r is the nominal interest rate (Recall (6.4) and (6.20)).

7.1.3 Equilibrium accumulation

In the present model, at stage 1, accumulated capital K is used together with non-production labor to provide the prerequisites of production at stage 2. The produced output can be consumed or is saved and used for accumulating capital. There is thus the following circle from investment to savings and savings to investment: Accumulated investments help to provide the capacity of production. Production within this capacity generates income which can be saved and the saved income can be invested. The interrelationship between accumulated capital (K) and accumulation of capital ($S = I$) is in equilibrium if capital K invested at stage 1 is consistent with the implied accumulation

I at stage 2. Since growth is not considered,[3] this means that I reproduces K so that capital endowment, the volume of organized work, production and the values of all other macroeconomic variables remain constant under equilibrium accumulation. Formally, this condition for equilibrium accumulation reads

$$\delta K = I, \tag{7.17}$$

where $0 < \delta \leq 1$ is the fraction of K that is used up (depreciates) in the provision of non-production prerequisites.[4]

Equation (7.17) requires that the amount of capital used up at stage 1 equals the volume of capital formation at stage 2. The following comparative-static analysis doesn't consider effects of variations in δ. For saving parameters, $\delta = 1$ is assumed. Thus, (7.17) simplifies to the following condition for equilibrium accumulation:

$$K = I. \tag{7.18}$$

The volume of capital that can be used in the economy for organizing production work must be equal to the amount of capital that is invested in this economy.

A macroeconomic equilibrium fulfilling the equilibrium conditions at stage 2 and stage 1 as well as the condition for equilibrium allocation (7.18) is determined by the *supply side*, if the causality behind (7.18) is as follows: Firms use any given supply of capital K to organize production work as analyzed in chapter 6. The production $\bar{X}(K)$ which can be organized with a given K determines aggregate real income and demand $X^D = \bar{X}(K)$. Moreover, it implies savings $S(K)$ and these savings are invested. In other words, capital supply K determines demand, income and savings. In equilibrium $K = I = S(K)$. Therefore, the equilibrium depends only on preferences, labor endowment and technology. By contrast, the macroeconomic equilibrium is determined by the *demand side* if the causality is the other way round: Firms have expectations about real demand X_E and choose their production so as to fulfill the expected demand. As a consequence, the macroeconomic equilibrium depends not only on capital supply K but also on the expected X_E as will be worked out in section 7.4. In particular, since $X = X_E$, we have $S = S_E(X_E, K)$ which implies for equilibrium accumulation $K = I = S_E(X_E, K)$. Hence, the equilibrium supply of capital depends on expected demand X_E. Before turning to the detailed exposition and comparison of the two types of equilibria, we confront the demand-side view of

[3] Growth by accumulation would require capital as a production input. Here capital is only used as a factor for producing the non-production prerequisites of organizing production work. Thus, a change in K affects production only insofar as the volume of organized employment is changed, but it has no effect on output for a given level of production labor.

[4] In a dynamic analysis condition (7.17) would describe a stationary state: The capital stock available at the end of period t is given by the sum $K_t = (1-\delta) K_{t-1} + I_t$. Thus, $K_t = K_{t-1} = K$ implies $I_t = I = \delta K$. Stage 1 and stage 2 are taking place in the same period.

macroeconomics with the supply-side view in the more familiar framework of the macroeconomic equilibrium at stage 2, in which supply is constrained by the capacity arranged at stage 1.

7.2 Supply side vs. demand side in the equilibrium at stage 2

At stage 2 capacity output $\bar{X} = \bar{L}^x/A$ is fixed. According to (7.10) - (7.12), the volume of capital K and non-production labor M employed at stage 1 for the provision of work places determine $\bar{L}^x$ together with $\bar{L}$ and κ. Moreover, also the interest rate $\hat{r}$ is determined by the cost-minimizing use of capital and non-production labor in the provision of the capacity to organize the $\bar{L}^x$ units of production labor, according to (7.16).

The purpose of this section is to discuss what it means that the macroeconomic variables at stage 2 are determined by the demand side as opposed to the supply side.

7.2.1 Full utilization of capacity

The supply side at stage 2 is given by the production capacity $\bar{X}$. Thus, in a supply-determined equilibrium we have $X^D = X^S = \bar{X}$ in (7.3). This implies, according to (7.2)

$$L^x = \bar{L}^x \tag{7.19}$$

for aggregate employment in production and $L = \bar{L}$ for total employment (including the fixed volume of non-production labor M).

The price level is determined by the condition that total nominal income $p\bar{X}$ must be equal to total money income Y. Thus, $p = \frac{YA}{\bar{L}^x}$ which together with (7.7) implies for the nominal wage rate

$$w = \widetilde{w} \equiv \frac{Y}{\mu \bar{L}^x}. \tag{7.20}$$

In sum, these are the equilibrium values which result in the perfect foresight equilibria analyzed in the basic model and its various extensions. Firms don't create wrong capacities unless there are unanticipated things happening at stage 2.

According to (7.4), aggregate savings is also determined by the capacity created at stage 1. Investment demand must absorb the saved output in equilibrium and we have

$$I = S = s(\hat{r})\,\bar{X}. \tag{7.21}$$

7.2.2 Underutilization of capacity when macroeconomic activity is constrained by effective demand

The theory of effective demand is based on the view that investment is not automatically adjusted to any given volume of savings but depends on uncertain exogenous circumstances. Suppose that investment demand is given by a function $I(\hat{r}, E)$ where E represents the exogenous state of expectations.[5] If $I(\hat{r}, E) > s(\hat{r})\bar{X}$ the investment demand cannot be satisfied with the given capacities. But if $I(\hat{r}, E) < s(\hat{r})\bar{X}$, then $X^D = C + I < \bar{X}$. Adjustment of supply X^S to demand X^D leads to the equilibrium income $X_E = \frac{I(\hat{r},E)}{s(\hat{r})}$, according to (7.6), and to savings $S = s(\hat{r})X_E$, according to (7.4). (Subscript E hints to exogenous expectations). Thus, investment determines income and savings. And, in contrast to (7.19), employment in production is given by

$$L_E^x = AX_E < \bar{L}^x. \tag{7.22}$$

Figure 7.1 illustrates this unemployment equilibrium in the usual Keynesian 45°-diagram.

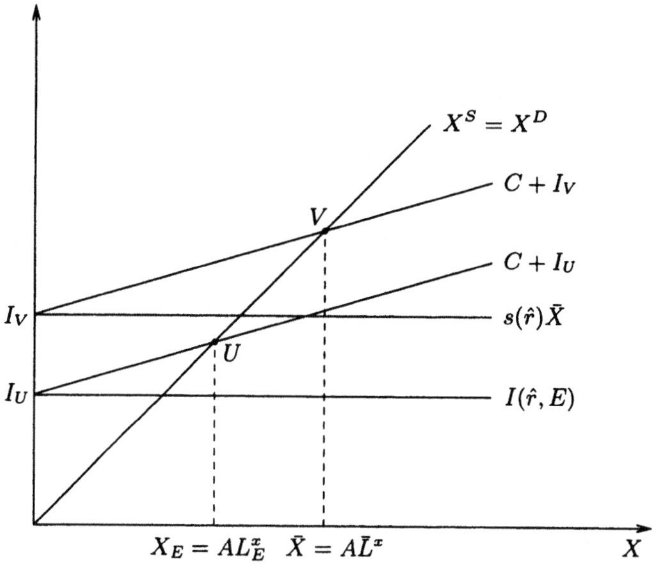

Fig. 7.1. Keynesian unemployment.

[5] Keynes' argument for why the state of expectations should be taken as exogenous was uncertainty. Instead of working with a shaky endogenous explanation for an uncertain variable it is better to keep in mind that the variable may change for unknown exogenous reason ("We simply do not know" was his warning against the idea that this uncertainty can be eliminated by the calculus of risks. See Keynes [38], p. 114).

The supply-determined equilibrium with full capacity utilization is represented by point V. If investment demand $I(\hat{r}, E)$ falls short of $I_V = s(\hat{r})\bar{X}$, then production, income and savings are reduced until they are consistent with $I_U = I(\hat{r}, E)$. This defines point U representing the demand-constrained equilibrium.

The problem with this kind of analysis is that price adjustments are not reflected. One aspect which cannot be addressed here, is the reaction of investment to the real interest rate, since $\hat{r}$ is fixed from stage 1 by construction of the model.[6] But the problem of price and wage adjustment can be seen by looking at labor demand L^x and the money wage w. As discussed in detail in chapter 2 and shown in figure 2.1 the equations $PX = Y$ together with $X = AL^x$ and $p_i = p = \mu w A$ for $L^x \leq \bar{L}^x$ imply for the demand of production labor

$$L^x = \begin{cases} \frac{Y}{\mu w} & \text{if } L^x \leq \bar{L}^x, \\ \bar{L}^x & \text{otherwise.} \end{cases} \tag{7.23}$$

Thus, if employment in production is L^x_E determined by (7.22), the nominal wage rate must be higher than the equilibrium value $\widetilde{w}$ defined by (7.20). This is shown in figure 7.2 where the wage rate consistent with L^x_E and (7.23) is denoted by w_E.

The fact that $w_E > \widetilde{w}$ raises the question why $L^x_E < \bar{L}^x$ should be an equilibrium unless wage rigidity prevents the wage rate from falling. After all unemployed workers are looking for a job and firms have unoccupied work places which they are willing to fill if a falling wage and price level allows to increase output. The argument of the demand-side view is that exogenous expectations, in particular the investment demand implied by these expectations, determine the macroeconomic activity level (see U in figure 7.1), and a fall in money wage and price level doesn't induce investors to increase their demand. In the picture of figure 7.2 this means that L^x_E determines w_E, and L^x defined by (7.23) is not a labor demand function but the condition determining the nominal wage and thus the price level which is consistent with given exogenous expectations. As a consequence, an increase in money supply so that Y is increased to Y' doesn't help to overcome the underutilization equilibrium shown by point U. If w_E were fixed by wage rigidity the shift of the labor demand curve to $L^x = \frac{Y'}{\mu w}$ would put the economy into point V' and eliminate the underutilization of $\bar{L}^x$. But if L^x_E is fixed by exogenous expectations the increase of Y to Y' leads only to higher nominal wages (w'_E) and prices at the new equilibrium point U'.[7]

[6] The reason is that no capital is used in production. So adjustments of $\hat{r}$ can only be discussed when we turn to the analysis of the two-stage equilibrium which is the true concern of this chapter. The purpose of the present section is after all only to show how the new approach of this study is related to traditional macroeconomic controversies.

[7] Note that goods prices $p = \mu w A$, nominal interest rate $\hat{r}p = \hat{r}\mu w A$ and wage rate w move in the same direction.

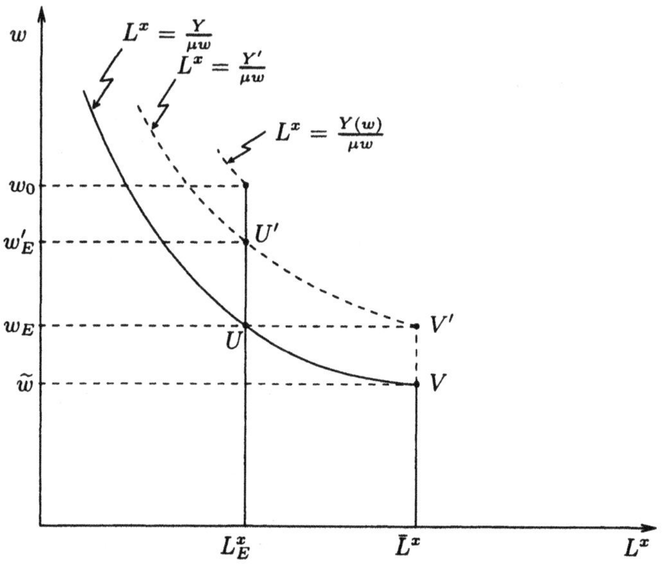

Fig. 7.2. Demand for production labor and labor market equilibrium at stage 2 $(Y' > Y)$.

Finally, it should be noticed that there is one possibility to reconcile the view that the macroeconomic activity level is demand constrained and employment is given by L^x_E with the view that underbidding of wages leads to employment along the labor demand curve defined by (7.23): Y is the amount of aggregate money income used for the transaction of consumption and investment goods. If this amount is endogenously adjusted to nominal prices, since money is also used for speculative purposes, then Y is not fixed by exogenous money supply but a function of w and $L^x = \frac{Y(w)}{\mu w}$.[8] Suppose now that $w_0 \geq w_E$ exists so that for all $w \leq w_0$ the aggregate money income used for transactions is always equal to $Y(w) = \mu L^x_E w$, since any additional money is hoarded for speculative purposes, then we have $L^x = \frac{Y(w)}{\mu w} = L^x_E$ for all $w \leq w_0$. This reproduces the idea of a liquidity trap.[9] In figure 7.2 it means that for $w \leq w_0$ the L^x-curve is vertical at L^x_E.

[8] Since the amount of money used for speculative purposes is a decreasing function of the interest rate r, the amount Y remaining for the transaction of aggregate output is increasing in r and thus in w (Remember $r = \hat{r}\mu w A = MRS(\kappa)\, w$).

[9] Note that $w \leq w_0$ corresponds to $p \leq p_0 \equiv \mu w_0 A$ and $r \leq r_0 \equiv \hat{r}\mu w_0 A$, where r is the nominal interest rate.

7.3 Equilibrium accumulation and equilibrium provision of jobs when firms are supply oriented

Supply orientation of firms means that they anticipate the supply-determined equilibrium at stage 2 when deciding about the provision of work places at stage 1. In other words, the behavior of firms at stage 1 is based on the expectation that any capacity of organized production work $\bar{l}$ that is consistent with the economy's endowment L^S and K can be fully utilized at stage 2. Thus, profit function (7.8) is equal to

$$\pi = (\mu - 1)\, w\bar{l} \tag{7.24}$$

and the firm's optimization problem at stage 1 is

$$\max_{\bar{l}} \pi^n = [\mu - 1 - AC]\, w\bar{l}, \tag{7.25}$$

where AC are the minimal costs of the necessary non-production inputs for organizing a unit of production work (According to (6.12), they depend on capital-intensity κ, on the aggregate level of employment L and on parameter γ). This corresponds to the two-stage equilibrium notion used throughout the study. Therefore, we know from the analysis of chapter 6 that in an economy with labor supply L^S and non-production requirements represented by γ the volume of total employment $\bar{L} = \bar{M} + \bar{L}^x$ organized with capital supply K is equal to L^*. That is, according to (6.23),

$$\bar{L} = L^* = \begin{cases} L_0(K,\gamma), & \text{if } K \le \hat{K}(L^S,\gamma) \\ L^S, & \text{if } K \ge \hat{K}(L^S,\gamma), \end{cases} \tag{7.26}$$

where $L_0(K,\gamma)$ is the level of aggregate employment resulting in an unemployment equilibrium. It is determined by (6.17), (6.18) and shown in figure 6.2. [10] $\hat{K}(L^S,\gamma)$ is defined by the condition $L_0\left(\hat{K},\gamma\right) = L^S$ (see (6.24)) and represents the amount of capital required for guaranteeing full employment. Moreover, we know from (6.25) that equilibrium employment increases with capital supply as long as there is jobless labor:

$$\begin{aligned} \partial L^*/\partial K &> 0 \ \text{ if } \ L^* < L^S, \\ \partial L^*/\partial K &= 0 \ \text{ if } \ L^* = L^S. \end{aligned} \tag{7.27}$$

Using this in (7.14), we obtain the capacity output as a function of capital supply K:

$$\bar{X}(K) = \bar{L}^x(L^*, K, \gamma)/A \tag{7.28}$$

[10] L^* depends also on the price-cost margin μ. But since no comparative-static analysis about the effects of μ was made in chapter 6, this parameter was suppressed for simplifying notation.

with

$$\frac{d\bar{X}}{dK} = \left[\frac{\partial \bar{L}^x}{\partial \bar{L}}\frac{\partial L^*}{\partial K} + \frac{\partial \bar{L}^x}{\partial K}\right] / A. \tag{7.29}$$

for $K < \hat{K}$.

The first term in the square bracket represents the effect of K working through the level of aggregate employment. According to (7.27), this effect vanishes if the labor force is fully employed. In an unemployment equilibrium, however, the zero-profit condition defining the equilibrium is met at a relatively higher level of total employment $L \left(= M + \bar{L}^x\right)$ if firms have access to more capital. And according to assumption (7.15) part of the additional employment falls on production work. Thus the first term in square brackets is zero in a full-employment equilibrium and positive in an unemployment equilibrium. The second term reflects the fact that for any given level of total employment L an increase in capital supply leads to a substitution of non-production labor. This sets resources free for expanding production. So the second term is always positive as noted in (7.14). In sum,

$$\frac{d\bar{X}}{dK} > 0 \tag{7.30}$$

With respect to the real interest rate we know from the analysis in section 6.3.1 summarized in figure 6.3 that $\hat{r}$ is a non-increasing function $\hat{r}(K)$ of capital supply K with[11]

$$\begin{array}{ll} \frac{d\hat{r}}{dK} \leq 0 & \text{if} \quad K < \hat{K}, \\ \frac{d\hat{r}}{dK} < 0 & \text{if} \quad K \geq \hat{K}, \end{array} \tag{7.31}$$

where $d\hat{r}/dK = 0$ holds in the case of homogenous labor.

So far we have only recollected the equilibrium results derived in chapter 6. The purpose of this chapter is to examine the circulatory relationship between savings and investment. That means, capital supply cannot be taken as given but one has to take into account that capital must be built up from the non-consumed part of the produced output i.e. from savings. Since $X = \bar{X}$ in a perfect-foresight equilibrium, we have

$$S = s(\hat{r})\,\bar{X}. \tag{7.32}$$

Total income and thus savings are determined by the supplied capacity output, and in the goods market equilibrium at stage 2 investment I exactly absorbs S, i.e. $I = S$. Under the assumption that the whole stock of capital is used up in production it must be renewed completely by investment. Then, as stated in (7.18), equilibrium accumulation must fulfill the condition

[11] No comparative-static analysis with respect to γ will be made in this chapter. Therefore, $\hat{r}$ is here considered as a function of K alone. L^S and γ in $\hat{K}\left(L^S, \gamma\right)$ are omitted for the same reason.

$K = I$. In other words, the amount of capital K that firms can use along with non-production labor to provide the prerequisites for organizing production work is equal to the part of produced output which is saved and invested. We have thus $K = s(\hat{r})\bar{X}$ as condition for equilibrium accumulation. But in the analyzed two-stage equilibrium $\hat{r}$ and $\bar{X}$ are functions of K so that finally the condition

$$K^* = S(K^*) \tag{7.33}$$

with

$$S(K) = s(\hat{r}(K))\,\bar{X}(K) \tag{7.34}$$

characterizes equilibrium accumulation K^* in the supply-determined two-stage equilibrium. (7.33) determines equilibrium allocation as a function of the exogenously given characteristics of the economy, namely, labor endowment, production and organization technology, preferences with respect to goods determining the price-cost margin and intertemporal preferences determining the savings propensity.

Equilibrium condition (7.33) can be analyzed by plotting the $S(K)$-curve and looking for its intersection points with the 45°-line. This is done in figure 7.3 for the case of a stable equilibrium. Before turning to this figure, one should observe that in general

$$\frac{dS}{dK} = s'\frac{d\hat{r}}{dK}\bar{X} + s\frac{d\bar{X}}{dK} \tag{7.35}$$

has ambiguous sign. The first term on the right side of equation (7.35) represents the interest-rate effect. According to (7.4) and (7.31), it vanishes if savings are completely inelastic with respect to the interest rate or if $K < \hat{K}$ and labor is homogeneous. Otherwise the effect is negative. The second term represents the income effect. According (7.30), it is positive. The ambiguity arising from these two opposing effects on sign as well as on magnitude of the slope of the $S(K)$-curve implies multiple equilibria as long as no further restrictions are made with respect to organization technology and savings behavior. (The former determines the relationship between capital supply K on the one hand and both interest rate $\hat{r}$ and total income $\bar{X}$ on the other hand. The latter determines for given $\hat{r}$ and $\bar{X}$ how much people save.) The intention of this discussion is not to present necessary and sufficient conditions for a unique stable equilibrium. The purpose of the chapter is to point out how savings and investment are interacting in the theoretical framework of this book. In particular, the supply-determined equilibria discussed in this section shall be compared to the demand-determined equilibria which will be considered in the next section. For this purpose, it is assumed that technology and preferences are such that a stable equilibrium exists. This means, condition (7.33) holds for some K^* with[12]

[12] Note that $dS/dK < 0$ is possible.

$$\left.\frac{dS}{dK}\right|_{K=K^*} < 1. \qquad (7.36)$$

Such an equilibrium is shown in figure 7.3.[13] It may be a full-employment equilibrium or an unemployment equilibrium, depending on whether $K^* \geq \hat{K}$ or $K^* < \hat{K}$.[14]

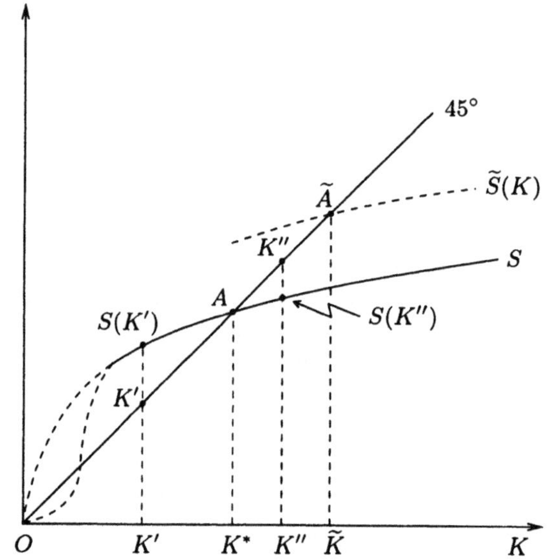

Fig. 7.3. Equilibrium accumulation in a supply-determined equilibrium.

Investment of capital $K' < K^*$ in the provision of jobs implies a two-stage equilibrium in which the level of organized employment and total income induces a volume of savings $S(K') > K'$ that more than reproduces the invested capital. Thus K increases. To the right of K^* savings $S(K'') < K''$ don't reproduce K'' and K shrinks. At the intersection point A capital investment K^* is consistent with savings. With a relatively higher inclination to save represented by an upward shift of the savings function from $S(K)$ to $\widetilde{S}(K)$ this intersection point moves to the right i.e. equilibrium accumulation increases. This corresponds to the usual supply-side view according to which a higher propensity of savings leads to a higher level of investment. The availability of more capital induces firms to provide more jobs if the economy was in an unemployment equilibrium at K^*. If the labor force is already fully employed the prerequisites for the organization of production work are provided

[13] $\bar{X}(0) = 0$ implies that $K = 0$ always fulfills equilibrium condition (7.33) if there is no autonomous savings, as was assumed in (7.4).

[14] Remember that $L^* = L^S$ for $K \geq \hat{K}$, according to (7.26).

with relatively higher capital intensity which sets non-production labor free for use in production. In any case, according to (7.30), the output which can be produced in the economy increases. In the demand-determined equilibrium considered in the next section a fundamentally different conclusion will result.

7.4 Equilibrium employment and equilibrium accumulation when firms have pessimistic demand expectations

For any given capital supply K, aggregate equilibrium employment is L^* if firms anticipate that they can sell at stage 2 any capacity they organize at stage 1, provided that it is consistent with the aggregate supply constraint of the economy. The resulting aggregate output level in such an equilibrium is $\bar{X}(K)$ determined by (7.28). The equilibrium was analyzed in chapter 6 and was called supply-determined equilibrium in section 7.3 where, in addition to chapter 6, the fact was taken into account that capital supply is related to savings. The purpose of this section is to compare the supply-determined equilibrium with the equilibrium resulting if firms are demand oriented when they decide about the provision of jobs at stage 1. First, the demand-determined two-stage equilibrium is characterized for a given volume of capital supply K. Then, the equilibrium accumulation implied by demand-constrained job provision is analyzed.

7.4.1 Demand-determined two-stage equilibrium

As a preparatory step we look at the consequences of a deviation of the organized aggregate output $\bar{X}$ from the supply-determined equilibrium level $\bar{X}(K)$. These consequences are independent of why $\bar{X}$ deviates from $\bar{X}(K)$. They follow from the general macroeconomic relationships discussed in section 7.1.2.

Denote by $\bar{L}(\bar{X}, K)$ the aggregate employment level which is consistent with capital supply K and production capacity $\bar{X}$. Since on the one side $\bar{L}^x = A\bar{X}$ and on the other side equation (7.14) must hold in any macroeconomic equilibrium, the function $\bar{L}(\bar{X}, K)$ is implicitly defined by the equation

$$A\bar{X} - \bar{L}^x(\bar{L}, K, \gamma) = 0. \tag{7.37}$$

Obviously, $\bar{X}$ is only feasible if $\bar{L}(\bar{X}, K) \leq L^S$. So the following statements concerning variations of $\bar{X}$ apply only to $\bar{X}$ within the feasible range, i.e., if $\bar{L}(\bar{X}, K) < L^S$. Implicit differentiation of equation (7.37) gives us:

$$\frac{\partial \bar{L}}{\partial \bar{X}} > 0 \quad \text{and} \quad \frac{\partial \bar{L}}{\partial K} < 0. \tag{7.38}$$

(Use $\partial \bar{L}^x / \partial \bar{L} > 0$ and $\partial \bar{L}^x / \partial K > 0$ from (7.14) and (7.15).)

Denote by $\widetilde{M}(\bar{X}, K) \equiv M(\bar{L}(\bar{X}, K), K, \gamma)$ the level of aggregate non-production labor consistent with $\bar{X}$ and K. This level is obtained if $\bar{L}(\bar{X}, K)$ is substituted into the function M defined in (7.13). Using (7.38) and (7.13), we get

$$\frac{\partial \widetilde{M}}{\partial \bar{X}} > 0 \text{ and } \frac{\partial \widetilde{M}}{\partial K} < \frac{\partial M}{\partial K} < 0. \tag{7.39}$$

The first inequalities in (7.38) and (7.39) state that with given capital endowment K a higher level of production work can only be organized if more labor, in particular also more non-production labor, is employed. The second inequalities in (7.38) and (7.39) say that a given level of production work $\bar{X}$ can be organized with less labor, in particular less non-production labor, if more capital is available. An immediate consequence of (7.39) is that the capital intensity, which is consistent with the organization of $\bar{L}^x = A\bar{X}$ units of production work in an economy endowed with capital K, is a decreasing function $\kappa(\bar{X}, K) \equiv K/\widetilde{M}(\bar{X}, K)$ of $\bar{X}$. Moreover, since $\widetilde{M}$ decreases with K, κ is increasing in K. We have:

$$\frac{\partial \kappa}{\partial \bar{X}} < 0 \text{ and } \frac{\partial \kappa}{\partial K} > 0. \tag{7.40}$$

Combining (7.38) and (7.40) with (6.12) and (6.19), we come to the conclusion that the minimal average cost $AC(\bar{X}, K)$ of providing a work place in an economy with aggregate capacity $\bar{X}$ and capital endowment K is an increasing function of $\bar{X}$. Thus,

$$AC(\bar{X}, K) \lesseqqgtr AC^*(K) \text{ if } \bar{X} \lesseqqgtr \bar{X}(K), \tag{7.41}$$

where $AC^*(K) = AC(\bar{X}(K), K)$ denotes the minimal average cost in the supply-determined equilibrium with production capacity $\bar{X}(K)$.

With these preparatory results we can now easily derive the implications of demand-oriented job provision behavior of firms. Suppose that firms expect at stage 1 that in stage 2 a demand-determined equilibrium with aggregate real demand $X_E = nx_E$ results as discussed in section 7.2. Demand-oriented job-provision behavior of firms means that they choose their capacity at stage 1 under the assumption that maximally x_E units of output can be sold at stage 2. This implies: Instead of (7.24) and (7.25), the relevant profit function at stage 2 is

$$\pi = (\mu - 1) w \min\{l_E, \bar{l}\}, \qquad l_E = Ax_E, \tag{7.42}$$

and the optimization problem at stage 1 is given by

$$\max_{\bar{l}} \pi^n = \begin{cases} [\mu - 1 - AC] w\bar{l}, & \text{if } \bar{l} \le l_E, \\ (\mu - 1) wl_E - ACw\bar{l}, & \text{if } \bar{l} > l_E. \end{cases} \tag{7.43}$$

(Note that the cost of providing the capacity to organize $\bar{l}$ units of production work is given by $ACw\bar{l}$ regardless of whether the provided work places are occupied or not at stage 2).

Thus, as long as $\mu - 1 > AC$ profit-maximizing firms wish to expand employment until $\bar{l} = l_E$ and the maximal net profit is $[\mu - 1 - AC]\, wl_E$. If $\mu - 1 < AC$ they reduce the organized capacity of production work. The average costs AC of providing a work place are composed of capital costs and wages for non-production labor. They depend on the aggregate demand for capital and non-production labor i.e. on the aggregate capacity $\bar{X} = n\bar{l}/A$ which all firms together want to organize. We know from (7.41) that $AC\left(\bar{X}, K\right) > AC^*(K)$ for any feasible $\bar{X} > \bar{X}(K)$. Now a feasible $\bar{X}$ with $\bar{X} > \bar{X}(K)$ only exists if $L^* < L^S$ i.e. if $\mu - 1 = AC^*(K)$.[15] Hence, $\mu - 1 < AC\left(\bar{X}, K\right)$ which means, it is not profitable for the firms to provide capacity $\bar{X}$. They reduce $\bar{l}$ as long as $\bar{X} = n\bar{l}/A > \bar{X}(K)$. As soon as $\bar{X} = \bar{X}(K)$, the known supply-determined equilibrium with $\mu - 1 = AC^*(K)$ is reached. However, for $\bar{X} < \bar{X}(K)$, we have $AC\left(\bar{X}, K\right) < AC^*(K)$. Therefore, $\mu - 1 > AC\left(\bar{X}, K\right)$, and firms expand employment until X_E or $\bar{X}(K)$ is reached.[16] In sum, profit-maximizing job provision of demand-oriented firms leads to

$$\bar{X} = X_E \quad \text{if} \quad X_E \leq \bar{X}(K) \tag{7.44}$$

and to $\bar{X}(K)$ otherwise. Thus, the equilibrium provision of jobs at stage 1 is demand-determined if firms decide about the organization of work on the basis of pessimistic demand expectations. In contrast to this, optimistic expectations with $X_E \geq \bar{X}(K)$ have no effect on the equilibrium. They always lead to the supply-determined equilibrium $\bar{X} = \bar{X}(K)$. In the further analysis, $X_E < \bar{X}(K)$ is assumed if demand-determined equilibria are discussed.

At stage 2, flexible wage adjustment guarantees that all provided work places are occupied. Thus, for $X_E < \bar{X}(K)$, we have

$$L^x = \bar{L}_E^x = X_E A \tag{7.45}$$

and

$$X^D = X^S = \bar{X} = X_E. \tag{7.46}$$

The provided capacities are fully utilized in the equilibrium at stage 2 and the pessimistic demand expectations are confirmed by the effective demand realized in stage 2.

In contrast to the usual view of the role of effective demand for employment, discussed in section 7.2, no additional assumptions like price rigidity or liquidity trap are needed to justify this demand-determined equilibrium at stage 2. The reason is that it is supported by the equilibrium decisions about the provision of work places at stage 1. In figure 7.4 this very important difference between underutilization at stage 2 and a demand-determined two-stage equilibrium is illustrated once more.

---

[15] According to (7.38), $\bar{X} > \bar{X}(K)$ implies $\bar{L}\left(\bar{X}, K\right) > L^*$. For $L^* = L^S$, this would imply $\bar{L}\left(\bar{X}, K\right) > L^S$ which is not feasible.

[16] Remember $\mu - 1 \geq AC^*(K)$ with equality holding if $L^* = L_0(K, \gamma) < L^S$.

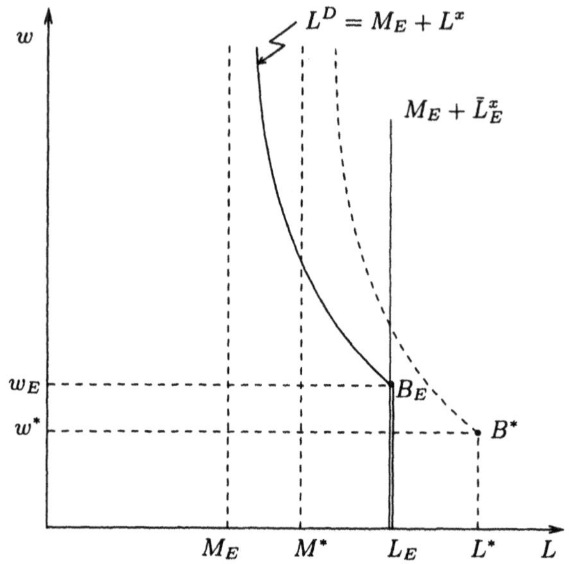

Fig. 7.4. Impact of pessimistic demand expectations on the equilibrium provision of jobs.

The supply-determined equilibrium is represented by B^* with respective equilibrium values w^*, L^* and M^*. Under pessimistic demand expectations $X_E < \bar{X}(K)$, firms organize work for $\bar{L}_E^x = X_E A < \bar{X}(K) A$ units of production labor by employing $M_E = \widetilde{M}(X_E, K)$ units of non-production labor. The maximally employable work force is then given by $L_E = M_E + \bar{L}_E^x$ ($= \bar{L}(X_E, K)$). According to (7.38) and (7.39), $L_E < L^*(= \bar{L}(\bar{X}(K), K)$, by definition) and $M_E < M^*$. Thus, there is necessarily unemployment in a two-stage equilibrium determined by pessimistic demand expectations. If wages are flexible and $L < L_E$, unemployed workers underbid wages and are hired at an organized job. However, as soon as aggregate employment reaches L_E, no places are organized for additional workers so that the remaining unemployed workers don't find a job whatever their wage. So nobody can effectively underbid the wage rate w_E at which all places organized at stage 1 are occupied. At equilibrium point B_E labor demand is equal to the labor force which is employable, given the prerequisites of organizing work that have been provided by demand-oriented profit-maximizing firms. Pessimistic demand expectations induce firms to reduce these prerequisites and thus the employable work force.

In sum, the macroeconomic equilibrium can indeed be determined by demand rather than by supply. Pessimistic demand expectations lead to a decrease in employment in a perfect foresight equilibrium with flexible wages. So there is a role for demand policy. If policy can raise the expectations to

$X'_E > X_E$, for instance by public investment, then firms create more jobs and aggregate equilibrium employment rises. As long as assumption (7.15) is fulfilled, this means a more efficient use of the economy's resources since aggregate output and thus income per head rises. However, whereas profits are raised or losses are avoided if underutilization is removed by demand policy, this is not guaranteed if demand policy changes the equilibrium level of organized work places. To the contrary, according to (7.41), $AC(X_E, K) < AC^*(K)$ if $X_E < \bar{X}(K)$. Thus, $\mu - 1 - AC(X_E, K) > \mu - 1 - AC^*(K) \geq 0$ and

$$\pi_E^n = [\mu - 1 - AC]\, wl_E > 0 \tag{7.47}$$

in a demand-determined equilibrium. If demand policy succeeds in raising X_E to $\bar{X}(K)$ and thus L_E to L^*, then the average costs of job provision rise to the level $AC^*(K)$. As long as $K < \hat{K}$ (so that $L^* = L_0(K, \gamma)$), this means that the firms' profits are completely eliminated.[17] The reason is that job creation is less costly if only a relatively low level of employment is organized. On the one hand, there is no need to integrate less able workers into the employed work force. On the other hand, more capital is available per organized unit of labor. So, reluctant job creation behavior is good for profits quite generally. In chapter 3, the power of firm owners to acquire a rent implied a lower level of organized employment for the same reason. If stimulating demand policy makes firms less reluctant, they demand more resources for organizing work and there is less room for pure profits.

7.4.2 Investment and savings in a demand-determined equilibrium

The preceding analysis showed that it is meaningful to consider the macroeconomic equilibrium as being determined by the demand side rather than by the supply side. The idea of a demand-determined macroeconomic activity level is consistent with the notion of perfect foresight of firms and involuntary joblessness in a competitive labor market. Unlike conventional Keynesian underutilization, the analyzed demand-determined two-stage equilibrium has no unoccupied work places. The employment problem arises because firms with pessimistic demand expectations provide relatively few jobs. This means, a smaller part of the labor force, in particular the relatively able part, is integrated into the work process organized by the firms. No job is provided for the rest of the labor force whatever their wage. The nature of the employment problem is the same as in the supply-determined equilibrium. But the size of the jobless labor force is the higher the more pessimistic are the demand expectations of firms.

The supply-determined equilibrium defines the upper bound of employment organized by profit-maximizing firms. According to (7.44), the two-stage equilibrium is demand-determined if $X_E \leq \bar{X}(K)$. Thus, it deviates from the

[17] Recall (7.25) and the fact that $\mu - 1 = AC^*$ at $L_0(K, \gamma)$.

supply-determined equilibrium if demand expectations are pessimistic relative to $\bar{X}(K)$. Since according to (7.30), $\bar{X}(K)$ is positively related to the available volume of capital K, the deviation of a demand-determined equilibrium from the supply-determined equilibrium depends on the level of capital supply. This is illustrated in figure 7.5.

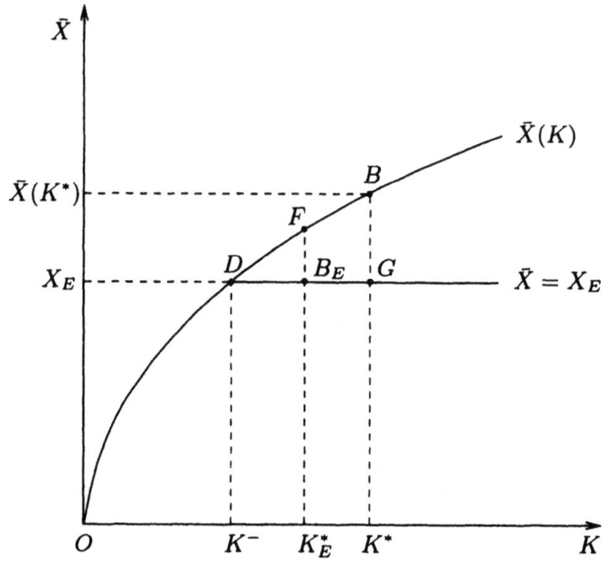

Fig. 7.5. Supply- vs. demand-determined capacity output.

For capital levels K to the left of the threshold value K^- , the supply-determined capacity output $\bar{X}(K)$ is lower than the exogenously given level of demand expectations X_E so that the equilibrium is determined by $\bar{X}(K)$ rather than by X_E.[18] But according to (7.44), for capital levels $K > K^-$ the equilibrium capacity output is equal to X_E if firms are concerned about demand when providing work places, whereas equilibrium capacity is $\bar{X}(K)$ if the firms' job provision is based on the assumption that any capacity can be sold as long as the labor force is not fully employed. If capital supply increases beyond the threshold level K^-, in a supply-determined economy, firms use the additional capital for expanding employment[19] as well as for increasing the capital intensity with which the prerequisites of production work are pro-

[18] Note that K^- is an increasing function of X_E defined by the equation $\bar{X}(K^-) = X_E$.

[19] Obviously, this is only true as long as $L^* = \bar{L}(\bar{X}(K), K) < L^S$ i.e. if $K < \hat{K}$. ($\hat{K}$ is the capital stock that guarantees full employment in the supply-determined equilibrium i.e. $L^* = L_0\left(\hat{K}, \gamma\right) = L^S$.)

vided. Both uses of capital increase the capacity output as shown by the derivation of (7.30) from (7.29). In figure 7.5 this effect of a capital increase corresponds to a move from point D towards point B along the $\bar{X}(K)$-curve. In contrast to this, with demand-oriented job-provision behavior of firms the economy moves from point D along the $\bar{X} = X_E$-line to the right. The additional capital is only used to organize work in a more capital-intensive way, i.e., to employ more capital per unit of non-production labor. Since output is fixed by X_E and the volume of production work $\bar{L}_E^x = AX_E$ doesn't increase, capital intensity is increased relatively more than in a supply-determined equilibrium in which $\bar{L}^x$ is expanded if more K is available. Formally, for $X_E < \bar{X}(K)$,

$$\kappa(X_E, K) > \kappa(\bar{X}(K), K), \tag{7.48}$$

according to (7.40). This suggests that capital accumulation is less attractive in an equilibrium which is determined by pessimistic demand expectations. And indeed, as will be shown below, the level of equilibrium accumulation K_E^* in a demand-determined equilibrium is lower than the level of equilibrium accumulation K^* in a supply-determined equilibrium.

The amount of capital K that can be invested by firms in the provision of work places depends on the volume of savings. And savings depend on the interest rate and on aggregate income. But in a demand-determined equilibrium, both the interest rate and total income are functions of demand expectations X_E. Put the other way round, pessimistic demand expectations affect savings and thus the supply of capital and the production capacity. What is the level of equilibrium accumulation in such a demand-determined economy?

Combining (7.48) with (7.16), we see that in contrast to the interest rate $\hat{r}(K)$ in a supply-determined equilibrium, the interest rate resulting in the demand-determined two-stage equilibrium is a function $\hat{r}_E(X_E, K) \equiv \frac{MRS(\kappa(X_E,K))}{\mu A}$ of demand expectations X_E as well. In view of the fact that $dMRS/d\kappa < 0$, we conclude from (7.48) and (7.40):[20] For $K > K^-$,

$$\hat{r}_E(X_E, K) < \hat{r}(K) \tag{7.49}$$

and

$$\frac{\partial \hat{r}_E}{\partial X_E} > 0, \quad \frac{\partial \hat{r}_E}{\partial K} < 0. \tag{7.50}$$

Using this and $s' \geq 0$ (see (7.4)), we obtain for $X_E < \bar{X}(K)$ and $K > K^-$ the savings function

$$S_E(X_E, K) = s(\hat{r}_E(X_E, K))\, X_E \tag{7.51}$$

with

[20] $\hat{r}_E$ is only defined for $X_E \leq \bar{X}(K)$, where $\hat{r}_E(X_E, K)$ coincides with $\hat{r}(K) = \hat{r}_E(\bar{X}(K), K)$ for $X_E = \bar{X}(K)$.

$$S_E(X_E, K) < S(K) = s(\hat{r}(K))\bar{X}(K) \tag{7.52}$$

and

$$\frac{\partial S_E}{\partial X_E} > 0, \qquad \frac{\partial S_E}{\partial K} \leq 0. \tag{7.53}$$

In an economy in which only that volume of capital is available which is saved and invested, equilibrium accumulation requires $K = I = S$. Thus, in a demand-determined equilibrium the equilibrium level of accumulation, denoted by K_E^*, must fulfill the condition

$$K_E^* = S_E(X_E, K_E^*). \tag{7.54}$$

$S_E(X_E, K_E^*)$ is only defined if the two-stage equilibrium is demand determined i.e. if $K \geq K^-$, where the threshold value K^- was defined by the equation $\bar{X}(K^-) = X_E$. Therefore, no demand-determined equilibrium allocation exists if $S_E(X_E, K) < K$ for all $K \geq K^-$. Since $\partial S_E/\partial K \leq 0$, according to (7.53), a necessary and sufficient condition for the existence of a demand-determined accumulation equilibrium is the inequality

$$S_E(X_E, K^-) > K^-. \tag{7.55}$$

Under this condition the equilibrium level of accumulation K_E^* defined by condition (7.54) is unique. The reason is that $\partial S_E/\partial K \leq 0$, in contrast to the ambiguous effect of K on $S(K)$ in the supply-determined equilibrium considered in section 7.3.[21] Moreover, implicit differentiation of condition (7.54) and use of (7.53) give us

$$\frac{dK_E^*}{dX_E} > 0. \tag{7.56}$$

Hence,

$$K_E^* < K^*, \tag{7.57}$$

if $X_E < X^* \equiv \bar{X}(K^*)$ and if X_E fulfills condition (7.55) for the existence of a demand-determined equilibrium. Figure 7.6 illustrates this comparison of equilibrium accumulation K_E^* in a demand-determined two-stage equilibrium with equilibrium accumulation K^* in a supply-determined two-stage equilibrium for the case of a stable K^*.[22]

In contrast to the ambiguous sign of the slope of $S(K)$, the curve $S_E(X_E, K)$, starting at $S(K^-)$ (point C), is always negatively sloped according to (7.53). Therefore, equilibrium point A_E is unique. Compared with

[21] There is only an interest-rate effect of higher K on savings but no income effect (compare (7.35)).

[22] Note that in the case of a stable K^* condition (7.55) for the existence of a demand-determined accumulation equilibrium is always met for K^- in the neighborhood of K^* (i.e. for X_E in the neighborhood of $X^* = \bar{X}(K^*)$). By contrast, condition (7.55) cannot be fulfilled in the neighborhood of an unstable K^* with $\frac{dS}{dK}\big|_{K=K^*} > 1$.

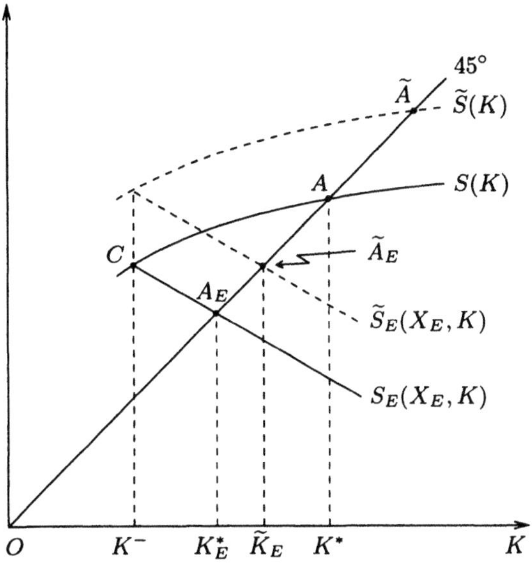

Fig. 7.6. Equilibrium accumulation in a demand-determined equilibrium (K_E^*).

A point A_E must lie closer to the origin, since $S_E(X_E, K)$ lies below $S(K)$ for all $K > K^-$. As consequence, equilibrium allocation K_E^* is lower than equilibrium allocation K^*. Suppose, for instance, that the economy initially is in the supply-determined equilibrium A with accumulation K^*. Then firms are seized by pessimistic demand expectations. They create less jobs. This implies less total income and a relatively high capital-coefficient per organized work place which depresses the interest rate. Both effects induce a reduction of savings and thus of the capital available for the provision of jobs. Only at point A_E the savings implied by the demand-oriented provision of jobs exactly reproduces the capital invested in the provision of the jobs.

For aggregate employment the switch from the supply-determined equilibrium A to the demand-determined equilibrium is bad. But, given that firms orient their provision by pessimistic demand expectations, the reduction of capital supply from K^* to K_E^* is good for employment. The reason is that employment of production labor $\bar{L}_E^x$ is fixed by X_E anyway. If less capital is available, the provision of the prerequisites for organizing the $\bar{L}_E^x$ units of production labor is less capital intensive. This means, more non-production labor $\widetilde{M}$ is employed. These effects can be seen very clearly by moving through figure 7.5. The supply-determined equilibrium with equilibrium allocation K^* is given by point B. (Thus, B corresponds to point A in figure 7.6.) The demand-determined equilibrium resulting at capital supply K^* is given by point G. At this point employment in production is low compared to B, while capital intensity κ is high. As a consequence, employment of non-production labor and total employment are low. According to (7.38) - (7.40): $\kappa(X_E, K^*) > \kappa(\bar{X}(K^*), K^*)$, $\widetilde{M}(X_E, K^*) < \widetilde{M}(\bar{X}(K^*), K^*)$ and $\bar{L}(X_E, K^*) < \bar{L}(\bar{X}(K^*), K^*)$. If the new equilibrium accumulation K_E^* is realized, the economy is shifted to point B_E. By this shift capital intensity is decreased while employment of non-production labor and total employment increases (see again (7.38) - (7.40)). So the move from point G to point B_E counteracts the effect of the move from point B to point G.

Does this mean that in the end, when equilibrium accumulation is adjusted, the switch from the supply-determined equilibrium at point B to the demand-determined equilibrium at point B_E has no employment effect at all? No, the described effects of the adjustment of the reduction of capital accumulation, i.e. the move from G to B_E, only partly compensates the effects of the reduction of production from B to G. This can be seen by moving in figure 7.5 from point B to B_E via point F. The effects of a move along $\bar{X}(K)$ are given by the comparative-static analysis of the effects of K on the supply determined two-stage equilibrium. We know from (7.27) that $L^*(K_E^*) \leq L^*(K^*)$ with equality holding only if the labor force is fully employed under both levels of capital supply.[23] If the economy is shifted from F to the demand determined equilibrium at point B_E, total employment is reduced according to (7.38), since only X_E is produced with the given capital stock instead of $\bar{X}(K_E^*)$. Hence,

$$\bar{L}(X_E, K_E^*) < L^*(K^*) = \bar{L}(\bar{X}(K^*), K^*). \tag{7.58}$$

If firms are demand oriented and their demand expectations are pessimistic so that the macroeconomic equilibrium is determined by the demand side rather than by the supply side, not only aggregate production, income and accumulation is reduced but also total employment. Employment of non-production labor may rise due to the reduction of capital supply but this cannot compensate the decline in the employment of production labor.

The discussed effects of demand oriented behavior of firms on job provision, production, employment and accumulation have far-reaching consequences for the impact of the people's propensity to save on the macroeconomic performance of an economy. Suppose that the propensity to save increases. As discussed in section 7.3, this shifts the $S(K)$-curve upwards to $\widetilde{S}(K)$ in figure 7.6. According to (7.51), also the $S_E(X_E, K)$-curve is shifted upwards to $\widetilde{S}_E(X_E, K)$. This increases equilibrium accumulation from K_E^* to $\widetilde{K}_E$ just as equilibrium accumulation was increased in the case of the

[23] Note that (7.27) and (7.38) are related as follows: $L^*(K)$ is the equilibrium employment that results if $\bar{X}$ approaches the equilibrium output $\bar{X}(K)$ realized in a supply determined equilibrium with capital endowment K. By definition, $L^*(K) = \bar{L}(\bar{X}(K), K)$. Thus $dL^*/dK = \frac{\partial \bar{L}}{\partial \bar{X}}\frac{\partial \bar{X}}{\partial K} + \frac{\partial \bar{L}}{\partial K}$. The first term of the sum is positive, whereas the second term is negative, because of (7.30) and (7.38). (7.27) tells us that the negative effect is never dominating.

supply-determined equilibrium considered in section 7.3. However, the increase of the equilibrium supply of capital has completely different effects. In the case of a supply-determined equilibrium the increase of capital supply leads to an expansion of production. This increases employment in production and, although at the same time non-production labor is substituted by capital, total employment increases if additional labor is available and it remains constant if the labor force is already fully employed. In sum, a rising propensity to save has positive effects on total production and income, a non-negative effect on employment, and it increases the ratio of production to non-production labor. In the case of a demand-determined equilibrium the effects are quite different. If more capital is available due to a higher savings propensity, the additional capital can only be used to substitute non-production labor, since employment in production is fixed by the reluctant job-provision behavior of the firms. Therefore, total employment declines to the same extent as non-production labor is substituted by capital. Formally, $\bar{L}\left(X_E, \widetilde{K}_E\right) < \bar{L}\left(X_E, K_E^*\right)$ and $\widetilde{M}\left(X_E, \widetilde{K}_E\right) < \widetilde{M}\left(X_E, K_E^*\right)$, according to (7.38) and (7.39).

A negative employment effect of a rising propensity to save, i.e. of a decline in the propensity to consume, is a familiar feature of the conventional Keynesian model considered in section 7.2.2. But the reason there was that for a given level of investment demand I, effective demand and thus employment in production L^x is depressed if a larger share of income is saved (see (7.6)). In the two-stage equilibrium considered here, employment in production always equals the organized capacity $\bar{L}^x$ of production work and this capacity is determined by the demand expectations of the firms. Not labor in production but non-production labor is harmfully affected if the share of output that can be used for providing a given number of work places increases.

To illustrate this difference between traditional Keynesian view and the two-stage equilibrium model presented in this book , suppose that the economy produces variants of computers which can be used by firms as capital goods as well as by consumers.[24]

If the savings propensity rises in the traditional Keynesian model, this means that consumers buy fewer personal computers for private use. And if the demand for computers by firms is given, total demand for computers declines and less computers are produced. Production workers will be fired, while the employment of non-production resources remains unchanged. As a result, there are unused capacities. They consist of the installed computer infrastructure, for instance, the capacity of the "docking stations" to which production labor must have access for being able to produce. Besides capital input there is also the non-production staff who is responsible for planning, financing, designing and marketing the produced computers, maintaining the

[24] Computers may be seen as the universal goods in an information-processing world, like corn was considered as the universal good in a world in which the production and consumption of food is the central element.

computer infrastructure, coordinating and supervising production work, or supporting and motivating production workers.

In the two-stage equilibrium in which the decisions about the employment of non-production resources determine the macroeconomic activity level the situation is different. In the supply-determined equilibrium discussed in section 7.3, the firms do two things when a larger share of computers is saved from consumption: They substitute staff work by computers and they expand production. In the demand-determined equilibrium considered in this section, only the first reaction is realized, since production is limited by the firms' expectations that there is no market for more computers. As a result, non-production labor is set free because there is more computer support for the staff work. This fits well to the observation of Breshnahan [13] mentioned at the beginning of this book, namely, that computerization has substituted middle-level white-color work. However, in the present model the non-production workers set free by the increased computer-intensity of staff work can find a job in production where they substitute less able production workers.

Thus, as far as individual persons are concerned, the negative employment effect of pessimistic expectations trickles down from middle-abled non-production workers to the least able production workers. While the first find a new job if they are ready to switch to production, the latter do not. But in terms of the volume of labor there is definitely a restructuring in the sense that the ratio of total non-production labor to total production labor declines if more capital is available in the economy. This finally leads back to the analysis of reorganization processes in chapter 4. Whereas there a new organization technology became available to firms by exogenous technical change, here the restructuring results from an increase in capital supply. Therefore, in terms of labor units a leaner organization can result, although the non-production requirements for organizing a unit of production work, given by the organization technology $g(L, \gamma)$, remain the same.

8. Summary

1. The transformation of human resources and non-human inputs into marketable products requires internal organization of economic activities. This remains true no matter how radically the forms of internal organization may change. Centrally organized traditional factories, disintegrated production and customer-oriented supply of goods and services based on modern logistics and communication technologies, or laboratories and networks dealing with the generation and distribution of information have in common that there is internal interaction of individuals as opposed to external transactions between economic subjects in markets. The most evident sign for this is the fact that firms and companies, not single individuals, are the important players in modern markets. In contrast to what some people seem to think, the role of internal organization is not disappearing but rather gaining importance. How else should one explain the many mergers or alliances observed in old as well as new economic sectors? And why else should it be reasonable for firms to expand their sphere of action by becoming a multinational or global enterprise?

2. Many branches of economics have contributed to a better understanding of why internal transactions exist in a market economy and how the structure of an organization, the methods of management or the design of incentives affect the performance of a firm and the behavior of the employed agents. However, a systematic theoretical analysis of the general equilibrium effects and the macroeconomic consequences of the internal organization of work in firms is missing. This book made an attempt to provide such an analysis. Economic analysis means to look at the economic means by which certain purposes are achieved. Therefore, this book introduced the notion of an organization technology describing in an abstract way the resources, in particular the input of non-production labor, which are required for organizing work in a firm. Macroeconomic equilibrium analysis looks at the aggregate consequences of the allocation of economic resources resulting in the interplay of factor and goods markets. In an economy with internal interaction of individuals in organizations (i.e. firms), in addition to external transactions in markets, the macroeconomic equilibrium does not only depend on the technology of production but also on the organization technology. This book developed a theoretical framework for analyzing macroeconomic equilibria of an economy

with internal organization of work and discussed the performance of macroeconomic variables in such equilibria. In particular, the equilibrium level of aggregate employment was determined. Due to the nature of the model, also the structure of employment, regarding the use of labor in production (i.e. production labor) and organization (i.e. non-production labor), respectively, is explained. Firms are symmetric in the considered macroeconomic framework, and the number of firms plays no role for the derived results.

3. Whereas in the standard model of a market economy full employment of the labor force results in equilibrium if no rigidities and frictions distort the labor market, this is not guaranteed in an economy in which internal interaction of workers in organized units (called firms) is a precondition of market transactions. The equilibrium volume of work organized by profit-maximizing firms may be smaller than the supplied labor force. Thus, workers may not be able to find a job whatever the wage they accept. In the basic theoretical framework of this book no rigidities or frictions hinder firms to hire and fire workers. So all work places organized by the firms are occupied in equilibrium. But firms possibly do not organize enough jobs. Neither full employment nor an efficient level of employment is guaranteed. The reason is that the organization of work requires resources the amount of which depends on the used organization technology but also on the interactive abilities of the employed work force. A higher level of aggregate employment implies that also less able workers have to be integrated into the employed work force. This raises the firms' costs of organizing the interaction of workers. Since these costs, although variable ex ante, are fixed when firms compete in the market they cannot be passed on to product prices but must be covered by the profit-margin earned in production. The equilibrium volume of work which is organized by profit-maximizing firms with perfect foresight is defined either by the available labor force, i.e. by labor supply, or by the condition that the costs of organizing the interaction of workers must not exceed the profit extracted from their work. In the latter case we have an unemployment equilibrium in which (after deduction of organization costs) firms earn zero profits.

4. The theory presented in this study explains employment in firms, i.e., organized employment. There may be individual earnings opportunities without any connection to internally organized interactions. But they do not affect the question of how many jobs are organized in the equilibrium of a market economy with a given supply of labor. Individuals whose outside opportunities are more attractive than a job in a firm do not belong to the relevant labor force. And that part of the labor force which is unemployed in the considered macroeconomic equilibrium would remain without job regardless of the wage. They want to work in a firm but there is no work place for them. Necessarily, they must have outside opportunities to survive. But these opportunities are less attractive than having a job. Also the statistical distinction between unemployment, measured by the number of people who

are actually looking for work, and non-employment, joblessness or inactivity of people who do not look for a work place although they want to have one, is irrelevant in this consideration. Whether they are searching or not, firms have no job for them. The studied unemployment is clearly involuntary. It concerns individuals with low interactive abilities who, even if they underbid wages, are not employed in the considered equilibrium of a market economy, since firms are not prepared to integrate them into their organization.

5. This kind of unemployment may be called unemployability. However, not nature but the organizational provision made by the firms determines the range of employable labor. Who is employable depends on how the internal interaction of workers in firms is organized and on how much resources are spent on the integration of workers into an organization. The achievement of this book is that it worked out a framework in which i) the way of how firms organize work, ii) the volume of resources spent on organizing work, and iii) the range of employment that is organized in the chosen way with the chosen organizational resources can be determined endogenously. The result depends on the feasible methods of organization and on the distribution of interactive abilities among the labor force. But in a market economy also the competitive pressure upon firms, reflected by the profit margin that can be achieved in the respective goods markets, is an important determinant of the equilibrium outcome. Equilibrium employment describes the range of labor considered to be profitably employable by profit-maximizing firms. It was shown that under reasonable conditions this range is smaller than the range of workers who are economically employable in an efficiency sense. That means, in an unemployment equilibrium output per head is lower than it would be if workers who are jobless were integrated into the work force employed in firms.

6. The derived macroeconomic equilibrium shows a rather fundamental employment problem. In practice, persistent non-employment of workers with low abilities is an example of the explained type of employment problem. The theoretical analysis is also suited to explain why, for instance, young people who have no experience with work in a firm, or older workers who have difficulties with new forms of work organization have particular problems to find a job. More generally, the theory presented in this book provides a rigorous framework for discussing popular concerns about the danger that modern economic life is restricted to relatively qualified and socially competent workers in their best years while the rest drops out of the organized economy. The analysis of the basic model showed that the minimal level of abilities, below which a worker is not employed by a profit-maximizing firm in the macroeconomic equilibrium, depends on the used mode of organizing work and increases with the competitive pressure upon firms in the goods markets. The extensions of the model showed that also wage rigidities, rents of firms owners, the supply of high-skilled workers, capital endowment and

pessimistic expectations of firms affect the equilibrium employment. The relevant effects are summarized below.

7. The employment equilibrium derived in the basic model is to be seen as a benchmark. It proves that unemployment is a possible equilibrium phenomenon in a macroeconomic framework which takes internal organization seriously but is otherwise as close as possible to an ideal market economy with flexible wages, perfect foresight and zero profits of firms. Conventional sources of unemployment like wage rigidity or unanticipated shocks lead to deviations from this benchmark. A less familiar deviation arises if firm owners have the power to extract a rent from their firms, for instance, because of capital market imperfections. This means that firms must earn pure profits in equilibrium. If no rents are required by the owners of the firms, employment is expanded until the full-employment constraint makes further expansion unfeasible or the zero-profit condition stops the desire of firms to provide more jobs. If firms must pay a rent to their owners, the expansion of employment stops before the zero-profit condition is reached. Starting from an unemployment equilibrium without rents the level of unemployment increases with the required rent. The reason is that, given the profit margin implied by the competitive situation in the goods markets, firms have to save non-production costs in order to bear the rent. The non-production costs arise from the resources required for the internal organization of work. They can be reduced if employment concentrates on a work force which is easier to organize, i.e., if firms do no longer provide work places for workers with low interactive abilities. An obvious application of this argument is the discussion about the pressure towards lean management caused by an increasing weight of shareholders for firm policy. The analysis in this book showed that shareholder orientation can indeed imply that a lower level of employment is organized by firms in the macroeconomic equilibrium, provided that shareholders have the power to acquire a rent and shareholder orientation means that this power is increasing.

8. Technical change comprises the whole process of transforming human and non-human resources into marketable products. This includes the way in which economic activities are organized. This study considered two stylized forms of organization technologies: The traditional mode of central coordination and a new mode called decentralized communication. The two forms of organizing work require different abilities of workers and imply for the firms different costs of providing work places. In the traditional way of organization with central supervision and coordination the interactive abilities of workers are not so important. To put it in an extreme way, each worker is told what to do, and quality control and communication among workers or between workers and customers is carried out by the central staff. This implies that each worker causes certain coordination and supervision costs which do not react very sensitively to the interactive abilities of the employed work force. In contrast to this, network-like forms of decentralized organization

require from the workers a high degree of self-organization. As long as only workers with high interactive abilities are integrated into the employed work force, this means rather low costs of non-production resources for organizing the interaction of workers. However, as soon as workers with low interactive abilities are included these costs are rising drastically. Actually, they will be prohibitively high if abilities fall below a certain levels. Not all workers who can be integrated into a traditional firm are capable of self-organization.

9. The discussion about the reorganization of work which is confined to the partial view of single firms or industries usually takes it for granted that versatile, autonomous, flexible and communicative workers can be picked. But how are things in the general equilibrium if all firms try to become self-organizing networks of able workers? Either only relatively able workers are employed in the equilibrium or the reorganization of work turns out to be less cost-saving than supposed, since the integration of workers with lower interactive abilities requires nonetheless increasing non-production resources. The theory developed in this book provided a natural framework to analyze these general equilibrium effects in a systematic way. The equilibrium adoption of organization technologies by the firms as well as the implied equilibrium employment effects were determined. If firms have the choice between the two described modes of organization, named "central coordination" and "decentralized communication", respectively, and if they decide simultaneously about which organization technology they adopt and which volume of labor they organize with the adopted technology, then the following equilibrium constellations can arise:

i) The new way of organizing work in a decentralized way may dominate the traditional form of central coordination in the sense that the whole labor force which is employed in the equilibrium using the old organization technology can be employed more effectively in the reorganized form. In this case all firms adopt the new mode of organization and equilibrium employment does not decrease, since the given profit-margin in the goods market allows to provide more jobs if the organization of work requires relatively less non-production resources. The assessment of whether the new organization technology is dominating depends on the abilities of the employed labor force. Obviously, a technology requiring high abilities is dominating more likely if all supplied labor is endowed with relatively high interactive abilities, but also if the macroeconomic conditions are such that the employment in firms is restricted to the relatively able part of supplied labor. As mentioned, rents for firm owners are working into this direction. Therefore, the incentive to reorganize work may be higher in an economy in which firm owners have the power to extract a rent from their firms.

ii) Completely different equilibrium situations result if the new organization technology is not dominating, i.e. if the organization of work in the decentralized way is easy as long as relatively able workers are employed but less effective then traditional central coordination when also less able workers are to be managed. In this case partial or total reorganization may arise in equilibrium and aggregate equilibrium employment declines compared to the equilibrium in which only the traditional organization technology was available. Partial reorganization means that only part of the firms switch to the new mode of work organization. They attract the relatively able workers. The other part of the firms is left with labor of lower interactive abilities. It is easier to organize their work in the traditional way rather than in the new way of decentralized communication. However, the fact that workers with lower abilities are left alone in the traditionally organized firms makes their organization more difficult than in the equilibrium in which only the old organization technology was available to firms and also the upper range of abilities was included in the work force organized in the traditional form. Therefore, compared to this equilibrium the range of employed abilities decreases in a partial reorganization equilibrium, although old firms are in operation parallel to the reorganized firms. The fact that firms which do not adopt the new organization technology are left with a less able work force may also completely drive out the old mode of organization. In this case we have a total reorganization equilibrium although the new organization technology is not dominating in the sense described above. Clearly, also in this case aggregate equilibrium employment is lower than it was in the equilibrium under the traditional form of work organization. In sum, this macroeconomic equilibrium perspective shows that current trends of reorganizing work in a way which is heavily relying on the interactive abilities of workers may reduce the provision of jobs for less able workers.

10. Often reorganization is associated with the notion of lean management. In the approach of this book the notion means a low ratio of non-production labor to production labor. So the question is if this ratio is brought down by the analyzed reorganization process. Again the macroeconomic equilibrium perspective showed that the answer suggested by the partial perspective of a single firm is misleading. For the individual firm the relevant criterion for adopting the new form of work organization under given macroeconomic conditions is indeed the lower amount of non-production labor required per unit of production labor. However, for the macroeconomic perspective two further aspects are relevant: First, the criterion guides the adoption behavior of *all* firms. Second, the ratio of non-production to production labor increases with the aggregate volume of work organized in the new way, since also less able workers have to be employed by firms that have adopted the new technology. Thus firms switch to the new organization technology until the ratio of non-production labor to production labor under the new technology is the same as under the old technology or all firms have adopted the new mode of organization. Moreover, firms expand employment as long as it is profitable to do so, i.e., until the zero-profit condition or full employment is reached. As a result, in an unemployment equilibrium all firms earn zero profits regardless of the adopted technology. This implies that the equilibrium ratio of

non-production labor to production labor is the same for all firms as long as there is unemployment in both the macroeconomic equilibrium before reorganization and the macroeconomic equilibrium after reorganization. If there was full employment before reorganization, the amount of non-production labor required per unit of organized production labor is even higher in the reorganization equilibrium. Only if the new way of organizing work is so effective that full employment is reached after reorganization, the equilibrium ratio of non-production to production labor is brought down in the reorganization equilibrium. Thus, organizational change is a weak candidate for explaining shifts in the aggregate ratio of non-production to production as long as there is unemployment. In the macroeconomic equilibrium approach of this book this ratio declines if the profit margin declines, i.e., when the competitive pressure in the goods market increases. Or imperfections are introduced so that unemployment equilibria with non-zero profits result. For instance, if firm owners have the power to extract a rent of their firms, the firms fire workers with low abilities. This indeed brings down the equilibrium ratio of non-production to production labor since less resources are required to organize work.

11. In the basic model only one type of labor was considered. This type of labor was heterogeneous with respect to interactive abilities but could be used in production as well as in the organization of production. The model was extended to consider the usually different role of skilled and unskilled labor differing in the formal education levels. It was assumed that skilled workers can be employed in both organization and production whereas unskilled workers can be employed in production only. In this extended model the macroeconomic equilibrium values of the aggregate employment of the two types of labor, the skill-intensity in production and the wage inequality measured by the wage of skilled relative to the wage of unskilled labor could be analyzed. The macroeconomic equilibrium values depend on the organization technology used by the firms and on the skill supply. The analysis showed that skilled labor is possibly a limiting factor for the employment of unskilled workers, since the internal organization of production work requires skilled non-production labor.

12. If wages are flexible, in particular also the relative wage rate, skilled labor was fully employed in the macroeconomic equilibrium. But unskilled workers may remain jobless. The reason is that skilled labor is becoming more and more scarce as employment of unskilled labor is rising. This depresses skill intensity in production and raises the costs of skilled non-production labor required for organizing production work. As a consequence, the gross profit (before deduction of non-production costs) earned per unit of unskilled labor employed in production declines if employment of unskilled labor increases, and the average non-production costs per unit of employed unskilled labor rise. Since firms stop expanding employment as soon as the return on a job equals the costs of providing the job, an unemployment equilibrium results

if the zero-profit condition is reached before the whole unskilled labor force is employed.

13. An immediate consequence of this argument is that a rise in the supply of skilled labor has a positive effect on the employment of unskilled labor. The reason is that skill-intensity in production rises and skilled non-production labor becomes less scarce. For any given level of employment of unskilled labor, this raises the return per unit of unskilled production labor and lowers the non-production costs per organized unit of unskilled production work. Thus, equilibrium employment of unskilled labor increases as long as the full-employment constraint is not binding. The net effect on the average non-production costs per unit of unskilled labor is ambiguous. The positive employment effect of an expanding skilled labor force is an equilibrium effect. This means the view that skilled and unskilled labor are competing for jobs and a rise in skilled labor drives unskilled labor out of employment can only be true temporarily or under particular distortions. However, there may be an indirect negative effect: If the increase in the supply of skilled labor is not feeded by exogenous sources like immigration but by education of unskilled labor the increase of skilled labor may go hand in hand with a decline in the interactive abilities of the remaining unskilled labor force. This raises the non-production requirements of organizing work. The effects are like those of a change in the organization technology. They are summarized in the next paragraph.

14. Skill-biased technological change usually means that the relative marginal productivity of skilled labor, compared to the marginal productivity of unskilled labor, is increased by a change in the production technology. In the framework presented in this book also changes in the organization technology may induce a change in the relative demand for the two types of labor. For instance, when firms switch to methods of organization that require higher interactive abilities, more resources must be spent for organizing a certain volume of work with given abilities. This means, skilled labor is shifted from production to non-production and becomes more scarce. As a consequence, it is less attractive for firms to provide jobs for unskilled labor. Also the usually considered skill-biased technological change of the production technology has a negative effect on employment of unskilled labor, provided that the economy was already in an unemployment equilibrium before the technological change. Contrary to the standard argument, according to which skill-biased technological change leads to a rise in the wage spread if wages are flexible and to unemployment of unskilled labor in rigid labor markets, the rise in the relative wage rate of skilled labor caused by the skill-biased technological change implies in the present model also changing conditions for the provision of jobs for unskilled labor. The reason is that the rise in the relative wage of skilled labor makes the organization of work by skilled non-production workers more costly. Obviously, this effect can only be seen

in a model in which the organization of work and the double role of skilled labor in production and non-production is explicitly taken into account.

15. The usual debate about wage rigidity concentrates on the role of rigid wages of low-skilled labor. In the model analyzed in this study also rigid wages of high-skilled workers may have negative effects on employment of skilled as well as of unskilled labor. The causes of wage rigidity were not examined in the analysis. But there is no reason why one should consider rigid wages for skilled labor as implausible in a world in which skills play a crucial role. In particular, the skilled non-production workers who are employed by the firm owners to organize work are in a powerful position. To be more concrete, manager salaries may possibly include rents. Two distortions of wages for skilled workers were considered: i) If the relative wage of skilled labor is higher than the market wage, then also skilled labor may be unemployed in the macroeconomic equilibrium. The effect of the rigidity of the relative wage of skilled labor on the employment of unskilled labor is ambiguous. A negative effect is possible. ii) If only skilled non-production workers have the power to acquire a rent, whereas the relative wage of skilled labor in production is flexible, skilled labor remains fully employed in the macroeconomic equilibrium. Nonetheless the skilled production workers bear a burden in form of a lower real wage. For unskilled labor a rent for non-production workers has the same negative employment effect as the rent for firm owners discussed above. The provision of jobs for unskilled labor becomes more costly if a rent is to be paid to the organizers of production work. In sum, if firm owners or skilled non-production workers get a rent whereas the wages of production workers are flexible, then a lower real wage of skilled production labor and a reduction in the work places organized by the firms' for unskilled labor is predicted by the analysis. If the skilled production workers successfully oppose the declining real wage, they too may experience a decline in employment.

16. Modern organization of work in firms heavily relies on the use of capital. The whole spectrum of information- and communication technologies are an obvious example. The basic model was extended to deal with this important feature of reality. The organization technology, describing how the prerequisites of organizing production work are provided, was generalized to include capital as an input, in addition to non-production labor. Capital as an input in the production technology was not considered. Profit-maximizing firms provide the prerequisites of production work by choosing the cost-minimizing combination of capital and non-production labor. This determines capital demand as a function of both the interest rate and the level of employment. On the other side, the amount of employed capital affects the costs of creating jobs and thus the level of employment. The macroeconomic equilibrium conditions are: Capital demand must equal capital supply, and the level of employment is equal to the size of the labor force or the costs of providing a job are as high as the profits earned from the provided job.

These conditions determine the interest rate and aggregate employment in the macroeconomic equilibrium.

17. In a first step, the macroeconomic equilibrium was derived for a given aggregate capital stock. It was shown that aggregate employment is an increasing function of the available volume of capital, as long as capital supply is not high enough to guarantee a full-employment equilibrium. The reason is that higher capital supply makes it less costly for the firms to provide jobs. The equilibrium interest rate as a function of capital supply is non-increasing as long as the economy is in an unemployment equilibrium and decreasing if the economy is in a full employment equilibrium. In the latter case, additional capital is only used to substitute non-production labor and to increase capital intensity in the provision of the prerequisites of production work. In the former case it can also be used do expand employment.

18. In a second step, the macroeconomic equilibrium effects of elastic capital supply were considered. This made it possible to deal with the employment effects of market power in the capital market and with the role of international capital mobility for the creation of jobs. Market power in the capital market reduces equilibrium capital supply and increases the costs of job provision. It has a negative effect on employment just like exogenous rents of firm owners in the basic model. For assessing the employment effects of capital mobility a small open economy as well as a two-country world were considered. The two countries were identical in every respect except factor endowments or organization technology. The following results were shown:

i) In the case of a small economy, fluctuations in the world interest rate induce capital flows which in the present framework cause employment fluctuations provided that there is unemployment in the considered economy. ii) In a two-country world in which countries differ only with respect to the size of their capital endowment, capital moves from capital-rich to capital-poor countries when capital markets are opened up. This capital flow smoothes employment disparities between the countries. iii) If the countries differ only in the endowment with low-ability labor, the opening up of international capital markets has no effect at all as long as unemployment prevailed in the closed equilibrium of both countries. The reason is that in this case neither at home nor abroad investors have an incentive to provide more jobs. If full employment prevailed in the country with the relatively small labor force, capital moves to the country which is "rich in low-ability labor". The country is attractive for investors, since more labor can be employed there. If unemployment prevailed in the closed equilibrium the capital inflow has a positive effect on employment in the host country, while labor in the home country remains fully employed. iv) Differences in the requirements of organizing work may induce capital flows between countries of identical size. In this case the pattern of capital flows and the employment effects depend on how scarce capital is in the considered world. If there is enough capital, then full employment prevails at least in the country in which job creation is easy, and capital flows to the other country in which the provision of a job requires more resources. This capital mobility is good for employment. However, if capital is so scarce that unemployment prevails in both countries, then capital moves in the other direction, namely to the country in which job creation is easier and employment is relatively high. In this case, free international capital allocation reinforces existing employment disparities.

19. Finally, capital formation by investment and savings, and its role for aggregate employment in a closed economy were considered. Capital is used to provide the prerequisites for organizing production work. Employment in production generates income. Part of the income is saved and invested. Since no growth was considered, equilibrium accumulation was defined by the condition that the saved part of income reproduces exactly the amount of capital that is used to provide the jobs which generate the income. This completion of the macroeconomic equilibrium analysis allowed a comparison of the theory developed in this book with traditional thinking about the macroeconomic circulation of national income. In particular, the long-standing debate about Say's Law and the controversy between supply-side and demand-side economics could be reflected in a new light.

20. The traditional theory of effective demand is based on the idea that pessimistic demand expectations lead to unemployment because of underutilized production capacities. In the framework developed in this book an unemployment equilibrium is possible in which the production capacities provided by the firms are fully utilized. The reason for unemployment is that the firms are not ready to employ enough non-production resources for organizing a higher level of production work. In a supply-determined equilibrium the firms base their decisions about the employment of non-production resources on the expectation that they can sell any production capacity they organize by employing these resources. In an equilibrium the expectation turns out to be correct. All conclusions presented so far have been based on the notion of a supply-determined equilibrium. In contrast to this, in a demand-determined equilibrium firms base their decisions about the employment of non-production resources on pessimistic demand expectations. These expectations are fulfilling themselves in an equilibrium. Reluctant job-creation behavior leads to comparatively higher unemployment than in a supply-determined equilibrium. Also the level of equilibrium accumulation is relatively lower, and the relationship between savings behavior and investment is fundamentally different. In a supply-determined equilibrium an increase in the savings propensity leads to higher equilibrium accumulation and has positive effects on aggregate income and employment. In a demand-determined equilibrium, in which output and employment in production are oriented towards pessimistic demand expectations, higher accumulation leads to a restructuring in the provision of the prerequisites of organizing production work: Non-production labor (e.g. work of middle-level clerks) is sub-

stituted by capital (e.g. information-processing machinery) reducing total employment.

A. Appendix to Chapter 2

If firms enter stage 2 with different investments m_i, for some firms the capacity restriction may be binding for others not. Let $\mathcal{J} = \{j \mid \nu_j = 0\}$ and $\mathcal{H} = \{h \mid \nu_h > 0\}$ be the index set of firms with a non-binding and a binding capacity restriction, respectively. Moreover, define $L_U \equiv \sum_{j\epsilon\mathcal{J}} l_j$ and $M_K \equiv \sum_{h\epsilon\mathcal{H}} m_h$. Thus, $l_h = m_h/g(L,\gamma)$ by definition, and (2.6) is equivalent to

$$L = M + L_U + \frac{M_K}{g(L,\gamma)}. \tag{A.1}$$

Budget constraint (2.8) can be written in the form (Use (2.18), (2.20), (2.21), (2.22))

$$Y = \mu w L_U + \frac{\mu}{g(L,\gamma)} \sum_{h\epsilon\mathcal{H}} \widetilde{w}_h m_h$$

with

$$\widetilde{w}_h = \left(\frac{D(P,L)}{m_h}\right)^{1/\sigma} / (\mu A). \tag{A.2}$$

This can be rewritten as

$$Y = \mu w L_U + \frac{D(P,L)^{1/\sigma}}{g(L,\gamma) A} \sum_h m_h^{\ 1-\frac{1}{\sigma}}. \tag{A.3}$$

Finally, the definition of P implies $P^{1-\sigma} = \sum_{i=1}^{n} p_i^{1-\sigma}$. Since $p_j = \mu A w$ for $j\epsilon\mathcal{J}$ and $p_h = \mu A \widetilde{w}_h$ for $h\epsilon\mathcal{H}$, according to (2.18) and (2.22), we can write

$$P^{1-\sigma} = \left[\mid \mathcal{J} \mid (\mu w A)^{1-\sigma} + (\mu A)^{1-\sigma} \sum_{h\epsilon\mathcal{H}} \widetilde{w}_h^{1-\sigma} \right]. \tag{A.4}$$

The four equations (A.1) - (A.4) define for the exogenous parameters Y,μ, A, γ and the given investments $m_1, ..., m_n$, the equilibrium values L_U, L, $L^x = L - M$ and P as functions of the wage rate w. When deciding about m_i at stage 1, each individual firm assumes that the aggregate values implied by the simultaneous choices of all firms are not influenced by the own decision. So they choose identical investments m_i.

B. Appendix to Chapter 6

Case a: $L^* = L^S$.

In this case, according to (6.17) and (6.18), the equilibrium values L^*, κ^* are given by $L^* = L^S$ and

$$f_1\left(\kappa^*; L^S, K^S, \gamma\right) \equiv K^D\left(\kappa^*, L^S, \gamma\right) - K^S = 0\,, \tag{B.1}$$

where, according to (6.15),

$$\frac{\partial K^D}{\partial \kappa} = \frac{L\left(1 + \left(q - \kappa q'\right)/g\right)}{\left(1 + q/g\right)^2} > 0, \tag{B.2}$$

$$\frac{\partial K^D}{\partial L} = \frac{\kappa\left(1 + \left(1 + \frac{\partial g}{\partial L}\frac{L}{g}\right) q/g\right)}{\left(1 + q/g\right)^2} > 0, \tag{B.3}$$

$$\frac{\partial K^D}{\partial \gamma} = \frac{\kappa \frac{\partial g}{\partial \gamma}\frac{L}{g} q/g}{\left(1 + q/g\right)^2}. \tag{B.4}$$

The sign of $\partial K^D/\partial \gamma$ depends on the sign of $\partial g/\partial \gamma$. Thus, $\partial K^D/\partial \gamma > 0$ if the convention $\partial g/\partial \gamma > 0$ is made.

Implicit differentiation of (B.1) gives us

$$\frac{\partial \kappa^*}{\partial K^S} = -\frac{\partial f_1/\partial K_S}{\partial f_1/\partial \kappa^*} = \frac{1}{\partial K^D/\partial \kappa} > 0, \tag{B.5}$$

$$\frac{\partial \kappa^*}{\partial \gamma} = -\frac{\partial K^D/\partial \gamma}{\partial K^D/\partial \kappa} < 0 \tag{B.6}$$

under the convention that $\partial g/\partial \gamma > 0$. Consequently, according to (6.22),

$$\frac{\partial \hat{r}}{\partial K^S} < 0 \text{ and } \frac{\partial \hat{r}}{\partial \gamma} > 0. \tag{B.7}$$

For later use, note that the derivation of $\partial \hat{r}/\partial K^S$ at $K^S = \hat{K}$ is given by

$$\left.\frac{\partial \hat{r}}{\partial K^S}\right|_{K^S = \hat{K}} = \frac{MRS'\left(\hat{\kappa}\right)}{\mu A}\left(\left.\frac{\partial K^D}{\partial \kappa}\right|_{\kappa = \hat{\kappa}}\right)^{-1}, \tag{B.8}$$

where $\hat{K}$ is defined by (6.24) and $\hat{\kappa}$ is defined by $K^D(\hat{\kappa}, L^S, \gamma) = \hat{K}$.

Case b: $L^* = L_0(K^S, \gamma)$.

According to (6.17) and (6.18), in this case the equilibrium values are implicit functions $\kappa^*(K^S, \gamma)$ and $L^*(K^S, \gamma)$ defined by the system

$$\begin{aligned} f_1(\kappa^*, L^*; K^S, \gamma) &\equiv K^D(\kappa^*, L^*, \gamma) - K^S = 0 \\ f_2(\kappa^*, L^*; \gamma) &\equiv AC(\kappa^*, L^*, \gamma) - \mu + 1 = 0, \end{aligned} \tag{B.9}$$

where the partial derivations of K^D are given by (B.2) - (B.4) and

$$\frac{\partial AC}{\partial \kappa} = \frac{g\kappa q''}{(q - \kappa q')^2} < 0, \tag{B.10}$$

$$\frac{\partial AC}{\partial L} = \frac{\partial g/\partial L}{(q - \kappa q')} \geq 0, \tag{B.11}$$

$$\frac{\partial AC}{\partial \gamma} = \frac{\partial g/\partial \gamma}{(q - \kappa q')}, \tag{B.12}$$

according to (6.12). (Remember $q - \kappa q' = \partial Q/\partial m > 0$.) The sign of $\partial AC/\partial \gamma$ is equal to the sign of $\partial g/\partial \gamma$. Thus, $\partial AC/\partial \gamma > 0$ under the convention $\partial g/\partial \gamma > 0$. For $L_0(K^S, \gamma) < L^S$, i.e. for $K^S < \hat{K}$, the impacts of K^S and γ on L^* and κ^* can be derived by applying the implicit function theorem to the system (B.9). We have

$$\begin{pmatrix} \frac{\partial \kappa^*}{\partial K^S} & \frac{\partial \kappa^*}{\partial \gamma} \\ \frac{\partial L^*}{\partial K^S} & \frac{\partial L^*}{\partial \gamma} \end{pmatrix} = -A^{-1} \begin{pmatrix} \frac{\partial f_1}{\partial K^S} & \frac{\partial f_1}{\partial \gamma} \\ \frac{\partial f_2}{\partial K^S} & \frac{\partial f_2}{\partial \gamma} \end{pmatrix} \tag{B.13}$$

with

$$A \equiv \begin{pmatrix} \frac{\partial f_1}{\partial \kappa} & \frac{\partial f_1}{\partial L} \\ \frac{\partial f_2}{\partial \kappa} & \frac{\partial f_2}{\partial L} \end{pmatrix} \tag{B.14}$$

and

$$A^{-1} = \frac{1}{\det(A)} \begin{pmatrix} \frac{\partial f_2}{\partial L} & -\frac{\partial f_1}{\partial L} \\ -\frac{\partial f_2}{\partial \kappa} & \frac{\partial f_1}{\partial \kappa} \end{pmatrix}, \tag{B.15}$$

where

$$\det(A) = \frac{\partial f_1}{\partial \kappa}\frac{\partial f_2}{\partial L} - \frac{\partial f_1}{\partial L}\frac{\partial f_2}{\partial \kappa}. \tag{B.16}$$

Using (B.2) - (B.4) and (B.10) - (B.12) in (B.9) and in (B.15) - (B.16), we obtain

$$-A^{-1} = \frac{1}{\det(A)} \begin{pmatrix} -\frac{\partial AC}{\partial L} & \frac{\partial K^D}{\partial L} \\ \frac{\partial AC}{\partial \kappa} & -\frac{\partial K^D}{\partial \kappa} \end{pmatrix} \tag{B.17}$$

and

$$\det(A) = \frac{\partial K^D}{\partial \kappa}\frac{\partial AC}{\partial L} - \frac{\partial K^D}{\partial L}\frac{\partial AC}{\partial \kappa} > 0. \tag{B.18}$$

Substituting (B.17), (B.18) and $\partial f_1/\partial K^S = -1$, $\partial f_2/\partial K^S = 0$, $\partial f_1/\partial\gamma = \partial K^D/\partial\gamma$, $\partial f_2/\partial\gamma = \partial AC/\partial\gamma$ into (B.13), and calculating the matrix product, we have the following impacts of K^S and γ on the equilibrium values κ^* and L^* in an unemployment equilibrium (i.e., for $K^S < \hat{K}\left(L^S,\gamma\right)$):

$$\frac{\partial\kappa^*}{\partial K^S} = \frac{1}{\det(A)}\frac{\partial AC}{\partial L} \geq 0 \tag{B.19}$$

with equality holding if $\partial g/\partial L = 0$,

$$\frac{\partial L^*}{\partial K^S} = \frac{1}{\det(A)}\left(-\frac{\partial AC}{\partial\kappa}\right) > 0, \tag{B.20}$$

$$\frac{\partial L^*}{\partial\gamma} = \frac{1}{\det(A)}\left(\frac{\partial AC}{\partial\kappa}\frac{\partial K^D}{\partial\gamma} - \frac{\partial K^D}{\partial\kappa}\frac{\partial AC}{\partial\gamma}\right) < 0 \tag{B.21}$$

and

$$\frac{\partial\kappa^*}{\partial\gamma} = \frac{1}{\det(A)}\left(\frac{\partial K^D}{\partial L}\frac{\partial AC}{\partial\gamma} - \frac{\partial AC}{\partial L}\frac{\partial K^D}{\partial\gamma}\right) > 0. \tag{B.22}$$

The signs of all effects except the last one follow immediately from (B.18) and the signs of the partial effects calculated in (B.2) - (B.4) and (B.10) - (B.12). (The effect of γ is based on the convention $\partial g/\partial\gamma > 0$.) For the sign of $\partial\kappa^*/\partial\gamma$, one has to show that

$$\frac{\partial K^D}{\partial L}\frac{\partial AC}{\partial\gamma} > \frac{\partial AC}{\partial L}\frac{\partial K^D}{\partial\gamma}. \tag{B.23}$$

In view of (B.3), (B.4), (B.11), (B.12) and $\partial g/\partial\gamma > 0$, this inequality is equivalent to

$$1 + \left(1 + \frac{\partial g}{\partial L}\frac{L}{g}\right)\frac{q}{g} > \frac{\partial g}{\partial L}\frac{L}{g}\frac{q}{g}. \tag{B.24}$$

By collecting terms, (B.24) can be rewritten in the form

$$1 + \frac{q}{g} > 0, \tag{B.25}$$

which is always fulfilled.

Moreover, applying (B.19) and (B.22) to (6.22), we have for $K^S < \hat{K}\left(L^S,\gamma\right)$:

$$\frac{\partial\hat{r}}{\partial K^S} \leq 0 \quad\text{and}\quad \frac{\partial\hat{r}}{\partial\gamma} < 0 \tag{B.26}$$

with $\partial\hat{r}/\partial K^S = 0$ if $\partial g/\partial L = 0$.

Finally, substitution of (B.19) in (6.22) gives us

$$\lim_{K^S\to^-\hat{K}}\frac{\partial\hat{r}}{\partial K^S} = \frac{MRS'(\kappa^*)}{\mu A}\left.\frac{\partial AC/\partial L}{\det(A)}\right|_{K^S=\hat{K}}. \tag{B.27}$$

Comparing this with (B.8), we get

$$\left.\frac{\partial \hat{r}}{\partial K^S}\right|_{K^S=\hat{K}} < \lim_{K^S \to^- \hat{K}} \frac{\partial \hat{r}}{\partial K^S}, \tag{B.28}$$

since $MRS' < 0$, $\det(A) > 0$, $\partial K^D/\partial \kappa > 0$ and $\det(A) > \frac{\partial AC}{\partial L}\frac{\partial K^D}{\partial \kappa} \geq 0$. (The latter inequality follows from (B.18) and the fact that $\frac{\partial K^D}{\partial L}\frac{\partial AC}{\partial \kappa} < 0$, according to (B.3) and (B.10). Moreover, $\partial AC/\partial L \geq 0$ and $\partial K^D/\partial \kappa > 0$, according to (B.2) and (B.11).)

References

1. Acemoglu, D. (2002), "Technical change, inequality, and the labor market", *Journal of Economics Literature XL*, 7-72.
2. Acemoglu, D. (1998), "Why do new technologies complement skills? Directed technical change and wage inequality", *Quarterly Journal of Economics* 113, 1055-1089.
3. Aghion, P., Garcia-Penalosa, C. and Caroli, E. (1998), "Inequality and economic growth", in: P. Aghion and J.G. Williamson (1998), *Growth, inequality and globalization. Theory, history and policy*, Cambridge: Cambridge University Press, 5-102.
4. Atkinson, A.B. (1997), "Bringing income distribution in from the cold", *Economic Journal* 107, 297-321.
5. Atkinson, A.B. (2000), "The changing distribution of income: Evidence and explanations", *German Economic Review* 1, 3-18.
6. Barro, R.J. and Grossman, H.I. (1971), "A general disequilibrium model of income and employment", *American Economic Review* 61, 82-93.
7. Becker, G.S. and Murphy, K.M. (1992), "The division of labor, coordination costs, and knowledge", *Quarterly Journal of Economics* 107, 1137-1160.
8. Berman, E., Bound, J. and Grilichis, Z. (1994), "Changes in the demand for skilled labor within U.S. manufacturing: Evidence from the annual survey of manufactures", *Quarterly Journal of Economics* 109, 367-397.
9. Berman, E., Bound, J. and Machin, S. (1998), "Implications of skill-biased technological change: International evidence", *Quarterly Journal of Economics* 113, 1245-1279.
10. Bhaskar, V. and To, T. (1999), "Minimum wages for Ronald McDonald monopsonies: A theory of monopsonistic competition", *Economic Journal* 109, 190-203.
11. Bolton, P., and Dewatripont, M. (1994), "The firm as a communication network", *Quarterly Journal of Economics* 109, 809-839.
12. Bound, J. and Johnson, G. (1992), "Changes in the structure of wages in the 1980s: An evaluation of alternative explanations", *American Economic Review* 82, 371-392.
13. Breshnahan, T. (1999), "Computerisation and wage dispersion: An analytical reinterpretation", *Economic Journal* 109, F390-F415.
14. Burda, M. and Dluhosch, B. (1998), "Globalization and European labour markets", in: H. Siebert (Ed.) *Globalization and labor*, Tübingen: Mohr (Siebeck).
15. Burda, M. and Dluhosch, B. (2002), "Cost competition, fragmentation and globalization", *Review of International Economics*, forthcoming.
16. Calvo, G.A. and Wellisz, S. (1978), "Supervision, loss of control, and the optimum size of the firm", *Journal of Political Economy* 86, 991-1010.
17. Clark, A.E. and Oswald, A.J. (1994), "Unhappiness and unemployment", *Economic Journal* 104, 648-659.

18. Clower, R.W. (1965), "The Keynesian counter-revolution: A theoretical appraisal", in: F.H. Hahn and F. Brechling (eds.), *The theory of interest rates*, London: Macmillan, 270-297.
19. Coase, R.H. (1937), "The nature of the firm", *Economica*, NS, 4, 386-405.
20. D'Aspremont, C., Dos Santo Ferreira, R. and Gérard-Varet, L.-A. (1990), "On monopolistic competition and involuntary unemployment", *Quarterly Journal of Economics* 105, 895-919.
21. Diamond, P.A. (1982), "Aggregate demand management in search equilibrium", *Journal of Political Economy* 90, 881-894.
22. Dixit, A. and Stiglitz, J. (1977), "Monopolistic competition and optimum product diversity", *American Economic Review* 67, 297-308.
23. Drèze, J.H. (2001), "Macroeconomics of uncertainty and incomplete markets", *Recherches Economiques de Louvain*, 67, 5-30.
24. Falkinger, J. (2002), "Employability and the costs of organizing work", in: A. De Grip, J. Van Loo and K. Mayhew (Eds.), *Understanding skill obsolescence*, Research in Labour Economics Series, forthcoming.
25. Falkinger, J. and Grossmann, V. (2001), "Skill supply, supervision requirements, and unemployment of low-skilled labor", *International Journal of Manpower* 22, 69-82.
26. Falkinger, J. and Grossmann, V. (2002), "Workplaces in the primary economy and wage pressure in the secondary labor market",Revised version of CESifo Working Paper No. 485.
27. Feenstra, R.C. (1998), "Integration of trade and disintegration of production in the global economy", *Journal of Economic Prespectives* 12, 31-50.
28. Gregg, P. and Manning, A. (1997), "Skill-biased change, unemployment and wage inequality", *European Economic Review* 41, 1173-1200.
29. Grossmann, V. (2000), Skilled labor reallocation, wage inequality, and unskilled unemployment, *Journal of Institutional and Theoretical Economics 156*, 473-500.
30. Hart, O. (1982), "A model of imperfect competition with Keynesian features", *Quarterly Journal of Economics* 97, 109-138.
31. Heckman, J.J., Lochner, L. and Taber, Ch. (1998), "Explaining rising wage inequality: Explorations with a dynamic general equilibrium model of labor earnings with heterogenous agents", *Review of Economic Dynamics* 1, 1-58.
32. Howell, D., and Wolff, E. (1991), "Trends in the growth and distribution of skills in the U.S. workplace, 1960-1985", *Industrial and Labor Relations Review* 44, 486-502.
33. Juhn, Ch., Murphy, K.M. and Pierce, B. (1993), "Wage inequality and the rise in returns to skill", *Journal of Political Economy* 101, 410-442.
34. Kahn, J.A. and Lim, J.-S. (1998), "Skilled labor augmenting technical progress in U.S. manufacturing", *Quarterly Journal of Economics* 113, 1281-1309.
35. Kalecki, M. (1939), *Essays in the theory of economic fluctuations*, London: Allen and Unwin.
36. Kalecki, M. (1954), *Theory of economic dynamics*, Revised second edition 1965, London: Allen and Unwin.
37. Keynes, J.M. (1936), *The general theory of employment, interest and money*, Vol. VII of The Collected Writings, London: Macmillan.
38. Keynes, J.M. (1937), "The general theory of employment", Vol. XIV of The Collected Writings, 109-23 (originally published in *Quarterly Journal of Economics* 51).
39. Kiley, M.T. (1999), "The supply of skilled labour and skill-biased technological progress", *Economic Journal* 109, 708-724.

40. Kremer, M. (1993), "The O-ring theory of economic development", *Quarterly Journal of Economics* 108, 551-575.
41. Kremer, M. and Maskin, E.(1996), "Wage inequality and seggregation by skill", NBER Working Paper No. 5718.
42. Lazear, E.P. (1999), "Globalisation and the market for team-mates", *Economic Journal* 109, C15-C40.
43. Lindbeck, A. and Snower. D.J. (1986), "Wage setting, unemployment and insider outsider relations", *American Economic Review* 26, 235-239.
44. Lindbeck, A. and Snower, D.J. (1988), *The insider-outsider theory of employment and unemployment*, Cambridge/M.: MIT Press.
45. Lindbeck, A. and Snower, D.J. (1996), "Reorganization of firms and labor market inequality", *American Economic Review* 86, 315-321.
46. Machin, S. and Van Reenen, J. (1998), "Technology and changes in skill structure: evidence from seven OECD countries", *Quarterly Journal of Economics* 113, 1215-1244.
47. Malinvaud, E. (1977), *The theory of unemployment reconsidered.* Oxford: Basil Blackwell.
48. Murphy, K.M. and Topel, R. (1997), "Unemployment and nonemployment", *American Economic Review Papers and Proceedings* 87, 295-300.
49. Nickell, S.J. and Bell, B. (1996), "Changes in the distribution of wages and unemployment in OECD countries", *American Economic Review Papers and Proceedings* 86, 302-308.
50. Nickell, S.J. and Bell, B. (1997), "Would cutting payroll taxes on the unskilled have a significant impact on unemployment?", in: D.J. Snower and G. de la Dehesa, (Eds.), *Unemployment policy: Government options for the labour market.* Cambridge: Cambridge University Press, 296-328.
51. Pasinetti, L.L. (1981), *Structural change and economic growth*, Cambridge: Cambridge University Press.
52. Phelps, E.S. and Zoega, G. (1997), "The rise and downward trend of the Natural Rate", *American Economic Review* 87, 283-289.
53. Pissarides, Ch.A. (1990), *Equilibrium unemployment theory*, Oxford: Basil Blackwell, (Second Edition 2000).
54. Rodrik, D. (1997), *Has globalisation gone too far?*, Washington: Institute for International Economics.
55. Rodrik, D. (1998), *Capital mobility and labor*, NBER workshop on Trade, Technology, Education and the U.S. Labor Market.
56. Rothschild, K.W. (1978), "Arbeitslose: Gibt's die?", *Kyklos* 31, 21-35.
57. Saint-Paul, G. (1996a), *Dual labor markets. A macroeconomic perspective.* Cambridge/M.: MIT Press.
58. Saint-Paul, G. (1996b), "Are the unemployed unemployable?", *European Economic Review* 40, 1501-1519.
59. Silvestre, J. (1990), "There may be unemployment when the labor market is competitive and the output market is not", *Economic Journal* 100, 899-913.
60. Silvestre, J. (1993), "The market-power foundation of macroeconomic policy", *Journal of Economic Literature* 31, 105-141.
61. Snower, D.J. (1999b), "The organizational revolution and its labor market implications", Keynote Address to the European Association of Labour Economists (EALE), Regensburg.
62. Solow, R.M. (1986), "Unemployment: Getting the questions right", in: C. Bean, R. Layard and S. Nickell, (Eds.), *The rise in unemployment*, Oxford: Basil Blackwell.
63. Sutton, J. (1991), *Sunk costs an market structure: Price competition, advertising and the evolution of concentration*, Cambridge/M.: MIT Press.

64. Sutton, J. (1998), *Technology and market structure*, Cambridge/M.: MIT Press.
65. Venables, A.J. (1999), "Fragmentation and international production", *European Economic Review* 43, 935-945.
66. Vogt, W. (1999), "Endogenously biased technological progress and the macroeconomic structure of employment", in: H. Wagner (Ed.), *Globalisation and unemployment*, Berlin et al.: Springer.
67. Walther, H. (1992), "Der Zusammenhang zwischen Bildungs- und Beschäftigungssystem vor dem Hintergrund strukturellen Wandels", in: J. Schmee u.a. (Hrsg.), *Strukturwandel und Bildung*, Ludwig Boltzman-Institut für Wachstumsforschung, Wien.
68. Weitzman, M.L. (1982), "Increasing returns and the foundations of unemployment theory", *Economic Journal* 92, 787-804.
69. Williamson, O.E. (1975), *Markets and hierarchies: Analysis and antitrust implications*, New York: Macmillan.
70. Williamson, O.E. (1976), "The economics of internal organization: Exit and voice in relation to markets and hierarchies", *American Economic Review* 66, 369-377.

Author index

Subject index

Contributions to Economics

Henri Capron, Wim Meeusen (Eds.)
The National Innovation System of Belgium
2000. ISBN 3-7908-1308-7

Tobias Miarka
Financial Intermediation and Deregulation
2000. ISBN 3-7908-1307-9

Chisato Yoshida
Illegal Immigration and Economic Welfare
2000. ISBN 3-7908-1315-X

Nikolaus Thumm
Intellectual Property Rights
2000. ISBN 3-7908-1329-X

Max Keilbach
Spatial Knowledge Spillovers and the Dynamics of Agglomeration and Regional Growth
2000. ISBN 3-7908-1321-4

Alexander Karmann (Ed.)
Financial Structure and Stability
2000. ISBN 3-7908-1332-X

Joos P. A. van Vugt/Jan M. Peet (Eds.)
Social Security and Solidarity in the European Union
2000. ISBN 3-7908-1334-6

Johannes Bröcker/Hayo Herrmann (Eds.)
Spatial Change and Interregional Flows in the Integrating Europe
2001. ISBN 3-7908-1344-3

Kirstin Hubrich
Cointegration Analysis in a German Monetary System
2001. ISBN 3-7908-1352-4

Nico Heerink et al. (Eds.)
Economic Policy and Sustainable Land Use
2001. ISBN 3-7908-1351-6

Friedel Bolle/Michael Carlberg (Eds.)
Advances in Behavioral Economics
2001. ISBN 3-7908-1358-3

Volker Grossmann
Inequality, Economic Growth, and Technological Change
2001. ISBN 3-7908-1364-8

Thomas Riechmann
Learning in Economics
2001. ISBN 3-7908-1384-2

Miriam Beblo
Bargaining over Time Allocation
2001. ISBN 3-7908-1391-5

Peter Meusburger/Heike Jöns (Eds.)
Transformations in Hungary
2001. ISBN 3-7908-1412-1

Claus Brand
Money Stock Control and Inflation Targeting in Germany
2001. ISBN 3-7908-1393-1

Erik Lüth
Private Intergenerational Transfers and Population Aging
2001. ISBN 3-7908-1402-4

Nicole Pohl
Mobility in Space and Time
2001. ISBN 3-7908-1380-X

Pablo Coto-Millán (Ed.)
Essays on Microeconomics and Industrial Organisation
2002. ISBN 3-7908-1390-7

Mario A. Maggioni
Clustering Dynamics and the Locations of High-Tech-Firms
2002. ISBN 3-7908-1431-8

Ludwig Schätzl/Javier Revilla Diez (Eds.)
Technological Change and Regional Development in Europe
2002. ISBN 3-7908-1460-1

Alberto Quadrio Curzio/Marco Fortis (Eds.)
Complexity and Industrial Clusters
2002. ISBN 3-7908-1471-7

Friedel Bolle/
Marco Lehmann-Waffenschmidt (Eds.)
Surveys in Experimental Economics
2002. ISBN 3-7908-1472-5

Pablo Coto-Millán
General Equilibrium and Welfare
2002. ISBN 7908-1491-1

Wojciech W. Charemza/
Krystyna Strzala (Eds.)
East European Transition and EU Enlargement
2002. ISBN 3-7908-1501-2

Natalja von Westernhagen
Systemic Transformation, Trade and Economic Growth
2002. ISBN 3-7908-1521-7

GPSR Compliance

The European Union's (EU) General Product Safety Regulation (GPSR) is a set of rules that requires consumer products to be safe and our obligations to ensure this.

If you have any concerns about our products, you can contact us on ProductSafety@springernature.com

In case Publisher is established outside the EU, the EU authorized representative is:

Springer Nature Customer Service Center GmbH
Europaplatz 3
69115 Heidelberg, Germany

Batch number: 10725973

Printed by Printforce, the Netherlands